Meeting the Living God

Meeting the Living God

(Revised Edition)

William J. O'Malley, S.J.

Paulist Press New York/Ramsey

Acknowledgments

The excerpt from "The Road Not Taken" is from *The Poetry of Robert Frost* © 1916, 1969 by Holt, Rinehart & Winston Inc. © 1944 by Robert Frost. Reprinted by permission of Holt, Rinehart & Winston Inc. The excerpt from "Wind and Silver" is from *The Complete Poetical Works* by Amy Lowell, copyright © 1955 by Houghton Mifflin Company. Reprinted by permission of Houghton Mifflin Company. The excerpts from *Markings* by Dag Hammarskjöld © 1964 by Alfred A. Knopf Inc. and Faber and Faber Inc. are reprinted by permission of Alfred A. Knopf, Inc.

IMPRIMI POTEST:
Vincent Cooke, S.J.
May 1, 1983

NIHIL OBSTAT:
Joseph M. Jankowiak, S.T.D.
Censor librorum

IMPRIMATUR:
Matthew H. Clark, D.D.
Bishop of Rochester
June 30, 1983

The Nihil Obstat and Imprimatur are official declarations that a book or pamphlet is free of doctrinal or moral error. No implication is contained therein that those who have granted the Nihil Obstat and Imprimatur agree with the contents, opinions or statements expressed.

Cover design by Jon Bauch.

Interior drawings by Kristin Malone.

Library of Congress
Catalog Card Number: 83-62014

ISBN: 0-8091-9565-8

Published by Paulist Press
545 Island Road, Ramsey, N.J. 07446

Printed and bound in the
United States of America

Contents

I shall be telling this with a sigh
Somewhere ages and ages hence:
Two roads diverged in a wood, and I—
I took the one less traveled by,
And that has made all the difference.

This book is for my friend
Bob Mooney
who has the wits and courage
to follow the unexpected roads.

Introduction

Worship him, I beg you, in a way that is worthy of thinking beings.

—*Romans 12:1*

This is a book about freedom. It is based on the truth that you can be free only when you *see* all the alternatives—not as you'd like them to be, but as they are.

It begins with what might seem at first to be a wild claim; these pages present the most crucial pair of alternatives any human being can face: either God exists, or he doesn't.

That may seem like a sheerly academic question, something to be debated long into the night at a party or in a college dorm, assessing the pros and cons, and then leaving it to go on to more pressing, more important demands on our time. However, if God doesn't exist—or if he is basically unimportant to our lives—don't go to a wake and console the bereaved by saying, "Well, she's in a better life now." If there is no God, she isn't in a better life; she has simply ceased to be real. If there is no God, don't expect anyone finally to do justice to retarded children. If there is no God, at death the Pope and the pimp receive exactly the same reward: annihilation. Each of us just accidentally happened, and one day we will just as accidentally un-happen. Ultimately, the God question is a question of our own value as human beings: are we immortal from the moment of our birth, or are we just so much potential garbage?

It's not just an academic question.

1

How Can We Be Sure of Anything?

1. Does God exist?
2. If so, what is he like?
3. How can we be sure?

When I was once a guest on the "Today" show, Barbara Walters leaned over to me during a commercial break and whispered, "You're obviously a very intelligent man. *How* can you be a priest?"

The greatest fear we have is the fear of being taken in, hoaxed, made to look like fools. We feel it when someone says, smilingly, "*Trust me*." We feel it when we're tempted to change jobs, try out for a team or a play, broaden our circle of friends, choose a college. But we feel it most intensely when the invitation involves a comprehensive life-commitment—whether it is the invitation to be a priest or to be a full-out practicing Christian. Before we choose a road, before we leave behind the warm cocoon we're sure of, we want some assurance that we are actually leaving behind something very good *in order to* have something better.

From that first betrayal at the kindergarten door, when Mummy deserted us and left us with all those strangers, we've learned to keep our guard up. We have been warned not to talk to strangers; we've entrusted secrets even to friends and been deceived; we're by God not going to be hurt that way again. And so we learn to live—or partly live—with a kind of low-grade paranoia.

This lack of apparent reliability has never been so strong as it is in

3

our day. We're cramped in smaller spaces with more and more strangers. Everything the ads tell us to buy seems programmed to break down. The media bombard us incessantly with new possibilities being opened and old myths being exploded. We begin to suspect that what was true for our parents and supported their lives is no longer true. Everything is changing too fast, too bewilderingly: the bomb, the economy, the terrifying enormity of the universe. It is what Alvin Toffler calls "future shock: the shattering stress and disorientation that we induce in individuals by subjecting them to too much change in too short a time."

What can you trust? Is there nothing which is *un*-shifting? It is almost easier to zip up the old cocoon and ignore it all, to raise up our hedges and turn on our security alarms, and let the rest of the world go by.

The trouble is that we were not made to hide in cocoons; it is against our nature. We were made to reach out: to know and to love and to grow. And when we act in defiance of our nature, we are—unavoidably—miserable.

Therefore, I would like to ask you, as it were, to clear the decks, to wipe out all pre-conceptions, to turn off all the contradictory voices inside your head—to become skeptical—and start over from scratch: how do we know—anything?

Epistemology

Epistemology is the study of the validity of knowledge and opinions. It comes from the Greek word *pistis,* which means "trust," and it examines the grounds on which one can say, "That statement or belief is trust*worthy.*" For the Greeks, who were highly speculative, a statement was trustworthy because it was logical and reasonable in itself and consistent with other already tested truths. It is what we will call in this book "notional knowledge"; it's "head-trip stuff."

For the Hebrews, who were highly inter-personal, a statement was trustworthy because the speaker had proven himself or herself trustworthy. Their word for trust was *'āman,* as in "Amen (truly)." It means "to be firm" or "to be solid." The Hebrew word for "know" is the same word used for sexual intercourse, the removal of all barriers. It is less speculative and more intuitive, as when the two disciples on the road to Emmaus after the resurrection "knew" Jesus "in the breaking of the bread." It is what we will call in this book "real or experiential knowledge."

To discover the truth of God—or any truth—we need both notional and real knowledge.

Knowing, loving and growing all require risk, trust, an act of faith—in ourselves and the power of our minds to contact and formulate the truth, and in the objects we study, and in the people who advise us, teach us, and test our ideas. Since we were made to know, love, and grow, the first nine chapters of this book will start right there, at rock bottom: what we can trust without any reasonable doubt. We will start with epistemology. In a sense, we will be going over the field with mine detectors before we start building a house on it. We will examine how we know what is true and the obstacles within ourselves and outside ourselves which deflect us from a clear vision of the truth and, by that very fact, twist our opinions out of congruence with reality, with things as they are.

Faith in God—or in anybody or anything—is a risk. But let it be a *calculated* risk.

Inner Obstacles to Truth

Where Do Opinions Start?

"My opinion's as good as anyone else's!"
Sez who?

A lot of years ago, I was teaching English to a class of eleventh graders, and the challenge for the day was a little poem called "Wind and Silver":

Greatly shining
The Autumn moon floats in the thin sky
And the fishponds shake their backs
      and flash their dragon scales
As she passes over them.
        —Amy Lowell (1874–1925)

Dutifully, I pointed out that it was just an image—a plain, straightforward little picture of ponds flickering in the moonlight. No deep symbols, just a picture. As Freud used to say, "Sometimes a cigar is just a cigar." But a lad over by the windows put up his hand.

"I have another interpretation," he said.

"Okay," I replied, a bit warily, "as long as you can back it up with evidence from the poem."

"I think it's about a U–2 flight over Red China."

The bright kids in the class whipped their heads quizzically in his direction. The rest continued to doodle and daydream. I tried to wrestle my gape into a benign smile. "Where's the evidence from the poem, Jerry?"

"It says 'dragon scales,' " he quoted, with indisputable accuracy and impregnable self-assurance.

"Wait a minute. You've taken two words, completely out of context—all the rest of the poem—and just written your own poem."

"That's your opinion," he replied, stoutly.

My neurons tried to untangle themselves; my jaw was beginning to grind a bit. "Well," I smirked smugly, "why couldn't it be a U–2 flight over medieval England. Apparently they had dragons back then, too."

I had him, boxed in and helpless. I knew it. But he said, "That's your opinion."

At that juncture, my fillings were starting to fuse, but I fought to keep a wise and teacherly smile. "Look at the bottom of the poem, Jer. See? It says 'Amy Lowell (1874–1925).' The poet died long before there were U–2's; Red China didn't even exist when she wrote the poem!"

He folded his arms, and set his own jaw, and said, "That's your opinion."

As I recall, several hefty football players had to pry my fingers from around Jerry's throat.

Opinions are only as good as the evidence that backs them up. And evidence comes *to* us from the object in question; we don't manufacture the evidence out of our imaginations, in defiance of the object. The alcoholic who is utterly convinced that pink elephants are romping around his bed is wrong. They're not there. Nor is the truth of an opinion established by majority vote; contrary to cliché, fifty million Frenchmen *can* be wrong. If you had taken a vote four hundred years ago about the shape of the earth, the flat-earth people would have won hands down. But the earth didn't flatten itself out to conform to their overwhelmingly unanimous opinion. Columbus discovered America not because he wanted to but because it was there. *It* got in *his* way. No matter how strong your belief or opinion, it can't make something real cease to exist.

At times, that's a bit hard to swallow. "I've got a right to my own opinion!" True, but you don't have an automatic right that your opinion be respected unless you've got evidence—weightier than just some vague "feeling"—to back it up. Bigots are of the opinion that all blacks, Jews, and Catholics are subversives or worse. But they're wrong. Students like Jerry are constantly asking teachers, "Do you want *your* interpretation or what we really think?" There's only one answer to that: does the evidence support any other interpretation? If so, then we do have two legitimate interpretations; if not, we're stuck with mine. Whenever I hear a rumor, like "Didja hear that the Assistant Principal battered Donny Driscoll to a pulp and sent him to the hospital?" my first question is always: "Were you there?"

Knowing anything is a humbling experience; we have to be vulnerable to the object. We don't make reality, i.e., the truth; we respond to it.

Distortion

When we're talking about first-hand knowledge—the beginning of an opinion—we have to begin with the senses. The thing—a tree, for instance—comes *to* us; we don't put it out there. Then the mind, in an almost instantaneous assembly line, processes the incoming data: categorizing it with other members of its class, evaluating the knowledge according to our own particular priorities at the time, putting it into words. In unique sightings, like encountering a pink elephant or a unicorn, it's rather wise also to check the object again and, if possible, see if anyone else sees the same thing.

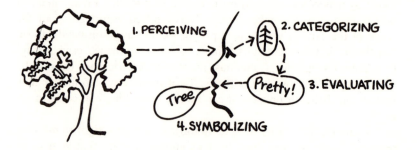

Distortion can occur at any one or all of those stages and, as a result, what comes out (the opinion) is nowhere near capturing what went in (the object).

Perceiving

On page 102 of this book there is a picture. Without looking at the questions below, turn to it and look at it for a count of ten. Then come back and see how many of the questions you can answer.

1. Discounting the tree itself, how many separate items were there on the tree?

2. How many non-living things can you recall?

3. What numbers were on the sides of the dice facing the viewer?

4. What was the least complex item in the picture?

5. There were three pairs of the same items? What were they?

6. How many birds were in the tree?

7. In the broadest sense of the word "animal," how many were in the tree?

8. How many were male?

9. How many were female?

10. What are the artist's initials?

At an accident, not too many people are accurate witnesses. We don't see most of what's there, simply because, as the event is occurring, we aren't aware that we're going to be questioned about it. Then, when the questions come, we hate to appear foolish or indecisive—much less honestly ignorant, so we often jump to conclusions on insufficient evidence. However, if the incoming data is very skimpy or inaccurate, the outgoing opinion will be worthless—like using the wrong sign at the very first step of an algebra problem.

Much of the reason that we don't see or hear what's there is also attributable to a kind of "protective disinterest." At every instant we're bombarded by skatey-eight zillion stimuli, and it's absolutely impossible to take in more than a tiny portion of them without burning out our mental circuits. Walking along a downtown street or even along the school corridor, I brush by hundreds of human beings, each of whom has a face and a name and dreams and problems, but I can't possibly perceive more than a few of them, even if I wanted to. Similarly, around about junior year high school, religious education students start moaning, "We *heard* all that before!" My response is, "Okay! If you've really heard it all before, let's have a pre-test." Groans, cries of "Unfair!" I wouldn't be self-destructive enough to say, "Take out a piece of paper and write down everything I said in the last five minutes!"

What's more, we're limited by what we're *ready* to see and hear. Sometimes we skew the actual evidence so that it "says" what we want it to say. For instance, one day when I first began teaching theology, the rector of the school hauled me rather summarily onto the carpet and growled, "What the hell's this I hear—you teach there's no such thing as mortal sin?" I gaped. "I never taught that because I don't believe it." But he replied, "I've had two different parents call up and say you told their kids today there's no mortal sin." Luckily, I had my class notes with me. What I'd actually said was: "I find it difficult to understand [*not* I refuse to accept] how *many* people *frequently* in their lives can *perfectly* fulfill the three requirements for mortal sin."

What had happened? All the qualifiers had dropped out. What those two (or more!) students had heard was the topic of mortal sin and some vaguely apprehended negatives and then *assumed* I'd said mortal sin didn't exist. Why? Because that's what they *wanted* to hear some priest say. As Fr. John Courtney Murray used to tell us in class, "I don't say what I say. I say what you hear."

Nor is this just a matter of being picky-picky. Take the case of abortion. A large number of people *assert* that the fetus is merely tissue, as much a part of the mother as her own appendix. Therefore, it can be removed with no more worry than any other justifiable operation. But how do they *know*? On what evidence is their opinion about this entity's non-humanity based? It's the product of two human cells; if you leave it alone, you don't expect to get a porcupine or a zebra in nine months. What is the fetus? Only the fetus can tell you, and it's not talking. Nor is there any litmus-paper test to tell when humanity "clicks on."

Then why the widely accepted opinion that abortion is not homicide? Because no one—not even the most ardent pro-lifer—wants any woman to suffer the torment of an unwanted pregnancy if there is any moral alternative. We don't *want* the fetus to be human—especially when the woman already has more children than she can care for properly, when it's the result of rape or incest, when there is a chance—or a certainty—that the child will be maimed or retarded. But the question remains: no matter what the situation, what are you killing when you kill a fetus?

Nor is the root question whether the operation itself is a competent one, done in a well-equipped hospital by well-trained staff, or an unspeakable butchery done in some back street by a criminal. If the object—the fetus—is indeed human, that question becomes: do you want your child murdered by a competent hit man or by a bumbling amateur?

The truth comes to us, sometimes painfully. But it remains the truth despite our pain or our denials or our assertions to the contrary.

In Robert Heinlein's futuristic novel *Stranger in a Strange Land,* the society has trained a class called "Fair Witnesses," whose function is to keep declarations strictly to the verifiable facts. One Fair Witness is asked, "What color is that house on top of the hill?" Her reply is, "The two sides I can see appear to be a shade of white." Pretty cautious, but her later judgments aren't going to be distorted by faulty original data.

The biggest possibility of distortion and closed-mindedness at this stage comes from using "is" when we mean only "seems." No one would ever get away with it in math, because in math "is" always means = , while "seems" always means ∼.

Our opinions of objective reality will never be comprehensive. Part of the object will always elude even the most careful study and definition, and therefore at best our knowledge of things will remain always slighty inadequate. All we can hope to do is train ourselves to see and hear as carefully as we can, especially in very important issues—like the nature of fetuses, like the motivations of the people we meet, like the questions about God.

Categorizing

It's the natural function of the mind, once it has taken in new data, to link things together. We try to put things under common heads: tree, box, jerk. When we play cards, most people arrange their cards in suits or pairs or some kind of related cluster. It's easier to handle multiplicity that way.

On the same basis, a child sees Lassie and is told Lassie is a dog. Then she sees Snoopy. They're different, but similar enough to go into the same general category for the time being. Then she meets chihuahuas and dachshunds and St. Bernards, and a pattern begins to emerge. Size is not particularly important or the precise shape, or the amount of hair, or the length of the ears, but each one fits into the same complex pattern of sights, sounds, and smells.

Again, distortion can creep into one's judgment if we categorize too quickly and bring home the nice black kitty with the pretty white stripe. But shoddiness in categorizing can be far more dangerous than that. We see a shabbily dressed woman reel down the street and collapse. Drunk, of course, so we pass by. But she could be an epileptic or a diabetic, and stopping could have saved her life. We see a thin, pale boy with a kind of mincey, twitchy walk. "Fag!" Based on what evidence? And the results on the young man's life can be as devastating as death.

In the same way, some scientists say, rather incautiously, that human beings are nothing more than a complex collection of chemicals and electricity or merely a more highly evolved species of animal. If that is the truth, however, one cannot criticize extermination camps, bombing civilian populations or any other homicide. You cannot commit a crime against a bag of chemicals or a high level ape. The same is true of over-quickly categorizing a fetus as mere "tissue."

Reality always eludes our categories, which is why after ten thousand years of trying, men and women are still probing the essence of love, aggression, individuality, society, and everything else.

Our craving for the security of certitude leads us to set up nice, clean, clearly labeled bins so that we can sort one reality from another. No problem there, yet. For one thing, that's the way our minds work; for another, there are indeed such clear similarities between one furry canine quadruped and another that we can legitimately put them in the "Dog" bin as a sub-grouping of the larger "Animal" bin. It helps us deal with our multi-faceted lives more easily and efficiently.

But there is a very real danger of oversimplification here, which can lead to injustice to the truth—and to persons. The "Egghead" and "Jock" bins, for instance, are not mutually exclusive. Nor are "Liberal" and "Conservative." Nor "Mortal (Deadly)" and "Venial (Trivial)." In such cases, the truth can't be so neatly divided up into bins; it is not a case of either/or but rather a case of more/less. There is a whole range of more and less "Serious" sins, for instance, which are not deadly to one's relationship to God and yet which are in no sense trivial either. In such cases, it is far more honest to think in terms of a *spectrum* between two extremes rather than two tidy bins in which greys are forced into becoming *either* black *or* white—again, in defiance of the truth. We will be speaking a great deal about spectrums in the course of these pages.

Again, one cannot hope to have absolute accuracy in categorizing many of the most important realities of our lives. We can hope only to judge them as carefully as possible and to guard our statements with careful qualifications: "it seems," "more rather than less," "close to," and so forth.

Evaluating

Once we've apprehended and categorized some new reality, we make a judgment about it according to our own particular list of priorities: interesting, neutral, dull; desirable, ho-hum, detestable; and so on.

Sometimes, because of faulty awareness or understanding in the first two stages, we misvalue the item. An ape, for example, pawing through a trash can, will sniff a $1000 bill and throw it away in favor of a verminous banana. Other times, the value judgment is conditioned by our need at the moment. A man stumbling out of the desert can choose between a voluptuous harem girl or the village well. What might seem irresistibly valuable at one time is not at another. More painfully, as we will see more fully in the next chapter, our needs and self-protectiveness very often give realities a value they don't objectively possess. An alcoholic thinks liquor is good for his depression; a boy or girl calls sex "making love" when it is really an act of selfishness; abortion is judged moral simply because carrying the child nine months is too shameful to consider doing otherwise.

Mention might be made here again of religious education. Unfortunately, even today, youngsters in grade school are given answers to problems which are not yet real to them (mortal sin, dirty thoughts, world hunger); they are forced to ingest information which is quite often utterly meaningless (the Trinity, the Virgin Birth, the dual nature of Christ). Like the ape sniffing the seemingly valueless $1000 bill, they drop it in the nearest waste basket or store it up in the attics of their minds like some junky piece of furniture bequeathed by a dotty old relative. Later, when the problems do become real or the information might be valuable, it is either long lost or just "that old stuff." But before getting rid of all that old stuff in the attic, it might be wise to give it one

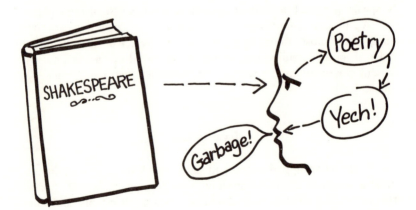

more honest appraisal. That old piece of junk from Aunt Fanny could be a priceless antique.

Once more, our value judgments will be inadequate, always. Again, one hopes to judge anyone or anything as honestly and fairly as he or she can. It takes a bit more time and effort, but one gets burned far less. One trustworthy norm is to place a reality squarely in front of the reality of death. Samuel Johnson once said that when a man realizes he is about to be hanged, it concentrates his wits most admirably. In the face of death, one's acne or the missed raise in pay or the casual thoughtlessness of one's children or siblings all dwindle down to their true perspective.

Symbolizing

"Oh, you know what I *mean!*"
No, I don't. I only know what you *say.*

In order to express a thing or category or value judgment—even to oneself—one has to use words or pictures or gestures or smoke signals or some other kind of symbol to focus and embody the idea. The great problem is to say exactly what you mean and mean exactly what you say.

Sometimes what's in our minds isn't at all reflected in what comes out of our mouths. Take a few examples:

This book stinks. [I don't really enjoy this book.]

She's a slut. [She seems pretty "loose" from what I can gather.]

Mass is a waste of time. [Nobody's convinced me it's worth it yet.]

Most people at Mass are phonies. [I'm looking for excuses not to go.]

I don't believe in God. [I'm confused about God. Help me.]

Words are tricky. That's why it's a good idea to become friends with a dictionary and the thesaurus. They have both *denotations,* the

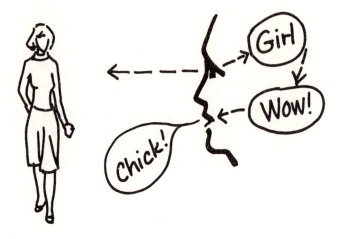

dictionary meaning(s), and *connotations,* the overtones those words ordinarily set up in a listener.

(1) *Denotations.* Words are chosen arbitrarily. There's nothing in
the picture "F-I-S-H" that mirrors the reality of ⊂⊃. You could
call it "GHOTI" if you like. But once you've chosen a label for a reality—and we all agree on it—you can't keep changing the code at whim.
It would be like changing your name every day. Maybe you think that's
a restriction on your freedom, but that's the way it is. You can write: "I
except your gift." Maybe you *mean* "I accept your gift," but don't expect to receive it. The word you used means: omit, cut out, reject.

People call themselves "lazy" when they really mean they're un-
motivated; they see no reason to do what they're expected to do. But if I
told a self-styled "lazy" boy there was a porno movie in the next room,
somehow he'd muster enough energy to overcome his supposed inertia.
A mother can call her daughter "high-spirited" and "popular" when
she really means the girl is scatter-brained, undependable, and promis-
cuous. Newspapers will frequently call Latin American Catholics "left-
ist" (read: communist) when they really mean men and women who
stand up for human rights against repressive governments. A boy and
girl use the words "making love" for what is actually just animal cou-
pling. Preachers condemn "pride in oneself" (which is a good thing)
when what they really mean is arrogance.

It makes a difference. Later, we will see a lot of descriptions of the "God" people believe in which, if "it" existed, would be no God at all.

(2) *Connotations.* Frequently, we use words which set up misleading overtones. "Average" and "mediocre" have the same denotation, but one is a neutral term and the other is loaded. Ads play on connotations all the time. (How can a car be "sexy"?) When you hear that Jesus was "meek and mild," what reality does that bring up in your mind: "prissy"? or "gentle"? or "unruffled"?

If you call somebody "my chick," you'll treat her that way. If generals use the word "casualties" when they mean maimed and dead human beings, they can afford to be more callous. When a "pacification team" obliterates a village and its inhabitants in order to "secure" it, the process sounds almost noble. If you call a fetus "it" (because its sex has not yet been determined), you find it easier to treat as an "it."

The words we use may be inadequate to the realities they stand for, but it makes a difference that we take care to make them as closely approximative—and fair—as we can. The person we're misleading, or kidding, is usually ourselves.

The first step toward wisdom is to call a thing by its right name.

Testing

When you were a baby, your father loomed like a giant over your crib. He *wasn't* really a giant, but he sure *looked* like one to you. Later, after sixteen or seventeen years of growing, you may even have been able to look down on your father, perhaps in more than one sense. Then he looked somewhat dwarfed in your eyes. But be careful. You were wrong about his stature before. Where does the truth lie? Not in your point of view, but in your father.

No matter how careful one has been in the process so far, it's wise to check and see if someone else has seen those flying saucers, too. More often than I'd like to admit, I've given an obnoxious student the benefit of the doubt for a couple of months; I've seen him on good days and bad, tried to probe around for some good points to balance off the mountain of negative evidence, and come to the seemingly unavoidable conclusion that he is, indeed, a total hemorrhoid.

But then, to my dismay, a student I admire happens to mention that the hemorrhoid has been a good, wise friend to him. Then I sit at a P.T.A. meeting and begin to see him through his parents' eyes. Then, the final blow, a fellow teacher comes up and says, "You know, that kid's terrified of you."

So much for my nice, secure, well-evidenced—one-sided—opinion.

To be fair—not only to the truth but to oneself—it really is wise to check one's opinions against others' before locking them in definitively. For instance, two young people who express their (very real) love for one another sexually can rightly claim that some outsider just "doesn't *really* understand" their situation. True, no outsider has the first-hand, inner experience of *this* situation. But the outsider very likely has been in a quite similar situation and—unlike the couple in question—has also experienced the *outcome* of that situation. Moreover, unlike the couple, he or she can look at the present relationship from a more objective, less prejudiced point of view. Quite likely what seems like a negative factor in the outsider (a cool, dispassionate, almost impersonal judgment) might well balance, laudably, the couple's own too warm, too tightly focused opinion of the wisdom of their sexual expression of their love.

The same is true of the God questions. Many people are shy about sharing their opinions about God. "That's too personal." Nor are they overly eager to ask anyone else's opinion. The first version of this text had a question for the notebook which asked students: "What does God look like from your parents' point of view? How do you know? If you've never asked them, try it tonight—without interrupting or arguing, just trying to find out what they think. If you can't bring yourself to ask them, can you say why it is too difficult?" Of the two thousand young men I taught over a dozen years, about a third of them preferred to guess; ten or fifteen a year left that page of the notebook completely blank. One can only guess why, but the ones who did guess said things like "it'd only be a hassle . . . we don't talk about those things . . . they'd think I was crazy."

And yet, if this question is as fundamental to one's ultimate value as I've made it out to be, if commitment for or against God should affect one's entire life, then surely one's opinion on the subject should be worth the effort of checking it against the opinion of as many others as one can find, even if they happen to be the two people you believe you know best.

Again, the truth is not a matter of vote. The existence of God isn't going to be proved conclusively by the "fact" that "everybody says" God exists. All one can hope for is that one's own carefully evidenced opinion on the God questions is *supported* or *balanced* (not proved) by the similar—and dissimilar—conclusions of others. That latter point is important. It's unwise, and unfair to the truth and to yourself, to check your opinion only with those people and books that agree with you. In every case, whether it's a judgment about persons, or morality, or buying a house, or worshiping God, it's worth the effort to study as open-mindedly as possible the reasons of people who violently disagree with your own opinion. Most reasoned opinions have at the very least a grain of legitimate truth in them; there have been genius unbelievers and genius believers, and in my own life nothing served more to strengthen my own commitment to belief—although it was a harrowing experience—than honestly entertaining the possibility that the atheists were right.

Opinion is an imperfect grasp of truth, and a wise man or woman spends a lifetime honing and fine-tuning and at times even rejecting opinions. But that is what it means to be fully human. Neither apes nor computers experience confusion too often; only human beings do. Instead of black-and-white, single-track certitudes, one has to get used to a world of multiple causes, to an imperfect grasp of data, to tentative conclusions and solutions which are certainly closer to the truth this time but which always leave more to discover. A high degree of probability is the best one can get.

Questions for the Notebook

Page 1. Is it fair to say, in your own particular case, that you still have a fifth-grader's view of God? If it is unfair, when was the last time you took a significant step forward in your relationship with God (remembering that one's image of a person is not the same as one's relationship with him or her)? If it is a fair picture, why has your image of God stayed where it was ten years ago?

Page 2. What kind of being is God from your parents'/spouse's point of view? If one is willing, just have one write the answer for himself or herself. If you can't ask, can you say why it's so difficult?

A Prayer

God, Father of Light, help me to see things as they are, not as I'd like them to be, not as people tell me they are. Teach me to be humble before the Truth. Help me to be more alive, more aware, more willing to be honest and fair in my judgments of all you have made. Amen.

Truth Blindness

They know nothing, understand nothing. Their eyes are shut to all seeing, their hearts to reason. A man who hankers after ashes has a deluded heart and is led astray. He

will never free his soul to say, "What I have
in my hands is a lie."
                                        —*Isaiah 44:18, 20*

You are free only when you see.

In the last chapter we saw that that isn't exactly as easy as it seems: perceiving that the object is *as* it is, categorizing it without pre-judgment, evaluating it without self-protectiveness, symbolizing it without hedging, sharing it with more than only those who agree with you.

Critics of the Church enjoy reminding us how infuriatingly closed-minded the Church has been to such daring minds as Galileo and Darwin and Freud, who broke open our horizons and changed our lives. And yet we ourselves, all of us, are just as repressive of new ideas. How many people "have time" to read challenging books once they've begun a career? How eager were they to read even when they were in school? How angry do they get when they're told, "Oh, all that's changed"?

Why that reluctance to open new questions or to reopen old ones? Because often unpleasant new discoveries (like Vatican II for some, like the Vietnam War for others) demand that we face the wrenching effort of completely rethinking "settled" viewpoints—and sometimes even of reorienting the whole future direction of our lives and values.

That process is called *conversion,* and it can more easily be avoided than faced squarely. "Don't bother me with facts; my mind's already made up." You can't be forced to believe what you won't allow yourself to believe. The less you know, the more certain you can be; the less you know, the safer you are from discomforting truth—and growth.

There are none so blind as those who will not see. That's a cliché we all accept—in others. For all our claims to open-mindedness, though, there are still people we can't abide no matter how hard those people try to be acceptable to us. We still break our necks to fit in, even with people whose values we secretly detest. We still blind ourselves to joy and cling to self-pity. We still stubbornly zip ourselves into our comfy cocoons and deny that the truth is the truth.

This chapter will cover a rather doleful (but perhaps familiar) list of manifestations of truth blindness, though all of them, I believe, grow from the same poisonous root: fear. The list is by no means exhaustive, but you may find one or two of them to be mirrors in which a truth blindness in yourself is reflected. If so, the mirror deserves to be smashed so that you can be free to see and do the truth.

Prejudice

"Hath not a Jew eyes? . . . if you tickle us, do we not laugh?
and if you wrong us, shall we not revenge?"
—*The Merchant of Venice, III, 1*

If this version of the book lasts another dozen years, I imagine Archie Bunker—or the memory of him—will still be around, too. If not, there will surely still be bigots aplenty from whom to draw a profile of prejudice. A bigot is a man or woman with unbreakably strong opinions, but opinions which are based on little or no real, first-hand knowledge and precious little reasoning. The bigot sees reality through pre-fabricated filters: no intelligent black, no generous Jew, no broad-minded Catholic can penetrate those barriers. Therefore the comforting stereotype can never be challenged.

We all feel somewhat condescending toward Archie Bunker and other bigots. They're so laughably sure of their prejudices, whereas we pride ourselves on generally living and letting live. However, in the interests of absolute honesty at least with oneself, are there really not a few "types" for whom I have no slightest whisper of fellow-feeling? What about fat, pimply girls with glasses who can't even dance? What about loud-mouthed know-it-all jocks? What about painfully shy people? What about homosexuals?

Are they persons—not just "objectively," but can I somehow, even from a distance, feel-with their pain? Do I sense their need for understanding—not my approval, merely my compassion for their loneliness? Have I ever bothered, as Atticus Finch suggests, to get into their shoes and walk around in them for a while to discover what makes them what they are? Am I, in a word, a Christian in their regard?

One afternoon after play rehearsal, I was sitting out on the soccer field watching the team practice, and one of the senior players who had twisted his knee shared the empty bench with me. I was troubled by the

fact that someone had told me that afternoon that a lot of the seniors really disliked the boy who had the lead in the play. I was puzzled; he seemed like a terrific kid to me. So I asked the sidelined soccer player if it was true. Without a second's hesitation to think it over, and with disarming forthrightness, he said, "Oh, yeah. He's a _____."

I was a bit taken aback by the quick and brutal offhandedness of the remark, so I said, "But what does that mean? I mean I *know* what a _____ is, but why is he one?"

With the same infuriating indifference, he answered, "He just is. He's been a _____ since sophomore year."

"But can't somebody *change* in two years?"

"I dunno. I haven't talked with him in two years."

Ah, the power we have! That soccer player and his pals would never dream of committing actual murder, and yet—as far as they were concerned—that boy they disliked was "dead." They'd negated another human being, condemned him to death with no hope of reprieve.

What would it cost to sit down at lunch with the _____ and find out if he—and I—have changed, or with the fat pimply girl with glasses, or with the boy who you know, even without asking, was the first one hit in the grade school dodgeball games? What would it cost to invite them to your next big party?

> Jesus said to his host, "When you have a party, invite the poor, the crippled, the lame, the blind. You are fortunate that they cannot pay you back, because repayment will be made to you when the virtuous rise again" (Luke 14:13–14).

We have the power to kill, and we have the power to give life. But we often prefer to blind ourselves to our power, and thus impoverish our lives. The nurds and creeps and outsiders are not the only victims of our cruelty.

Herd Need

Adolescence can be a painfully lonely time. (So can adulthood.) Your body has become unfamiliar and embarrassing; your parents and siblings seem to have been created with the sole purpose of ruining your life; you are smothered in other people's unfair expectations. In a kind of perverse paradox, everybody seems to be staring at you all the time, and yet nobody pays you the slightest bit of the attention you deserve.

There is a need to hide in the herd. But the group gives more than a place of refuge. It's a collection of people who share the same interests, the same unspoken fears, the same gripes. But more importantly, my "crowd" relieves me of the burden of thinking for myself. I never have to decide what kind of clothes to wear, who the acceptable people are, where I'm going Friday night.

It's perfectly natural—and healthy—for people to be attracted into groups: the football team, the poker club, the sorority, the parish, the garden club. We need the sense of belonging to an entity larger than our own skins, different and more variously enriching than the family we've known all our lives. The more talented members of the group spark hitherto unknown talents in us and challenge us to reach further than we'd thought ourselves able.

There's only one very real danger: cliques tend to grow exclusive. They start to define themselves not just as "us" but also as "not them."

In a sense, they can become a kind of organized prejudice. And this is not only painful to outsiders, it is also stifling and impoverishing to the insiders. There is no chance to be cross-fertilized by different ideas, no chance to be challenged to broader, richer, more varied horizons. The group can become one more set of blinders.

Every year at the school where I teach, the seniors have a kind of authorized skip day on one of the last Fridays of the spring term. They go to a park, play ball, cook hotdogs, drink beer—and talk. And every year, as predictable as graduation, they come back beaming: "God! I talked to So-and-So for the first time in four years. I always thought he was an idiot. But he's a great guy! I really gotta get to know him better."

Too late.

Protective Indifference

Nobody really forgets dentist appointments or filling out college applications. We merely choose to be unaware of them. If we ignore them, they'll get bored and go away.

We can shut out the whole world in the same way. Thirty years ago, before Our Town exploded and then imploded into Our Global Village, the human agonies came more or less one at a time; they were heart-rending but manageable. However, since the Electronic Eye took up residence in every living room and began to tyrannize over our time, the length and breadth and height and depth of man's inhumanity to man has become so enormous, so heart-breaking, so insupportable that, in order to hold onto our sanity, we have had to erect barriers of indifference. Perhaps it began when the first uncensored pictures began to come back from Vietnam, but now deaths on the news are no more real or arresting than deaths in a cowboy movie. The unrelenting dark glacier of human suffering became "inadmissible"—wars, famines, fires, urban degradation, drugs, battered children, and on, and on, and on. And always the atomic sword hanging by a hair over our heads. The only haven was in self-induced psychological denial and repression. As Eliot wrote more than once: humankind cannot stand too much reality.

Only a few hardy souls want to open themselves widely to the truths of human life. We'd prefer to drink and drive and not remember that we've heard of people who've killed themselves—and others—that way. We'd prefer to deny that we are capable of sinning, that our actions have consequences. All that guilt is so . . . stifling. We'd prefer not to comprehend that we, as individuals, occupy only an insignificant space on a bit of cinder floating in the endless cold of cosmic space. Better to pretend. Better to zip up a cocoon in which I loom very large. It's not the truth, but it's . . . comforting.

The difficulty with admitting all those truths is that it makes us very small, very vulnerable. We lose our protective "cool." We find ourselves in need of God.

But if you violate the truth—the way things are—the truth will sooner or later rise up and take its revenge. Count on it.

False Humility

At the opposite end of the spectrum from the arrogant blindness of indifference is the paralyzing blindness of humility.

There's only one Gold Medalist in any event; all the rest are merely different shades of loser; even the Silver and Bronze are also-rans. There's only one Prom Queen, one Top Salesman, one Most Popular. The rest of us are just, oh well, so-so.

Whenever I hear confessions, I usually end up by saying, "You're a good person, do you know that?" (After all, bad people don't go to confession; only good people do.) But the response—almost without exception—is something like: "Well, I try to be," or "Uh, I'm not *bad*," or "Oh, I dunno."

Don't expect such people to set the world on fire.

The cause is a fear of being—or at least a fear of being *considered*—proud. One has been told by parents and teachers and above all homilists that pride is a sin, and that good boys and girls do their damnedest to act like unprofitable servants. What's more to the point, we all have ample evidence of our indisputable mediocrity: report cards, College Board scores, blank dance cards. We didn't lead the Little League in batting average; we don't have cover girl complexions; we don't take the garbage out as soon as we're asked. All those mirrors can't be wrong, right?

There's a pernicious self-blinding there, a masochistic concentration almost exclusively on one's shortcomings, and all in the name of a virtue: humility. The trouble is: if you don't trust the vehicle, it's never going to take you (or us) anywhere.

You can change the world!

Right.

How many people vote? How many write a letter to an editor or a congressman? How many put up their hands in a class or a meeting? How many complain to the pastor about boring Masses? How many ever say, "Now wait a minute! You can't *do* that!" Oh, uh, I'm nobody.

All that's needed for the triumph of evil is that good men and women be silent.

Franklin Roosevelt once said, "No one is irreplaceable." He should have added: "But everyone is important." Who can tell that you might be the last straw, the one that broke the camel's back?

There are, of course, other forms of truth blindness than those we've considered here. There is, for example, the tunnel vision we adopt to defend our privilege, our position, our being spoiled—even in the face of glaring injustice to the exploited, But in my opinion, the most paralyzing and evil truth blindness of them all is false humility.

The Root: Fear of the Cost

To be truly open-minded means to be *both* unprejudiced *and* receptive—willing to consider new ideas, even those threatening to my own. In fact, in the best sense, being open-minded means going out in search of new ideas. It's not all that easy. Trying out a new idea is a threat, a risk. Often it's uncomfortable at first, like trying out a new pair of shoes. Often you begin to suspect that tinkering with this tiny new idea may well be pulling a thread that will unravel the whole fabric of your life. Often it's a matter of finding new and fresher ways to look at old facts you "settled" so long ago that they seem lifeless and dull—like, does God really exist? What's he really like? How can I really get to know?

Conversion means a shattering of comfortable certitudes *in order* to open oneself to wider, more enriching horizons. But we all have an understandable resistance to conversion. There's no question that it is painful to leave the warm cocoon behind, to lose something good in the hope of something better. It happened to Abraham when he was called from the security of Ur to discover the Promised Land. It happened to Moses when, on the way back to the Land, his people moaned, "Were there no graves in Egypt that you had to lead us out into this wilderness?" It would have been far easier for Jesus, and the apostles, and generations of missionaries to stay where they were and mind their own business. It would have been far easier for Lincoln and Harriet Tubman and Martin Luther King to settle for things as they were. It would have been far easier for Galileo and Darwin and Freud never to have published what the world would demand they defend.

But something dies in a man or woman who turns from the truth. Blinding oneself to the truth is a violation of one's human nature, because we—of all the inhabitants of the earth—were made to *know*. To deny that hunger, or to palliate it with comforting illusions, is to live a life far smaller than the one to which we were invited. The late actress Rosalind Russell put it about as well as anybody could: "Life's a banquet, and most poor bastards are starving to death."

An open mind, surely, is a terrible risk. It means being vulnerable to the truth, no matter into what new and precarious roads it leads us. It means making peace with uncertainty. It means leaving behind the dull security of the cocoon for the excitement of flight. But that's what we were born for.

Examining the God questions for oneself—for the first time or once again—is that kind of risk. It refuses to pre-judge the outcome by the people one thinks he finds in the Church or by the listlessness of its liturgies or by the apparent divergence of its doctrines. It refuses to hide in the herd and say, "Oh, well, *every*body believes that," or "*no*body believes that." It refuses to protect itself with dodges like, "Oh, we've heard all that before," or "I settled all that long ago." It refuses to defend inertia by denying that God would have any interest in somebody as insignificant as myself. It means, in a word, to be curious, and if you dare to reach for the heritage of your humanity, many people will think you very curious indeed.

Be assured, it will cost. Whichever way you decide the God questions, it will change your whole life. And not to decide *is* to decide.

Questions for the Notebook

Page 3. Think of one "outcast" in your year or office, someone you honestly do feel a twinge of compassion for but to whom you never really had the courage to reach out. (a) Without giving any names, describe him or her. (b) Concretely, today or tomorrow, what could you (and perhaps others) actually do to make him or her feel even a little more . . . welcome?

Page 4. Jesus warned us not to "hide your light under a bushel basket." Do you? In what concrete ways? Could anyone help you to trust yourself more?

A Prayer

God, my Father, there are things I'm afraid to see. You know them far better than I do. Help me to see them honestly, without bias, without fearing what others will think, without kidding myself. Help me toward the true self I was born to be. Amen.

Truth = The Natures of Things

"Truth?" said Pilate. "What is truth?"
—John 18:38

You can't treat a scorpion like a pal or gin like gingerale. Not for too long anyway. Whether you see it or not, or even if you purposely choose *not* to see it, both the scorpion and the gin have a stinger. And if you play around with either of them incautiously, you're inevitably going to get stung.

Whether you know it, or like it, or approve, or agree, that stinger *exists*. What's more, whether you know it, or like it, or approve, or agree, the *nature* of stingers is to inflict pain.

We have seen that our ideas of things will never be exact or exhaustive mirror-images of the things themselves. We can only hope they are as good as they can be for the moment. Previously, examining the way our minds work, we saw that incautiousness at any of the stages can skew opinions. Also examining tunnel vision and our defenses against what is really "out there," we saw that our reluctance can also skew opinions. In this chapter, we'll consider how you can "un-skew" opinions. When opinions differ, what is the test of which opinion is right?

The test of whether something really exists or what it's really like is, of course, the truth: what's out there. And yet most people, even on both sides of a completely contradictory question, honestly believe *they* have the truth and the other side is completely wrong. For instance, little Katy insists that Santa Claus exists; her older brother sneers that he doesn't. How do you find out who's right? Simple: buy a ski plane. Go and see. Similarly, Columbus swore that the world was, by nature round; his detractors sneered that if he sailed west he'd drop off the edge. How do you find out who's right? Simple: climb aboard the Santa Maria. Go and see.

Evidence

The answers to questions about the existence and natures of things comes from evidence. Anyone's opinions—no matter whose—are only as good as the evidence that backs them up. (And an act of faith is an *opinion,* based on evidence, to which one is committed.)

Evidence is what one knows about the object—in a courtroom, a lab, a classroom, an Off-Track Betting Parlor. And there are two kinds of knowledge: (1) *Real* knowledge is first-hand, experiential, and therefore certain. I have no need of logical proof or witnesses to the fact that my hair is graying a bit faster than I'd wanted it to. (2) *Notional* knowledge is second-hand, academic, and therefore not certain but probable. I'd be taking the word of so-called experts—chemists and ad men—that

Grecian Formula would not make my hair look like a circus clown's if I used it.

(1) *Real Knowledge.* Seeing is *not* believing. Seeing is *knowing.*

(a) *First-hand observation* is what we were considering in the first chapter. I know, for instance that I exist; I know that the desk I'm writing on is (or at least seems) oak-solid. I don't need anyone to come in periodically and reassure me I'm here, nor would I have a tough time convincing anyone else I'm here. Simply bop him in the nose; evidence enough.

However, the alcoholic who claims he talks to a giant white rabbit or the husband who tells his wife there's a unicorn in the garden eating a lily makes the same claim: first-hand evidence. But no one else can have it; one eyewitness is pretty slim.

(b) *Common sense* tells me that the corridor outside my room is still there, even if I don't have direct evidence of it at the moment. I never met you, most likely, but I'm certain beyond doubt that you had parents, one male, one female. I saw moon landings only on TV, but I'm confident they were real and not faked in some Hollywood studio. I know you can't get blood out of a turnip, that you can't have an effect greater than the complex of its causes.

(2) *Notional Knowledge.* There is a measure of faith here, with varying degrees of probability in each case.

(a) *Reason* is the process by which the mind moves, step-by-step— sometimes with a leap or two—from *certain* data (evidence) to a *probable* conclusion. Reasoning is not restricted to the science lab or to the math text. All of us use it every day, in highly complex ways, even without our being aware of its complexity.

Induction is a generalization (categorizing) from a fair number of typical examples to a conclusion about all members of that group: water freezes at 32°F; fire burns; green apples give you a bellyache. I'm confident by induction that what goes up must come down, that three martinis get me drunk, that because my friend has never betrayed me before she won't betray me now. Induction counts on a certain amount of observed regularity in the world.

Deduction is a process that moves in the opposite direction: from a generalization about a whole group to an application of that truth to a particular member of the group:

All humans will die;	Three martinis get me drunk;
Edna is human;	This is my fourth martini;
Edna will die.	Oh-oh!

The task is to show that this particular object or case is indeed a typical member of this group, e.g., this water will freeze at 32°F (*if* it isn't laced with antifreeze).

Analogy tries to explain something the listener doesn't understand *in terms of* things he or she does understand. For example, when a metal is heated, the molecules spread—like people spreading out in an overheated room; when the metal is chilled, the molecules huddle together "for warmth," and the size of the metal contracts. Is that the way it *is?* No, but that's what it's *like.* Jesus used this method all the time: "If you can't understand the Kingdom of God, it feels like being at a big party."

(b) *Testimony* gets a trifle shakier. One is depending on the generalization that most people tell the truth when they have no reason to deceive. Because of this, testimony always has to be accepted with a critical eye. When Chicken Little comes up and tells me the sky is falling, I tend to be somewhat dubious. Ads alone are proof enough that not everything in print is truthful or trustworthy.

Eyewitnesses, as we saw before, are not always accurate. Nonetheless, although I've never been to China or met the president, I trust that both of them exist and are, more or less, the way they are described. The more witnesses, the better. If a whole army of people tell me they've actually communicated with God, I may be skeptical, but I tend to believe them—even though I myself haven't had that same experience.

Expert opinion has an authority based on long experience, careful study, and the corroboration of fellow experts. I've never seen an atom; nonetheless, I'll deny the evidence of my own senses and affirm that the desk I'm writing on is not oak-solid after all but rather aswarm with galaxies upon galaxies of moving particles—and most of it is empty space. I do this as an act of *trust*—an act of faith in the lifetime reasoning (inductions and deductions) of physicists, who apparently have nothing to gain by conspiring to deceive me. One might say the same about saints and theologians.

One has to be careful, however, that the expert is talking *in his field* of expertise. There's no reason why I should automatically accept a football player's opinion about a breakfast food or a razor blade, or a theologian's opinion about physics, or an astronomer's opinion about religion. Moreover, even in the same field, two psychiatrists can appear as expert witnesses at a trial and hold absolutely contradictory opinions: sane and insane.

Consider, then, the quandary of *The Exorcist.* The existence of the symptoms was undeniable: levitation, talking in languages never learned, reading minds, moving objects without touching them. (This is true not only in a novel and movie; it's actually happened in real life.) But what was the *nature* of those phenomena? What caused them? Was the cause psychological? Physiological? Extra-terrestrial?

Consider, too, the quandary of the universe. It's undeniably there. But what caused it? There are only two possibilities: either some Mind intended it to exist and to exist in this way, or its existence and nature are the result of an infinite series of accidents.

Establishing Existence

When we were in the first year of the seminary, there was a very old lay brother in the infirmary who was rather a long way round the bend. Every night at dinner, he'd sit there glowering, arms folded high on his chest, refusing to eat because someone had put nuts and bolts in his food.

The only way we could keep the poor man from starving was actually to *put* real nuts and bolts in his food, carefully pick them one by one out of his mashed potatoes and peas, and say, "There, brother. They're all gone." Then he'd eat.

The first set of nuts and bolts actually existed in that old man's mind. But they didn't *exist.* Therefore, there are really two kinds of existence: a kind of *secondary* reality in the mind—which is dependent for its verification on a *primary* reality outside the mind.

On the one hand, ultraviolet rays and love and personality exist, even though we can't see them. We can only reason to their existence from their effects, which we can see. On the other hand, Santa Claus doesn't exist, even though little Katy believes in him with all her heart, chats amiably with him in a department store, and sees very tangible results of her belief around the tree on Christmas morning.

But there's a kind of unconscious arrogance in us that fights against that. We'd much rather be a touch more "in charge" of reality. It's still a bit hard to accept that reality doesn't move from room to room with me; the room I just left is somehow "less real" because it's ceased to be important to *me*. There's also the old conundrum: does a tree falling in the woods, when no human is around, make a noise? The same low-grade arrogance declares that a country wasn't properly "discovered" till some white European arrived there. On the contrary, even though it's rather humbling, that country existed before any human discovered it. Did dinosaurs once roam the earth? Of course. We've got all those fossil bones as evidence. But no human being ever saw a live dinosaur.

It's pretty clear that the existence of things doesn't depend on me. The existence of things may come from God, or it may come about through evolutionary accident, but it's certain that it didn't come from me. I wasn't there, for one thing. For another, things I want to keep around cease to exist, and things I want to get rid of keep hanging around. That's more than proof enough.

There are two important points here. First, the thing either exists or it doesn't; there are no in-between, sort-of realities. Second, my *awareness* doesn't make a reality exist (Katy and Santa Claus), nor does my lack of awareness make a reality cease to exist (Columbus' critics and the New World).

REAL (TRUE) ≠ REAL (TRUE)-FOR-ME

One more absolutely essential point: first-hand evidence is not the only way of establishing a reality's existence. Sometimes reasoning is the best we can get; sometimes we have to accept the testimony of others, and both reasoning and testimony are probable, not certain; they are acts of faith to some degree.

No one has seen an atom; no one ever will; our eyes are just not fast enough. Scientists observe certain effects and determine that atoms must be "there" or else those effects couldn't occur; operating on that conclusion over the years, with predictable results, they can be reasonably sure that the atomic theory is tried and true.

Similarly, no one has ever seen love. It really exists, but you can't produce a bushel of it. You can't clamp an ammeter on somebody's head or heart and measure the degree of love or calibrate the amount of truth in the statement "I love you." Not all "receivers" need to be metallic to be trustworthy. Like the scientist, you can only observe certain effects and determine that love is "there" or else these effects couldn't occur; operating on that conclusion over the years, with predictable results, you can be reasonably sure that your friend's love is tried and true.

And what about God?

The Existence of God

The *idea* of God is certainly real in the mind, in that secondary sense. No existentialist or Hottentot or atheist would deny that. The question is whether God has any existence *outside* the mind.

Is God just another fantasy like Santa Claus, with reality only in your imagination, made up both to make you happier and get you to be good? This is where the atheist stands.

Is God just another impractical question like ghosts and Martians, one that can get you scared in your off-moments, but whose existence outside the mind is sheerly an academic discussion? One can live life happily and prosperously without him. The unquesting agnostic stands here. (Notice that I said "unquesting." This in no way includes the man or woman who is still sincerely searching.)

Is God actually "there"— as real (though not visible) as atoms and love? Is it possible that the problem is not with God but with our vision? The theist, regardless of his or her religion, stands here.

Establishing Natures

Freedom to do the truth depends on seeing the truth, the real natures of things. That truth is primarily in the object, but also secondarily (and at least slightly inadequately) in one's mind.

Take the example of ethical or moral behavior. The law does not make an action evil; it only makes the action illegal. A law forbidding me to hide Jews from the death squads does not make me evil when I hide them or good when I turn them over to be shot. Jews are human beings, no matter what any law says. Therefore, I must treat them as human beings, even though I'm shot myself for doing it.

The Constitution doesn't *give* me the rights to life, liberty, and the pursuit of happiness; it acknowledges that I have those rights—because I am a human being. I have those rights whether the Constitution chose to acknowledge them or not; as a human being, I have them even if I live in Siberia or El Salvador or South Africa, no matter what the accidental color of my skin or shape of my eyes or degree of my intelligence.

Nor do the Commandments make an act sinful. It was a sin for Cain to slay Abel, even though the Commandments weren't going to be written down for thousands of years. Murder, arson, rape—such actions were anti-human and therefore immoral long before the civil law made them punishable or the Judaic Commandments spelled them out. They were sinful because they violated the human nature not only of the victim but of the criminal. Anyone who robs me or burns me or rapes me lessens me as a human being by treating me as less than himself, and in so doing also lessens himself as a human being. He has turned me into a sheep and himself into a wolf. We're both de-graded.

Therefore, morality is not based on laws; laws are based on morality, and morality is based on human nature. You can use a human being as a paperweight, or as a guinea pig, or as an entree at dinner, but it's wrong simply because that is not what human beings are *for*. Whether one believes in God or not, an act is immoral *solely* because it is act against human *nature* in both the perpetrator and the victim.

Here, too, there is a real distinction between the objective evil of the act (because it is anti-human) and an individual's *awareness* of the nature of the act—or even of the nature of the human being. Just as babies are objectively male or female without their knowing it, so also murdering female babies is evil even if the Chinese acted otherwise in the last century, and mercy killing the retarded is evil even if the Nazis acted otherwise. Whether the child killer or the mercy killer subjectively acknowledges it or not, the victim has objectively lost something very real: his life. An evil thing has been done.

REAL (TRUE) ≠ REAL (TRUE)-FOR-ME

Therefore, it is simply idiotic to say: morality is "up to the individual." The individual does not make unicorns or atoms or death or humanity (morality) *exist,* and the individual does not dictate the *natures* of unicorns or atoms or death or humanity (morality). They come to us; we adapt to them. *Awareness* of morality may depend on the individual; he or she may be ignorant of it, or be self-blinded to it, but the existence and nature of morality doesn't vary from individual to individual. And again, if you violate the truth—the natures of things—the truth will eventually rise up and take its revenge. The house always wins.

And what about God?

The Nature of God

No one has seen an atom, but atoms exist whether we want to acknowledge them or not. And their natures—the composition of the nucleus, the number of electrons, the ways they interact—come *to* us. We may manipulate them, "tell them what to do," but only on *their* terms. We can't make them do things of which they're not capable, and we judge the nature of an atom by fiddling with it, and watching its effects, and reasoning to its nature from that.

Similarly, no one has seen God, but if he exists, he comes to us on *his* terms. We don't dictate his nature or his likes and dislikes any more than we dictate the nature of humanity or the personalities of our other friends. For one thing, he's the Host; he set up the party, supervised the decorations, invited each of us to attend, and—whether we like it or not—establishes the departure time when, for us, the party is over. None of us can complain that we have to leave the party. Who said we could come to the party in the first place?

What's more, we have no real right to criticize the accommodations at the party. "How could a good God set up a world where there are hurricanes and wars and deformed children?" If God exists, and if he set things up this way and set us in the middle of them, and if he gave us wits, apparently he wanted us to figure that out for ourselves.

We discover the nature of God just as we discover the nature of anything or anyone else: first-hand experience (praying), reasoning (theologizing: induction, deduction, analogy), testimony (Scriptures, lives of saints), and expert witnesses (theologians).

One final point. As we saw before, there is a difference between the object itself (the primary reality) and our awareness of that object (the secondary reality). Religions all over the world and down the ages have perceived God in many different ways and through the prisms of their own cultures and times: very distant and aloof, very warm and near, unspeakably holy, tenderly merciful, and so on. The pagan aborigine has one vantage point, the Buddhist another; the speculative theologian sees him though his particular eyes, and the old charwoman through hers. But it is the same God.

What's more, each of those vantage points has a truth which can balance and enrich my own. Each of those perceptions of God—like all human perceptions—is inadequate to the reality it describes. But that does not diminish God. If he exists, he made us to find him. That's what we're for.

Questions for the Notebook

Page 5. Who or what do you honestly think God is? — That's a tough question, one for which you'll have to settle for an imperfect answer. But give it an honest try.

Page 6. At this moment, what *evidence* do you have to back up your belief or disbelief in God: first-hand experience, common sense, reason, testimony?

A Prayer

God, if you are out there—or in here—or wherever, give me some kind of sign, some kind of realization of your presence. At this time of my life, when everything is changing, shifting into new perspectives, give me a little help, Lord, that I may see. Amen.

Whom Do We Seek?

It is a terrible thing to fall into the hands of
the living God.

—*Dorothy Day*

Before leaving behind the obstacles inside ourselves to seeing truth, and
moving on to the obstacles outside ourselves—not only to seeing truth
but even desiring to look—it is well to clarify the three questions we're
asking, just so we don't miss one another in the dark: does God exist
(existence outside the mind), what is he like (nature outside individual
or cultural limits of vision), how can we know (real and notional knowledge)?

Does God Exist and How Can We Know?

We begin with one incontrovertible fact: *either* God exists outside
the mind, *or* he doesn't. There is no other alternative; you can't "sort
of" exist, any more than you can be "sort of" pregnant or "sort of"
dead.

However, there are four—and only four—possible *opinions* about
that set of alternatives:

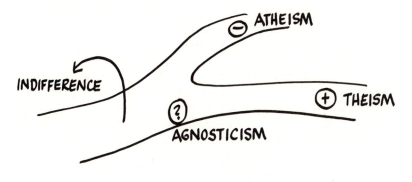

Indifference: for a whole variety of reasons, a decision on the alternatives is simply not worth the effort.

Agnosticism (Gr. *a-gnosis* = not-knowing): a decision on the alternatives seems honestly impossible, because neither set of arguments seems to outweigh the other, and the question is too fundamentally important to judge lightly or on whim.

Atheism (Gr. *a-theos* = no-God): the evidence for the non-existence of God—or more likely the lack of sufficient and acceptable evidence to the contrary—leads to the definite choice of the negative alternative and a life lived accordingly. This is an act of faith—a reasoned opinion, not a certitude.

Theism (Gr. *theos* = God): the evidence for the existence of God is of such high probability that it outweighs arguments to the contrary and leads to a definite choice of the positive alternative and a life lived accordingly. This, too, is an act of faith—a reasoned opinion, not a certitude.

Indifference: "I can't really get excited about it."
It is my belief that all the other positions on the question of God's existence are honorable—except this one. To persons taking this "stance," the question simply is irrelevant compared to keeping busy, keeping up the pretenses, keeping up with the Joneses. It is not so much a denial of either alternative as an avoidance of the question altogether—or at least of its importance to human meaning. Since the level of evaluation depends on the previous steps of perceiving and categorizing the data, such blindness to the seriousness of this question is often attributable to some of the vision problems we saw previously.
In this category, I would lump most of the people I call "cocktail-party atheists and agnostics"—the sort drawn by a priest's collar at a social gathering, like some divine retribution for priestly partying: "Well, *dah*-ling, I'm *a*theist, you know. All that guilt is so *sick*-making!" At such moments, I must control the devil in my censorious and un-Christian tongue which yearns to growl, " 'Witless' would be closer to the truth." Take one of these Indifferents to the funeral of a seven-

teen-year-old, or seduce him or her into an afternoon of teaching the mentally retarded to dress themselves, or strand one of them in a foxhole at night under mortar fire. Then the alternatives would be less easily avoided or judged beneath consideration. Then the question becomes very real, because it becomes unavoidably real-to-them.

Thinking Agnosticism: Charles Darwin wrote: " . . . the whole subject is beyond the scope of man's intellect. . . . The mystery of the beginning of all things is insoluble for us, and I for one must be content to remain an Agnostic."

As we have seen, I can judge what Darwin means only from what he says. It seems he is saying that, if God does indeed exist, we can know absolutely nothing of him, not even from his effects in the artwork he (might have) created: the universe. He says that this inability springs not from any defect in God (if he exists), but from the inability of the human "intellect."

Were he alive, one might argue terms with Darwin on that last word. To my mind, there is a difference between the realities identified by the two words "intellect" and "intelligence," a difference we will return to frequently in these pages when we speak of "the human mind" and "the human spirit." Perhaps it is a distinction based merely on connotations personal to me, but "intellect" has always meant to me the power to manipulate data efficiently, cleanly, and without bias; it is associated with the very laudable processes of science, mathematics, grammar, and general academic precision. "Intelligence," on the other hand, has always meant to me a human power of greater scope and therefore of less precision as a word. It includes the powers of "intellect," but goes beyond them to apprehend realities which aren't testable by precise logic: "vision," art, literature, honor, love—and most especially "educated hunches." Love, for example is not rational. And yet it is not *ir*rational, like running amok, nor *non*-rational, like breathing. Like God in Darwin's statement, love is "beyond the scope of man's intellect"—but it is not totally beyond the scope of human intelligence.

My problems with the statements of thinking agnosticism focus around what seems to be the "least common denominator" agnostic stance: I can't believe what I'm not sure of. On the one hand, that statement is understandable when "believe" means an honest commitment of one's life, based on uncertain evidence. On the other hand, it seems to be a position taken only on the God questions but on no other fundamental and pressing questions of one's life.

For example I don't understand—in any but the vaguest way—my doctor's explanation that the cause of my shortness of breath is an occlusion of my heart valves. I have to take his or her word that the conclusion is justified. I haven't the knowledge to look at my own X-rays and come to a trustworthy judgment; nor do I know whether my doctors and their consultants all may have graduated last in their classes from medical school. And yet I will go through tests and operations—and hazard my very life—based on the doctor's *belief*—which I have no way of verifying with certitude, even with a second or third opinion.

For most of us, the same is true on questions of the government's economic theories which may endanger one's very livelihood, on nuclear increase/decrease which could endanger the life of the entire planet (either way), or on something as seemingly commonplace as two people making a life commitment (perhaps fifty years of living together) in marriage based on only a year or so of knowing one another.

Perhaps the most realistic stance on all these questions—including the God questions—is that:

It's difficult to believe what I'm not sure of.

A student wrote it well: "Oh, God, I wish I knew. Everything tells me he can't exist but, honest to God, I wish he did." But perhaps my favorite agnostic/atheist, Albert Camus, said it best: "He doesn't exist, the bastard." If God existed, everything would make sense. But the evidence is too inconclusive, Camus maintains; therefore, with iron logic, nothing makes sense.

This is not an ignoble stance, provided it doesn't devolve into the first "stance" of indifference or lapse into either atheism or theism from sheer fatigue.

Thinking Atheism: The thinking atheist's position is summed up quite well in the first sentence of Carl Sagan's book, *Cosmos:* "The Cosmos is all that is or ever was or ever will be." Later he writes, "By definition, nothing we can ever know *was* outside [the physical universe]." This seems, at least to me, somewhat arbitrary, especially from a man who pleads so eloquently for open-mindedness. "By definition," he says. Whose definition?

The "definition" is the presupposition of the scientific method: nothing can be asserted as existent or true unless its existence or truth can be verified by painstaking research in a lab. For science, that is a praiseworthy drawing-of-the-boundaries—for "intellect," but not necessarily for "intelligence." It seems, at least to me, to restrict human intelligence to solving problems, at which Dr. Sagan is extraordinarily gifted. But it seems to leave out of all human understanding other exclusively human modes of acting which less scientific folk associate with the human spirit. There is no place, as far as I can judge, for the very real difference between information and wisdom, between being interested and being moved, between shrewdness and love. Is it merely electrons traveling along his neurons that explain the almost palpable awe Dr. Sagan shows in his television program when he looks at the stars? I am left unconvinced.

Freud held that belief in God is illusion, a regression to the helplessness of childhood, a product of wish-fulfillment. Marx believed belief in God was the "opiate of the people, numbing their capacity for outrage" at the inhumanity of the exploitative upper classes and delaying the day of the great revolution; rather than rise up and shake off their chains, the poor submit to them as "the will of God."

Undoubtedly, these three men are geniuses in their fields. And yet my life seems to have dimensions *outside* the lab and classroom (Sagan), the bedroom (Freud), and the boardroom or union hall (Marx). What each says has a basis in experience and a logical completeness to it. But each seems too exclusive; each seems to leave out very real and important human experiences simply because such experiences don't fit their initial "definitions."

Thinking atheists are not naive. They realize that, logically, if there is no God, the universe is, literally, mindless—since God, if he existed, would have been precisely that "Mind behind it all." Therefore, the only "purposes" that things—and human beings—have are dictated by one's own particular needs and desires at the moment. Morality, for instance, is very definitely "up to the individual." Moreover, the closest thing to a deity is the *human* mind, and such atheist humanists often come close to deifying humankind, exaggerating the human capacity to control the universe through science and technology. One hears a watered-down version of this atheism in such assertions as, "Sooner or later, given enough time and government funding, we will have wiped out disease, old age, war, suffering, and death." I wish them luck. As I wrote those words, I had just finished writing a funeral homily for a twenty-year-old friend killed in a boating accident. Their utopian claims failed to impress me.

My most fundamental quarrel with atheism, however, is that its proponents *start* from the proposition that God *can't* exist. That seems highly anti-intellectual and closed-minded to me. No scientist sets out to test a theory by presuming it is false.

And yet they could be right, and I could be wrong. Only the evidence will justify the better of the two choices.

Thinking Theism: Sagan and other atheists rest their claims on the fact that an almost infinite series of accidents is sufficient to explain the existence of the universe and an intelligent humanity. I find that hard to accept, although I don't deny it's possible. I can see how accident can produce the endless *variety* of the universe, but I can't see how it could produce the *order* of the universe. Without a Mind behind it all, I can't comprehend how we could have the exquisite arrangement of the Periodic Table or the iron predictability of the laws of physics. How does one get *inevitability* out of an unpredictable series of *accidents?*

My belief is also based on more than reason. I truly believe I have experienced God. (All receivers need not be metallic in order to be trustworthy.) And I've tested my belief by living it out. Moreover, as with the atheist's, the thinking theist's belief is not naive. He or she is well aware not only of the arguments of the other alternative, but also of the "loopholes" in his or her own arguments. For instance, no one has ever *seen* God; like Thomas, our fingers itch for the chance to probe those nailholes. Most glaringly, there are all those arguments which begin, "How could a good God allow . . . ?" The theist's response can only be that, if there is no God, then there is *no one* to blame. No one has a purpose for human suffering.

To the reader, however, my arguments and experience are merely notional knowledge—testimony—and as such they are precarious. God's existence—or non-existence—cannot be established beyond all doubt. My experience of God could be no better than the experience of the man who saw a unicorn in the garden eating a lily.

What's God Like and How Can We Know?

God. The Supreme Being; the eternal and infinite Spirit, Creator and Sovereign of the universe.
—*Webster's New Collegiate Dictionary (Sixth Edition)*

Assuming the *possibility* God exists, what is he like? Whom are we seeking?

There is no question here of "proving" the specific nature of God as seen by Christians, or by Buddhists or Jews or Moslems or pagans. Rather we are seeking evidence about the entity who *underlies* all those varied perceptions of him. And there are two different aspects to that search: the first is God's *nature,* his role in the universe and in our lives; the second (on which the various religions differ more strikingly) is God's *personality,* his purposes in creating a flawed humanity, the things he cares about, his likes and dislikes.

This whole book is an attempt to probe all those questions, and it can't all be done here, on one page. For the moment, then, rather than answering those questions, let me *eliminate* some descriptions of God in order at least to narrow down the field of search. These are brief descriptions of a "god" by people who say they believe in him. But if their descriptions are accurate, then the God described above by the dictionary—the definition of God which both theists and atheists accept—does not exist.

Nature: False Gods

"God is a useful creation of humankind, a fantasy which gives our lives direction and purpose and keeps human beings in line."

"God is a feeling I get, like my conscience. It's a feeling that you have to do right and help mankind."

"God is an ideal, the personification of all those virtues human beings strive for but never achieve: power, peace, justice, love."

"God is 'the Force,' a non-personal essence of energy that powers the universe but makes no demands on us."

"God is human love, the summation of all the love in the world at any given time."

Whatever the five beings described above are, they are not what all human languages mean when they say "God," that is: a personal Being greater than all humankind on whom we depend for our existence and nature, not the other way around. The reason these descriptions of "God" are called atheistic is simple: each one of the beings described is *less than* a man or woman. Each of them is dependent on man for "its" existence and "its" nature. Whatever God is, he is not *less* than human.

God is either a *personal* Being—that is, with the intelligence to see goals and a will to choose among them—or he is an *impersonal* being (like "the Force") with neither intelligence nor will. If "it" is the latter, we need give it no more thought than we give the law of gravity. "It" is not God. If "God" is an impersonal being, there is no such thing as God.

Personality: Strange Gods

"God is there when I'm in need. Otherwise, when things are going okay, he doesn't intrude on my life."

"God is the Good Shepherd who pats our woolly heads and makes everything right again."

"God is a judge whose sole purpose is to condemn and forgive; we do not encounter him until we die."

"God is an infinitely distant and holy perfection. He is the reason behind things, but he is too pure to muddy himself in human life and its concerns."

"God is the pal at my elbow who goes along with anything I choose to do."

As we have seen, if God exists he comes *to* us on *his* terms. The "gods" described here do manifest some insight into the divinity, but each of them is one-faceted—in contradiction to the experience of a multi-faceted entity testified to by men and women of all religions. God does exist when I need him; he is, in a most humble way, my servant. But—logically—he must also exist when I don't need him; otherwise his existence would depend on me, like letting a genie out of a bottle. What's more, human experience of the entity we believe is God has shown him to be *not only* the merciful Good Shepherd *but also* the just Judge; he not only cherishes us, but he also challenges us. Further, human experience also testifies that he is not only infinitely distant from us in holiness but also closer to us than our own skins; he is not only "out there" but he is also "in here"—as Bonhoeffer describes him: "the beyond in our midst."

The "god" described in these statements seems also to have less life, less color, less enthusiasm than the Creator whose personality we can infer from his creation—just as one can "read" the differences in the personalities of El Greco and Van Gogh and Picasso from their paintings, even though we have never met them directly. From the varied order of the universe and from the logical and curious human intelligence which God created, we can find a far more exciting personage than the ones described above.

What seems to underlie these and other far *too* inadequate concepts of God is that they seem self-serving. They are attempts to "have their cake and eat it, too," to "play it both ways." On the one hand, they preserve the Mind behind everything—which even the atheist wishes were true, while on the other hand relieving the individual of any need to deal with him in any significant or consistent way—in worship and prayer, in assuming a personal responsibility for one's own actions and for stewardship over the earth. On the contrary, every "is" implies an "ought." If God *is* the source of our existence—and everything we enjoy because of our existing—he *ought* to have a very important and central and visible place in our everyday lives.

Unfortunately, as we will see more fully later, most of our ideas of the personality of God come from well-meaning but very third-rate propaganda: so-called Biblical movies, plaster statues and treacly art, over-simplified and childish explanations of God—even long into adulthood. We are too shy to ask one another about our profound and personal experiences of this Person who, if he exists, is the most important Person in the universe. There is a tragic and blind irony there. We are too "busy" with more pressing matters to probe for God's personality even in our own Scriptures—much less in the records of the experience of Buddhists or Moslems or Hindus with this overwhelming personality. We are also too busy to pray, to try to experience him directly.

In the end, the reason for this puzzling ignorance about a Person we claim to be at the root of our very existence may be the same reason we saw earlier at the root of all the truth blindnesses: fear of the cost.

Every "is" implies an "ought."

Questions for the Notebook

Page 7. Reread your description of God's nature and personality on p. 5. Considering what's been said in this chapter, is there anything significant you left out?

Page 8. If God exists, and if he is as important as believers—and unbelievers—describe him, one's belief or disbelief in him should be obvious in one's daily living and one's concrete, personal choices. How is your belief evidenced concretely in your life?

A Prayer

God, they tell me you're hiding in plain sight. But I don't see you. Help me at least to care, at least not to be so busy with what seems important that I ignore the one Person who gives "importance" its meaning. If you're there, help me take the time to pick you out from behind your disguises. Amen.

Outside Obstacles: Propaganda

Fools need no enemies.

—*Victor Steele*

The word "propaganda" has a very positive denotation, but a very neg-ative connotation. Its root meaning comes from the verb "to propa-gate," which is the positive act of increasing and multiplying, spreading a truth, publishing. But over the years, the word "propaganda" has been weighted with negative associations: misleading, deceiving, hoax-ing, brainwashing.

The same is true of the word "bias." On the one hand, it can mean something very positive: a commitment to a position after very long study. I was biased—brainwashed, if you will—by my parents to be po-lite, continent, truthful and kind. I am biased *against* people who are impolite, incontinent, untruthful, and nasty. On the other hand, "bi-ased" can mean all the closed-minded blindness we saw before when we spoke of bigotry: chauvinism, racism, intolerance. We are in danger once again of saying a word and having the exact opposite meaning heard.

The front page of the newspaper attempts, inadequately, to be as non-propagandistic as possible—though even the judgment on what sto-ries are newsworthy betrays some kind of "bias." The Opinion-Editorial pages, however, are very definitely written from a bias—a reasoned point of view for or against a particular issue.

In the next sections I would like to restrict the word "propagan-da," initially, to mean: a vehicle for embodying a view of life in concrete symbols and practices. Each view of life is "biased": it believes it has the answer to human fulfillment, what will make people truly happy. Each, unabashedly, touts its own merits and tries to cover up its shortcomings, while trumpeting its opposition's shortcomings and soft-pedaling its merits.

Political speeches, Army and Peace Corps recruitment posters, homilies and the Gospels, novels and songs and commercials, and every class you've ever sat through—all of them have been propaganda. Some propagate the truth; some propagate illusion and lies. The touchstone, as always, is the truth: is this a true picture of humanity? The point is that you can't escape propaganda or education. If you did, you'd have to start from scratch, trying to figure out everything for yourself, like Tarzan. However, one must be vigilant, if not at times downright skeptical. Everybody is trying to sell you his or her viewpoint. But the even more basic point is that you are free (if you're willing to pay the price of thinking for yourself) to accept what is true and reject what is false in these sales pitches—a choice based not on mere feelings or whims, nor on what's easier or more difficult, but on what is more consistent with what you believe human beings really are and what will really fulfill them.

There's a whole discordant chorus of voices today shouting for your attention, your approval, your allegiance. We will deal with only five major groupings: the System, the counter-culture, the Church, the school, and your parents and peers. They are separable, but they are also intermingled. Rock stars, the heroes of the counter-culture, become millionaire taxpayers; schools, which are intended to open minds, often serve only as sorting houses of workers for the System; the Church often pays less attention to cultivating the lilies of the field than it does on raising money; many parents' opinions are echoes of the System and many peers' opinions are lifted from TV.

It would be foolish and unfair to caricature each of these value systems as some kind of conspiracy to enslave your will. Each somehow reflects a real ingredient of human fulfillment: we need to work and eat (System), to relax and play (counter-culture), to worship and serve (Church), to stretch our minds and solve problems (school), to be with others and get along together (parents and peers).

The problem arises when one of these voices dominates to the exclusion or erosion of the other balancing values: one becomes a slave to the System and never relaxes, or a slave to the counter-culture and loses all ambition and spine, and so on. As long as the message is propaganda, no problem. The critical man or woman can assess what's true and reject what's false. The difficulty arises when we start accepting the message uncritically, when it becomes brainwashing. And the best brainwashing is the brainwashing you don't realize you're getting.

Each of these value systems can become a kind of cult—a religion substitute—with its own scripture, its priest-experts, its "saints" to imitate, its "holy" places and activities guaranteed to give human fulfillment. Each offers a prize, but at a price.

Therefore, these pages are an attempt to offer you the freedom to choose—which comes only from the willingness to perceive clearly what a life–view is actually offering (and its price), to categorize it, evaluate it, form an opinion of it, and test that opinion by sharing it with others.

The alternative is to be a sheep, driven in one direction and then another by conflicting and externally imposed values. You can deceive yourself into believing: "I am keeping all my options open," which is just another way of saying: "I have no biases, no convictions, no spine."

The odd thing about freedom is that the only time it actually comes into play is when you actually *do* make a choice—and ironically, in that very act, surrender your freedom to choose the *other* alternatives.

But freedom is what we were born for. And your freedom depends on what you know, on how willing you are to think things through for yourself.

Slavery is far easier.

The Plastic Paradise

Give me your tired, your poor,
Your restless refuse yearning to breathe
    free. . . .

Send these—the homeless, tempest-tossed—
   to me.
I lift my lamp beside the golden door.
                              —*Emma Lazarus*

. . . a land of sullen people, bored, phlegmat-
ic, nasty in their emptiness; a land of subju-
gation to pre-fabricated things and
pleasures; where the television set and juke-
box have replaced humans as the center of
energy in the room.
                              —*William Stott*

In the beginning, the New World of the United States and Canada was
the Land of Opportunity. Except in the shameful case of the original
owners, the native American Indians, it offered a haven from religious
persecution, from inhuman poverty, from societies in which blood lines
determined who would live the good life. The land opened up before
them, wide and rich and seemingly endless; cities began to mushroom
up along its coasts and rivers. Here, there was little aristocracy, and the
wise Constitution guaranteed equality of opportunity for all (white)
males and their families, regardless of any previous situation. Here, the
norm for rising to the top was not the accident of breeding but one's
own courage, wit, ambition, and hard work. Here, anybody—even a
gangly railsplitter from a log cabin in Illinois—could aspire to the very
leadership of the nation—and achieve it.
    Stories stirred the heart to hope. Horatio Alger wrote endless tales,
like *From Rags to Riches,* about penniless bootblacks who, through tire-
less effort, thrift, pluck and luck, rose to be giants of industry. As late as
the 1930's, it was still hearteningly commonplace to hear the success
story of a young Jewish boy leaving his father's small tailor shop on the
Lower East Side of Manhattan on his relentless climb to fame, money,

and glamor as the president of a great Hollywood studio. Then such stories became rarer. Perhaps everybody had "arrived."

America succeeded largely because of the so-called Puritan ethic: God rewards those who work hard; our lives will slowly improve, and our children's lives will be paradise. Nor was this ethic restricted to our first English, Protestant, Pilgrim fathers (and mothers); it dovetailed perfectly with the hardworking, flinty, orthodox peasant faiths of the Irish, Jews, Poles, and Italians who followed them. At that time, hard work needed no defense. In the first place, it was the only alternative to starvation; but of equal importance, hard work was the source of a man's or woman's sense of dignity. And, slowly, it prevailed. It cleared the land, built the cities and industries and universities, defended freedom both here and all over the world. America became the richest and most powerful nation on earth.

We are the grandchildren of those men and women. We have achieved paradise. Uh . . . now what? Well . . . uh . . . *more,* of course! By definition, the Myth of Progress can have no final goal. There is always more.

Subtly, around the time of the incredible boom economy associated with the mass production of World War II, things—expectations, values, even morality—began to change, like windows being turned into mirrors. Time, education, and prosperity began to erode the invisible walls of ethnic and religious ghettos. No one really paid much attention anymore to whether your name began with an "O' " or a "Di" or to whether you were Protestant or Catholic or Jew. With both positive and negative results, those things seemed peripheral now. The influence of religion on everyday and everyweek affairs began gradually to shrink from complete dominance back into the church building—and that only once a week, if at all. All of us were becoming more sophisticated, more cosmopolitan, more "worldly."

Whatever the connection to the lessening of ethnic and religious values, "democracy" began to edge toward becoming synonymous with "monopoly capitalism." "What's good for GM is good for America!" In a kind of perversion of the God-centered Puritan ethic, a good American was one who had made a lot of money and could now afford to aspire to the presidency. With equal irony, "economy," which had always denoted thrift and caution, was now divinized into a kind of idol that demanded bigger spending for its survival. The farm boy who rose from nowhere to eminence was no longer Abraham Lincoln but Elvis Presley.

In dizzying spirals, everything began to get out of hand: higher salaries meant higher prices, but then higher prices called for higher salaries, but then . . . "Things" had exploded so far outside the effective control of individuals and their families that people could no longer blame themselves or their neighbors for local problems, nor did they look to a town meeting for their solution. That was in the hands of "the System"—the "they" who make decisions, with which we comply for our own good and for the general welfare. Concretely, "The System" means the government and big business—and which has the greater influence on the other is becoming more and more difficult to determine.

The Headlong Quest for Mediocrity

Values had changed dramatically. The yearning for novelty had replaced any sentimental attachments to old goods or locations; speed, efficiency, and therefore lower prices replaced quality; appearances and "image" replaced substance; work became only a means to goods and a vacation, not an end in itself which gave pride to the worker and quality service to the neighbor.

In a word, almost every important aspect of human life had been *trivialized:* work, sex, politics, entertainment, even death. And almost every trivial aspect of human life had been given an importance it doesn't objectively merit: gossip, bodies and complexions, styles, athletics.

One very clear manifestation of this topsy-turvying of values is its effects on athletics. Formerly, sports were sportive; they were for fun, a challenge in which skill, intelligence, and concentration could be brought to bear on utterly useless activities. But such scorn for profit bothered both social reformers and businessmen. For them, useless was the same as valueless. Thus, sport was co-opted. It must promote either fitness in the devout citizen or the expenditure of money by the devout consumer.

A team, whether professional, college, or high school, became no longer an organic group, sinewed together by loyalty—and even love— but a collection of insulated individuals out to aggrandize themselves, with either the fans or the front office or the college scouts. The purpose of the game became not sport but economics, and thus now winning is not the most important thing; it's the only thing. Wrong. There is also losing.

The Live-In Brainwasher

To my mind, next to the boom economy at mid-century, the single most important agent in this transformation of values has been television: both by its programming and by its commercials.

No Marine drill instructor, no Siberian interrogator, no voodoo spell-thrower ever had so much power, such sophisticated methods, or such compliant subjects. Never in the history of humankind has there been such a powerful teaching tool—such an ability to affect opinions and expectations and the meaning of human fulfillment—as television and its support: commercial advertising.

Programming. There are good—even overwhelmingly good—TV programs. The regular fare, however, almost without exception, is as shallow as a contact lens and as challenging as unflavored yogurt. Quiz programs are screaming orgies deifying greed, and the "story" shows— soaps, sitcoms, cops/doctors/cowboys/lawyers—are almost all perversions of the truth, which are in turn the poisonous seeds of false expectations of human life and human fulfillment. What doctor is never wrong, never loses a patient, chases runaways down the street, and solves all problems in one hour? Is it any wonder the number of malpractice suits has skyrocketed, with people thinking: Why can't my doctor be as good as the real doctors on TV? Most everyday policemen may draw their revolvers once or twice in a *career;* their daily work is most often dull, unrewarding paperwork, and most crimes are not solved, much less brought to justice. But the real cops on TV fire more slugs in one week than were fired in the American Revolution, and if they don't get their criminal this week, they surely will in the "To Be Continued." How many kids, sitting most of their days and nights in front of the Electronic Nanny, look at TV lives and then at their own lives, and find the latter unjustly dull? Locked in their self-disdaining walnut shells, they extend themselves by identifying with the Beautiful People in whom celebrity (i.e., being talked about) replaces accomplishment.

Where's *my* big break? How am I gonna get where it's *really* at: the Super Bowl, Vegas, Hollywood, New York? The Tonight Show! That's *really* living!

REAL (TRUE) $\neq$ REAL (TRUE)-TO-ME

Advertising. It's not only the TV commercials. Where can you go to escape ads? Behind a bus? On the top of a building? Along a country road? In a phone booth? But TV is where the big bucks go.

Ever since you were old enough to sit up on the living room rug, the Electronic Guru has been telling you the *real* secrets of human life, and every ten minutes (every three minutes on the radio)—no matter what the product—the kindly voice has told you, "The more things you have, the happier you'll be. We don't want to be like those poor children, do we? They don't have chocolate cake and new toys. Why don't we talk to Mommy and Daddy and see how much they love us? The more things you have . . . "

Oh, Brave New World! We have arrived!

Tie a carrot to a stick, and tie the stick to a donkey's head so the carrot dangles just outside the donkey's reach. That jackass'll run for you forever. Or until he drops dead. Or goes insane.

Notice that the ads always use the comparative adjective: new*er*, bett*er*, whit*er*, cream*ier*, soft*er*. Never -*est* words. In those two letters is the promise of still *more*. Got to keep them paying the System's pew rent at the counters. But it's worth it! A fountain of youth in every bottle, spray can, chassis, and on and on. No previous religion ever dared promise so much, convinced so many, delivered so impermanently, enslaved so deeply.

Again, appearances paradoxically outweigh substance. The critical point is not whether something is true but whether it sounds true. Consider the statement: "No fluoride toothpaste fights cavities better than Grinn!" which is a rather devious way of saying that all fluoride toothpastes are exactly the same. Nothing succeeds like the appearance of success.

Don't get me wrong. I don't believe a group of fanged business people and ad executives gather periodically in some Madison Avenue office to conspire how to undermine our values and rubberize our spines even further. They're out to make a buck; they give us what we (think we) want. If truth, thrift, and intellectual challenge sold, they'd be only too happy to supply those.

Whenever I ask my classes what content the word "success" has to each of them as individuals, the usual answers are sublimely vague, like "to achieve my goals" or "to fulfill myself." One great problem: they can't achieve an unfocused goal. What the hell does "human fulfillment" *mean?* Another problem: in the *concrete,* how much does success in their minds assume living at least as materially well as their parents: two cars, a pool, and so forth? Nothing wrong with any of that, provided you're running toward it with true freedom, provided you're honestly aware of the existence and appeal of other alternatives, provided you've chosen that material goal and aren't chasing a carrot because the Electronic Guru told you to.

Don't run from that possibility too quickly. The best brainwashing is the brainwashing you don't realize you're getting.

$ $ $

In order to have all those "nice things" which even Mother Teresa would find pleasant—and which we have been relentlessly urged to desire perhaps out of all proportion—we have to work, beg, borrow, or steal. Nothing wrong with money. Man may not live by bread alone, but we can't live without it either. There's no reason to feel guilty about having enough money; nor would anyone in his right mind assert that people with money can't be happy. If money were really the root of all evil, why do Church organizations spend so much effort trying to harvest more o'them roots?

Having money is not evil—unless the need for it gets out of hand, unless it dominates all other human values and becomes anti-human, unless it takes away one's freedom to see and do the truth.

Once on a retreat, I spoke several times with a highly "successful" man who was anguished over his job. He hated to get up for work, and he spent all weekend dreading Monday. His wife's life was tormented, too, because she could do nothing to help him. I asked when was the last time he'd been happy working, and he said it was in the job from which he was promoted. So I asked if, without losing face with the company, he could get his old job back. He said of course. What was he making in the previous job? $75,000 a year. What was he making in the new job he hated? $90,000.

"Simple," I said. "Just ask for your old job back. It's not exactly as if you're going to be impoverished."

"But that's a $15,000 loss!"

"Pretend you're paying it to a very expensive psychiatrist. Is fifteen grand worth all this anguish to you and your wife and your family?"

He didn't answer. He never came back. I never heard from him again.

Effect on Ability To See the Truth

Dehumanizing Goals

It's hard to convince someone so strongly persuaded to the contrary that a large paycheck (and all it can buy) is not a reliable indicator of success as a human being. It's almost a foregone conclusion that if you ask "How much is he worth?" you're going to get his bank balance, as if human value could be measured in dollar-signs.

At a wedding reception, a girl who had heard I'd been right up there on the big old silver screen, and that I knew lots of famous and influential people, gushed up to me as starry-eyed and breathless as if I were Cinderella's Fairy Godmother. Her first words were not "Hello," or "I'm So-and-So," but I swear: "How do I make it to the top?" I sidestepped a bit, danced a bit, and finally got around to asking what talents she thought she had. Answer, quick and simple: "None. I want the money."

What made that girl believe—unlike her Pilgrim and immigrant and Horatio Alger and Depression forebears—that "success" (money, happiness, fulfillment) was going to drop out of the sky if she just said the magic word, pressed the right key, met the right connection? I've seen the same thing in students who planned to be wealthy engineers, in defiance of the fact that their math SAT scores were not high enough to boil water. If I can only get a car . . . if I can only . . . Life becomes like a video game. If I can only knock 'em all down, then I'll be important, like the people in the *Guinness Book of World Records.*

When I was in that now-forgotten movie, I was something of a puzzle to the people I was working with. One day the director asked me, "Bill, we've been friends for a while; can I ask you a personal question? Do you honestly mean you don't get laid?" And I told him, no, I don't get laid. And he said, "Then how can you be so at ease? How can you be happier than we are?"

He wasn't the only one. Actors, make-up people, hairdressers, carpenters—all of them, like my interviewer on the "Today" show, saw me as a contradiction. All the things by which they defined "success" I not only lacked but happily walked away from: money, fame, sex, and power. And yet, by their own admission, I was happier than they were. And when I walked away from the big silver screen, to teach high school in Rochester, New York, without a qualm . . . unthinkable!

On the one hand, my starry-eyed friend at the wedding didn't realize that, if you have a $100,000 job, you have $100,000 headaches. There is no free lunch. On the other hand, she doesn't realize that money is a deceptive gift, as King Midas found to his peril. Another friend, whose monetary value was far in excess of eight figures, once told me, "When I was making a decent living, I knew when a girl went out with me it was because she liked *me*. Now . . .?"

What's the difference between living and making a living?

It's only recently, too, that we've unearthed what is commonly called the "mid-life crisis," men and women who have bought the whole blueprint in high school and college, achieved "success" even by the most sneering standards, and suddenly realize their years are numbered. What have I really *done?* I have only about a third of my life, more or less, left. Why do I feel so unfulfilled?

Take it from another angle, the point of view of such people's children. I couldn't count the number of fathers who have said to me: "I waded through such crap as a kid! I *vowed* my kids would never have to endure what I had to—work, worry, fear, going–without. And by God I *did* it. I gave them everything I didn't have. Everything . . . except what I *got* from going through all that: spine."

One of the true geniuses of the American theatre, Arthur Miller, has captured the corrosive falsehood of the promises of the American Dream in his play, "Death of a Salesman." Willy Loman, a nice, limited, hard-working man, has also bought the whole blueprint. If only you're "popular, well-*liked*," you can't miss. Buyers will come to *you,* and when you die, the funeral will be breathtaking. But it didn't work out that way—not for Willy or for his two sons. Willy's only true success was to crack up in his car so that, at the very least, his wife could have his insurance money.

Why? Because the American Dream—unbalanced, alone—is anti-human.

Consider Marilyn Monroe. Consider Elvis Presley. Consider Howard Hughes. Or Janis Joplin, John Belushi, William Holden. And tell me what "success" means.

The American Dream is an empty illusion because its promises are as false as the first advertisement: "Eat this, and you'll become like God."

Dehumanizing Attitudes

Narcissus was a fabled Greek boy who fell in love with looking at his own reflection in a pond. And he fell in and drowned. It needn't be one's beauty or bulging bank balance that hypnotizes the modern narcissist. His or her ugliness or poverty will do as well. As long as one turns all windows into mirrors, the effect is the same: to center the universe on oneself.

There is only one radical difficulty with that: it is not the truth. In fact, even the whole earth is not the center of the universe.

Narcissism did not begin with the advent of television and commercial advertising. But it is beyond dispute that advertising has not only given narcissism a good name; it has made narcissism into a life-view. Ads stimulate infantile cravings and encourage us to remain on that level till we die. Even aging and death become un-truths. There will be transplants, drugs, changed social structures so that I can beat them. I'll learn the new dance craze; I'll buy a wig. I'm still young, dammit. I'm still attractive. I'm still fighting the facts, the way things are, the natures of things. And while I'm elbowing others out of the way on my run to the lifeboats, life passes me by.

Every commercial is a mirror, a reminder. We must keep checking, just to be sure, forgetting that if you plant a radish and keep pulling it up to see if it's grown, it will never grow. In a world where "image" tyrannizes, one is afraid of giving oneself away—in both senses. Surely, one so shackled can't even *hear* a voice which says, "Unless you lose your life, you will never find it."

When one becomes God, it is a very tiny universe indeed.

Something goes out of kilter when—despite the fact that I'm not the center of the universe—I act as if I am. Other people obviously don't give me the deference I deserve; they don't yield to my wishes; they won't let me play quarterback, have the lead, get that raise. It's therefore all *their* fault; it's the System's fault, and my parents, and my teachers, and . . .

Even when you do achieve "success" and find, as so many do, that it doesn't deliver fulfillment as promised, what is left? Trying to get more? When you don't make it to the top, as so few can, the result can be cynicism, emptiness, at times even suicidal despair. With loss of perspective, with loss of vision of the true natures of things—human beings, money, fame, material goods, power—frustration is inevitable. The truth rises up and takes its revenge. Because one can't see the truth, one can't live the truth. One can't be human.

The great question, then, still remains buried deep in the hearts of even the most fanatic cultists of the plastic paradise: is there, anywhere, a permanent world? Is there anything in us that won't wear out and die?

Questions for the Notebook

Page 9. Can you think of a job at which (if your spouse were willing) you suspect you could be extremely happy—even though the paycheck would not allow you to live in great comfort and would not be something you'd brag about at the alumni reunion? If so, what would it be? If not, can you explain why such a job would be unacceptable?

Page 10. Except for the relatively few hermits among us, we are all going to have to work in some way "in the System" and under the very strong and pervasive influences of the System's propaganda. Is there any way you as an individual can counter—and balance—the influences of that propaganda?

A Prayer

God, help me to find myself and stay myself, despite all the very inviting calls to a life that is easier, quicker, cheaper, smaller. Haul me up short every once in a while, and make me ask myself whether I'm striving for what I really want. Help me be human. Help me to find me. Amen.

The Love Machine

I tell you solemnly, unless you change and become like little children, you will never enter the kingdom of heaven.
—*Matthew 18:3*

There has always been a counter-culture, and there always will be. Why? Because, as we saw in the last section, the System is oversimplified, and people are complex. By our human *nature,* we become dissatisfied and then disillusioned by an unrelieved diet of the plastic values of wrinkle-proof suburbia.

One hero of the anti-phony counter-culture is Holden Caulfield, the central figure in J.D. Salinger's novel, *The Catcher in the Rye.* Something inside Holden rebelled against the unnaturalness of the up-tight masks of pseudo-adulthood he found all about him; something yearned to cling to the world of childhood, to his sister Phoebe on the carousel and his brother Allie writing poems on his baseball mitt; something told him to be "just a nice guy," standing in a field of rye, protecting little children. For twenty years, I've seen that novel capture the minds of students as no other has: "That's the way it *is!*" Indeed, that is the way it is—and not just in the 1980's or 1970's or 1960's, but always.

Because *The Catcher in the Rye* was written about *my* generation; in 1981, both Holden Caulfield and I turned 50.

A hundred years before that, Mark Twain immortalized that natural human refusal to put up with too much fuss-and-feathers in a boy named Huck Finn, for whom even shoes were too constricting. In the 1960's we had campus radicals and college blitzkriegs; in the 1940's they were called Beatniks; in the 1920's they were called Bohemians; in the last century they were called Romantics. Across the centuries they are united by the one dream of returning to the simplicity of childhood. Off with the Puritan sexual restraints! Off with shoes and touch the good earth! Off with the uniforms and into a costume! Off with everything that smacks of competition and therefore of inequality. Competition is the law of the jungle; cooperation is the law of humankind.

Especially today, as the future becomes less and less certain, only an imbecile would postpone till tomorrow the fun he or she can have today. Live now; pay later—if later even comes.

If the System deifies the collectivity and uptightness, the counter-culture deifies the individual and spontaneity. If we can only get rid of "middle-class" or "bourgeois" taboos, anchors, responsibilities, and poses, they claim, then we will achieve paradise: spiritual freedom. It would be good to understand what those two words "spirit" and "freedom" mean.

Spirit: In my Puritan younger days, I always regarded my spirit or "soul" like one of those locked black boxes of pilots' voices that they dig out of plane wrecks. Nothing you put in there could ever be sneaked out or changed; it could be opened only when you die; only God had the key. Pretty sick, huh? On the contrary—in both the religious and counter-cultural use of the word—one's spirit or soul is one's *self:* all that it is to be *me,* not merely my mind, but all the things one associates with the "heart"—love, poetry, music, art; ambition, spiritedness, vulnerability; hope, honor, peace, pride. And religion. They all spring from and feed the same inner human energy source. The real meaning of the human soul is captured about as well as anywhere in the "old Negro spirituals" and in "Soul music." Its opposite is seen in "the soul-less System": the rat race, the treadmill, *1984.*

Freedom: Ironically, though it is one of the most positive human values, "freedom" can be defined only in negative terms: *not* subject, *in-*

dependent, *un*chained. Further, there is no such thing as *total* freedom; it can't exist. You will never be free from the force of gravity, from your genetic code, from your past. You are not free from the natures of things or from the natural consequences of choices. You are free to drink a pint of gin, but you have already ingested the consequences; you are free to avoid risk, but in that very choice you have rejected joy; you are free to reject knowing, loving, and growing, but the inescapable consequence is to die as a specifically human being.

There is a difference, too, between freedom *from* outside coercion and freedom *to* act. When men and women leave home for college, for instance, they are free from nearly all external constraints on their behavior: they can sleep in on Sunday, go to bed with anyone who strikes their fancy, get bombed every night if they want—and if the money holds out. But will they be free to get up and go to Mass on Sunday, while everybody else is snoring or sneering? Will they be free to be chaste and sober? All chains are not clamped on from outside.

Thus, any life-view that promises total freedom is offering an appealing lie.

Let me be clear before we examine three manifestations of the counter-culture. There is nothing wrong with sex or music or booze—just as there is nothing wrong with having enough money. They make good servants, but bad masters. When any one of them dominates other human values, it dehumanizes. What I want to examine here are ways in which the counter-culture oversimplifies. Just as human beings are not just worker-consumers, they are not just Playboy/Playgirls. But these alternate life-views are worth scrutinizing honestly, especially since—like the System—they have the media and slogans and megabucks to surround us with their gospel, to make the counter-culture appealing, and even to bring it very profitably (if ironically) into the mainstream of the System.

Playboy/Playgirl

Thirty years ago, when Hugh Hefner put out the first issue of *Playboy,* he seemed something of a doomed Prophet of Porn. Critics said he'd be bankrupt in a year: most Americans are decent, hardworking, controlled folk (the Puritan ethic); nobody is going to walk up to a counter and buy that erotic filth. Alas, the authentic gift of prophecy is rare. Hefner—and a host who have followed his lead—have built a billion-dollar empire based on our most secret fantasies. Within a decade, Hefner had legitimized lust.

When I was a kid not *that* long ago, if you wanted to see what a n-a-k-e-d person of the opposite gender looked like, you had to sneak a guilty peek at a sculpture book or hope that this month *The National Geographic* took another intellectually stimulating jaunt to Africa. Now, thirty years later, one has only to go to the family drugstore to discover a cornucopia of lust varied enough to sate a satyr. It's undeniable that we paid a price for our purity: ignorance, guilt, simplicism, rigidity, and the lopsided conviction that there were in reality only two serious commandments. However, neither extreme, puritan or prurient, hovers near the truth.

Not many, one assumes with slight fear of error, pick up both *Playboy* and *Playgirl* at the same time, or that they do so in order to analyze recurrent themes in the articles, pictures, and ads. I, heavily disguised in dark glasses and fake moustache, did precisely that.

Few of the articles, at least in the two issues I goggled at, were too many degrees below "sensationalism," though the women's intelligence seemed to be more openly insulted than the men's: "What Co-Workers Think (and Say) About Your Office Affair," "Warm Bodies," "The 30-Minute Orgasm." With the exception of the business and political articles (the "System pages") in *Playboy,* most qualified for what Freud said about religion: wish-fulfillment, a chance to fantasize about the perfectly fulfilling quickie, with no strings, no personal involvement, no cost. As Charlie Brown is wont to observe, "Good luck."

The pictures were a gorgeous array of well-structured nude bodies, airbrushed of any defects, perfect, and as impersonal and uninvolving (non-human) as an encounter with a male or female prostitute. Wish-fulfillment again. On the one hand, there is the conviction that lurking somewhere inside me is *really* someone just like him (or her), if only I could find the magic incantation or diet plan or sex manual to release it. (Those are all in the ads, by the way.) On the other hand, she *is* looking lustfully and invitingly right at *me,* isn't she? Oh, God if only . . . Again, good luck. More likely the viewer will remain haunted by a quietly masochistic and helpless envy.

The ads are made more appealing, of course, by the pictures. In the woman's magazine, most ads offered guaranteed bust builders, love oils, and erotic underclothes—all the things that make a real *woman,* one guesses. In the man's magazine, they touted expensive beer and booze, stereos, athletic clothes and equipment, sports cars, and cigarettes—all the things that make a real *man,* one guesses. Both magazines had more than a few ads promising to rearrange *your* embarrassing flesh.

Thus, sex is also trivialized in a spiritless and impersonal world, without mystery or awe. We begin to wonder if religion was shouting against promiscuity not just because it was fun, but because it made something beautiful into something commonplace.

These two magazines and their imitators are for singles and people who wish they were. *My* spouse or friend sure doesn't look like that. But singles' bars are very spirited and spiritless places, and single is a very lonely number. They are free, to be sure, but with all the inescapable consequences of being unattached. *Playboy* and *Playgirl* know that. They're offering what they believe is the answer to it, and millions of magazine buyers can't be wrong, can they? If chastity sold, they'd give us that.

Pop Music

I don't want to challenge you,
Marry you, or remember you.
I just wanna make love to you.
         —Rod Stewart

People tell me they don't listen to commercials. But why is it that when you're brushing your teeth a voice in your head tells you where to go next time to get your glasses fixed or your tank filled? And why do companies pay megabucks for TV time that *doesn't* affect people's behavior? Likewise, people who listen to the radio and records for at least a couple of hours a day tell me they never listen to the lyrics. So how could the lyrics affect their attitudes and behavior? But why is it they can sing along so easily with so many songs? People don't listen to commercials or lyrics, but they sure seem somehow to hear them.

It follows, I'm pretty sure, that the people who deny listening to the words can't possibly have analyzed the recurrent themes in the lyrics they haven't listened to. In a minor way, I have, not only while driving in the car but, since I'm an old fossil and can't hear them very well, I bought copies of *Hit Parade* and *Smash Hits* in that same tremulous excursion in which I purchased the two mini-porn magazines.

Before I begin, let me first GRANT, in capital letters, that in MANY cases pop lyrics are (a) neutral or (b) positive. But anybody I've ever known who has made an honest attempt to find themes in contemporary lyrics has said that there are such recognizable themes and they do present a consistent life-view.

Since the beginning of time, a great deal of music and lyrics have been about love—much of it being "lament" for true love scorned, pleading , and near despair. But the lyrics of the past twenty years seem to give a different twist to the unchanging problems of being not-a-child, not-an-adult but still "desperately in love."

Innuendo: When I was a lad, radio stations banned "The Blue Tango" (no lyrics) simply because it *sounded* "dirty." Today, however, the insinuation is far more explicit—if that's not a contradiction. "Baby, let's *do* it!" (play catch, right?) "Let's go down!" (To the ol' St. James Infirm'ry, huh?) "Let's get physical!" (Maybe a little hot-and-heavy handball.)

Honesty: I found it perversely refreshing when The Rolling Stones walked away from saying "I love you" and very forthrightly said, "I want *It!*" The Rod Stewart lyric which opened this section may sound harsh, but at least it's in some way honest; it offers no commitment, just a roll in the hay to release physical and psychic tensions. I do get angry, though, when the lyric goes on to say, "I just want to make love to you." Clearly, Rod Stewart and I mean something quite different when we say "love." I find a similar recurrent theme that says, in one way or another, "Baby, it's all over, but let's do it just once more for old times' sake."

Emptiness: Many lyrics lament the fact that I'm just one more number, just one more statistic; who knows my name? These are more directly against the unfairness and dehumanization of the System: I'm lost in the crowd; I work from nine to five, Monday to Friday, and then I'm gonna *explode!* Cut loose! Really *live!* "Plenty of women and plenty of booze!" (The two seem to be equated.)

The Rock Priest: If you read the Old Testament, you discover that the appeal of *Playboy/Playgirl* and many rock lyrics is not a recent invention. The Israelites were surrounded by these Canaanites whose religion was, to be sure, considerably more appealing than bowing in an empty room to an invisible Yahweh, no matter how much incense. The Canaanites thought you worshiped the god by "engaging" with temple prostitutes. There was no head-trip, no theology, no System to bog things down.

Let the celebrants of Sunday Mass take note.

At a dance or concert, you are in a kind of sacred communion with the whole body of fellow believers. There, or alone with the radio or stereo, you are also in silent communion with something that's very deep inside yourself. In a group there is what Mick Jagger rightly calls "a dialogue of energy" between you and the band, concelebrating. Furthermore, the vocalist is not up there with the bored correctness of the Sunday priest. Vocalists are up there *sweating* with commitment to what they believe is truly important. In communion with them, you can release some of those nameless forces everybody tells you to hold in, and somehow you can feel fulfilled.

On the contrary, people tell me Mass is boring because "you hear the same old prayers all the time." And yet songs *become* pop (popular) simply because they are repeated over and over. The problem with Mass, I suspect, is not the fact that it seems repetitive, but the fact that it sends messages we'd prefer not to hear.

Just as the core of *Playboy/Playgirl* is lust, the core of many pop songs at least seems to be loneliness. At times the lyrics seem to say that being lonely together is at least better than being lonely alone. Again we're back in the singles' bar, "between relationships," and solitary confinement is a sentence worse than death.

Drugs/Booze
IS ≠ SEEMS

One of the escapes from the inhumanities which the System can provoke is narcosis: stupor, the arrest of involvement, dropping out. Just as narcissism didn't begin in Greece, and sex-worship didn't begin in Canaan, escape-to-the-instant-paradise didn't begin with the repeal of Prohibition, nor will it reach fulfillment with the legalization of marijuana. It is intriguing that the Greek root for both "narcissism" and "narcotics" is *narkē:* stupor.

There has been more than one Friday night when, after a week of classes, circling spelling errors which no one will ever notice, running play rehearsals, incinerating hotdogs for football games, showing up at parents' meetings, faculty meetings, hospitals, funeral homes, and talking to strangers who show up at the front door looking for "that priest who knows about exorcisms"—I myself have honestly gone to the liquor cabinet in our residence and poured myself more than one narcosis with water and ice. I just wanted—like Jesus surrounded by the lepers in "Jesus Christ Superstar"—to have them "leave me alone!" I wanted to sleep Saturday morning till I woke up. I wanted to heal.

When one does that occasionally at home (where there is no need to drive), I personally find no problem, though others would. The operative word, of course, is "occasionally," by which I mean, oh, maybe every few months or so. But when it's every week or every day or every weekend, the escape becomes serious. The frequency belies not an occasional escape from the rat race of life, but an escape from life, truth, things as they inescapably are.

My friends who justify frequent narcosis—not just grass but beer and booze—offer me the following justifications, in which I can find no truth.

They expand the mind: They expand the feelings and perceptions, surely—though on the following day I'm hard pressed to remember what those great liberating insights were. The ability to perceive is there already; otherwise, the chemical couldn't release it. What's inhibiting that release during the rest of the week? (There's the real question.) Does the chemical give insight, or only the *feeling* one would have from a real insight? Isn't the chemical's aftermath at least comparable to the laugh we can't resist when we're tickled? Nothing's funny; it's just that nerves have been artificially triggered. Composer Paul Simon says, "I used to listen to my music when I was high and say, 'Wow, that's great.' Well, it wasn't always great. Sometimes it *stank.* It only seemed great because I was high, and I got tired of being fooled."

They solve personal problems: Solve or postpone? The next morning

I wake up with the problems—plus a hangover. Unless one is going to spend most of his week on drugs, doesn't that mean he really lives only a bit of every week? One could surmise that life *really* begins at 2:30 on Friday and ends at 8:30 Monday morning. If that's true, those people are living only two-sevenths of their lives. The rest of the time they are zombies: the living dead.

We all need escapes. Perhaps everybody deserves to get stinko every once in a while. But the person who has to get high every Friday and every Saturday—no matter on what—has a problem that neither booze nor pot is likely to resolve.

They help me to be myself: Drugs/Booze are capsulized courage. When I'm high, I am (seem) unusually charming, open, unafraid of what anyone thinks of me. But, as with the insights that narcosis stimulates, that ability to be open is inside all week long or the chemical couldn't trigger it. The real, unfaced question is: what are the obstacles to one's being charming, open, and unafraid seven-sevenths of the week?

They combat conformity and dehumanization: Conformity, yes; in many cases drugs/booze are even against the law. But dehumanization? We're all victims of mass education, mass production, mass organization, constant criticism, constant competition. But does getting strung out really make one *more human?* Insofar as it makes us less aware of reality, it makes us *less* human.

They don't hurt anybody else: Even if I don't go off the road and kill someone, chemical narcosis keeps me from facing myself, from growing. And that impoverishes all the people who love me or could love me. Moreover, drugs and (at least for teenagers) booze are illegal, and in taking that risk one is equivalently saying (whether you mean it or not) that you don't really care whether your parents have to face the shame of bailing you out if you get caught.

Another (admittedly arguable) contention is that one reaches a plateau at which this particular stimulant no longer does the trick, and the user is drawn *inevitably* to something with a stronger kick. It's undeniable that a great many heroin addicts did begin with milder drugs. But who can prove that *I* can't hold at the lower level? No one. However, it's beyond dispute that almost all illegal drugs come to us courtesy of organized crime. Therefore, even if my purchase of grass isn't contributing to my own heroin addiction, it certainly helps supply the money to help others become heroin addicts.

Effect on Ability To See the Truth

Dehumanizing Goals

"Hedonism" is the belief that pleasure is the sole goal in life, and human fulfillment comes only from the gratification of impulses. But if the pursuit of pleasure is the dominant motivation in one's life, it is doomed from the start. We're back again, smack-dab up against the natures of things. On the one hand, you can't become a good little System ant, toiling away relentlessly to assure a blissful retirement; you may never reach retirement. On the other hand, no matter how rich you are, you can't fritter away your days like a carefree grasshopper singing, "Eat, drink, and be merry, for tomorrow we die!" You may get cirrhosis of the liver first.

Paradise on earth is a contradiction in terms.

Dehumanizing Attitudes

When the voices of the counter-culture give rise to expectations in us that, in a just world, life would be fun all the time, they are selling us maps for a treasure that doesn't exist. The work week is inescapable—whether it's the nine-to-five job or the school day to prepare us for a better nine-to-five job. We have to eat, and unless we have the courage to go off to a commune in the hills, we have to deal with the System, because the System generates the money to enable us to eat. You can "drop out" of the rat race, but you still have to stand on the street and cadge quarters from System types, or put the arm on old Systematized Dad, or get an unemployment check from the System.

What's more, for all their rigidity, the Puritans weren't all wrong. Retired men and women can testify that, when they stopped working, something very important was lost from their lives. In the first place, there is a life-giving cameraderie in almost any job. Even more important, work gives a shape and a direction to one's days and weeks and years. Little kids may say they hate school, but how often on a rainy Saturday do they whine, "Mommy, what can I *do?*"

Granted, there are jobs which of their very nature are deadening—assembly line work that will sooner or later be done by robots, picking up other people's garbage, selling candy corn in Woolworth's. One of the most basic purposes of education is to give men and women at least the opportunity to be free of such spiritually numbing work. And yet, no matter what the job, the work week becomes a rat race only when the people involved approach their jobs with all the willingness of rats in a maze. Martin Luther King once said, "If your job is to sweep streets, sweep those streets the way Michelangelo would have swept them!" Whatever the job—cleaning the attic, writing an essay, washing diapers—if you do the job all-out, with pride, with verve, you won't dread Monday morning and spend the rest of the week yearning for Friday afternoon. People rarely need to escape lives that are already exciting.

Another poisonous flaw in the fantasies projected by the counter-culture is that, just as the ideal families on television can make us despise our own visibly flawed family, the Never-Never Land of *Playboy/Playgirl* can make us despise who we are and prevent us from coming to terms with the truth of ourselves and moving onward from there. Escapes into illusion, whether into unrealizable erotic fantasies or into drunken forgetfulness, detour us from laying claim to our integral selves.

Thus, the basic flaw in the counter-culture as a dominant life-view is that it promises spiritual freedom, and it can deliver only the opposite of both. On the one hand, its devotees seem visibly dis-spirited. There is no focus to their lives; they drift; life happens to them in a series of one-damn-kick-after-another. Because the kicks by their nature can't satisfy for long, they have to get hott*er,* fast*er,* loud*er,* kinki*er.* The hedonist has forgotten the taste of bread. On the other hand, as we have seen, there is no freedom from the work week. But even on the weekend there seems to be no freedom for the hedonists. They seem as enslaved to impulse on Saturday and Sunday as they were to regimentation from Monday to Friday.

In the end, the Love Machine is not about love. It is about its direct opposite: selfishness.

Questions for the Notebook

Page 11. In what ways has the life-view described in this chapter affected your personal ideas of what "loving" means?

Page 12. To what extent do you think you personally have settled for the "five-sevenths/two-sevenths" split of the work week, that is, drudgery from Monday to Friday, aliveness on the weekend? If so, how could you get aliveness into the entire week? If not, what do you do to accomplish that?

A Prayer

God, help me to live and work as a human being. I need to work, and I need to relax. Help me to find ways to take pride in my work and pride even in my fun. Help me to understand why there are really no shortcuts to laying claim on my own integral self. Amen.

The Un-Ideal Church

Christianity will go. It will vanish and shrink. I needn't argue about that; I'm right, and I will be proved right. We're more popular than Jesus now; I don't know which will go first—rock'n'roll or Christianity.
                                        —*John Lennon*

Like the System and the counter-culture, the Church is—at least in part—a vehicle for propaganda, a way of embodying a view of life in concrete symbols and practices. It is an institutionalized ideal. The view of life comes, at its core, from Jesus Christ; most of the concrete symbols and practices which embody it come from human beings. Every human society is an imperfectly realized ideal, whether it is the Church, or the United States, or the Boy Scouts, simply because it is an ideal carried out by fallible human beings. Because of that, there are many who believe that the original ideal of Jesus Christ was much closer to the concerns of today's counter-culture, but that its actual embodiment—the present-day Church—is much closer to the concerns of the System.

It is surprising that, after eight-twelve-sixteen years of what many call intensive "brainwashing" by the Church, that propaganda seems to have had so little effect on the individual Christian's theoretical knowledge and concrete practices.

Few Church members I know seem able to sum up in a paragraph the *core* of what "the Church" or "Christianity" is. Answers to "What is the Church?" range from something as cynically limited as "the building" to something as comprehensive and comfortingly vague as "the people of God." In such statements as, "The Church is old-fashioned and closed-minded," the actual content of the word—the evidence which backs up the assertion—often really is "my parish" or very often only "my pastor."

In reading about two thousand notebook responses to the question: "What is the basic core of Christianity?" I've found that more than half described a kind of "ethical niceness" to the neighbor—without a word about Jesus Christ or even about God; the descriptions would equally well describe the Lions' Club or the Brownies. Charity, after all, is not an aim exclusive to Christians. Other religions are equally dedicated to it. Even the state encourages it; after all, generous children don't ordinarily grow up to be anti-social burglars and rapists.

As for its effect on concrete Christian practice, the so-called "brainwashing" seems to have been just as remarkably unsuccessful. In comparison to the effectiveness of the propaganda from commercials, it is plainly ludicrous to claim that the Church indoctrinated so many little automatons. If Christian education were indeed "brainwashing," why aren't people lined up at Communion every morning the way

they're lined up at the sales counter? Why is the number of actual Christian volunteers such a small percentage of those who sign "Catholic" when asked their religion on a questionnaire? Why are there more nominal Christians who aspire to be pop musicians than to be priests and nuns?

Propaganda, to be sure, but hardly brainwashing.

Perhaps the reason for this vagueness on a subject supposedly studied for years is too much propaganda, too soon—with the result that, after labeling and cataloging each and every tree, one can no longer see the forest.

The Ideal of the Christian Church

The Greek word for "Church" is *ekklesia:* "those who are called out." From what? To what? Jesus never used the word "Church."

When he spoke of that reality, he used the words "the Kingdom (or Reign) of God" and, speaking to an unsophisticated audience, he explained it by analogy—to a group of people enjoying a banquet, to a mustard seed that dies in order to grow, to a flock of sheep and goats, and so forth. In fact, it would be fair to say that every verse of the Gospels is an attempt to explain the nature of the Christian community, its membership, and their call. But how to distill out the irreducible essence, the "non-negotiables" at the core of Christianity? Even in such summaries as the Apostles' Creed, some doctrines are more important than others; some doctrines are not even mentioned—for example, the Eucharist. What is "The Mustard Seed," if you will, *before* it grew into the complex of doctrines and practices we have now, two thousand years later?

Let me try, inadequately again, to formulate the core of Christianity in the fewest words I can:

1. Jesus and Yahweh are one.

2. Jesus/Yahweh died *in order to* rise and share immortality (the aliveness of God) with us.

3. If you want to be part of the mission of Christ—Gospel/Kingdom/ Church—you must be converted (turned 180° around) *from* the goals and values of "the world" (materialism, "me-first," competition) *to* the goals of the Gospel/Kingdom/Church, namely: (1) love God more than you love *any* creature, and (2) love the neighbor, especially the outcast.

4. In everyday life, that belief is *embodied* in a community of people, missioned to bring the liberating message of Christ to the world, who celebrate their unity of faith in that message at a literal re-enactment of the Last Supper.

That was the mustard seed the apostles took first to the Jews in Palestine, then to Jews in settlements around the Mediterranean, and finally to the world. Over the course of twenty centuries, that message has been expanded, argued, reinterpreted, and applied to countless new and unexpected developments the original messengers and interpreters could never have foreseen. What we have today is a whole—sometimes bewildering—forest of doctrines sprung from that first seed: doctrines on sacraments, the legitimacy of St. Christopher, other religions, the natures of Christ, sins, the rosary, birth control, who can be priests, how to bless holy water.

It is important to realize that these doctrines are not all of equal importance. Again, there is a whole *spectrum* of them ranging from the essential to the peripheral. At one end of the spectrum you have doctrines that no one can deny and still call himself or herself a Christian—such as the resurrection of Jesus. At the other, you have doctrines that can be denied, changed, or forgotten completely, without affecting one's belonging to the Church—such as the authenticity of the appearances of Our Lady at Lourdes or Fatima. Between those two extremes there are thousands of doctrines that range from "heavy" through "serious" to "trivial." How to determine the difference? Find yourself a trustworthy theologian or, more practically, invest in a good encyclopedic work like Richard McBrien's *Catholicism* (2 vols; Winston Press) or less expensively, *A New Catechism,* often called "The Dutch Catechism" (paperback; Seabury Press). They are easily readable, unprejudiced, and approved.

It is also important to realize that the core *truth* of the Christian message doesn't change from age to age, although our way of *talking about* the the message changes. The Church is in a constant effort to reperceive, recategorize, re-evaluate, resymbolize, and retest; Vatican II was only the most recent dramatic example. The Scriptures explained the message in metaphors and symbols, but as the Church grew more sophisticated, it began to re-examine the message with the highly technical methods of the Greek philosophers; more recently, due to the "knowledge explosion" of the last hundred years, we have been able to go back and re-examine it with the even more sophisticated tools of psychology, anthropology, literary criticism, and so on—tools, again, undreamed of by those who first heard and interpreted the message.

Even the "official" language of the Church can change: from Aramaic, to Greek, to Latin, to the vernacular, and the words of the consecration are still effective.

The point is that—with the exception of that core—the Church and its doctrines are not a house of cards, such that if you can say, "Aha! I've found a doctrine that is undeniably *false!*" the whole structure falls apart. The official Church could change its mind about St. Christopher, about the morality of eating meat with blood in it or of lending money at interest or of owning slaves, or even about birth control, and it would still remain intact.

The *truth* can never harm the Church.

It began as a mustard seed. Over the years, a lot of doctrines have grown out of that seed, and a lot have been artificially grafted on. If the Church realizes that a graft is inconsistent with that initial truth, it simply lops it off.

The Real Church

Many major events affected the growth and shape of the Christian Church between 30 A.D. and today, but we will consider only one, since it has a strong effect on our ability to perceive the truth—and value—of the Church. It concerns the relationship between people inside the Church, their "roles." I hope I can simplify it without falsifying it.

Originally, the Church was twelve men and Jesus. Since they were to be imitators of Jesus, they were fundamentally teachers. As the group grew, the teaching began to diversify—but they were *all* called to teach: the Gospel. This diversification came about simply because individuals were more gifted at one aspect of teaching than at another. As Paul divides them (1 Cor 12:28),

> In the Church, God has given the first place to apostles [the Twelve, plus Paul, Barnabas, and one or two others], the second to the prophets [inspired preachers who encourage, warn, and stimulate the community], and third to teachers [theologians]; after them miracles, and after them healing; helpers [service people], good leaders, those with many languages [to act as interpreters].

I restrain myself from reminding my principal that administrators come second last in the line of teachers! However, even Paul says, in that same chapter, "The eye cannot say to the hand, 'I do not need you,' nor can the hand say to the feet, 'I do not need you.'" (12:21) *All* are important, and in the often-quoted following chapter, 1 Corinthians

13, Paul says that the love which motivates the teaching is more important than *any* specific gifts.

Over the centuries, however, at least partly because of (sometimes literal) battles over interpretations of the Gospel, other offices became subordinate to pastor-administrators: pre-eminently the Pope, bishops, and general councils of bishops, with learned theologians as their advisors. As McBrien puts it: "The church divided according to those who taught (and presumably no longer had to learn) and those who learned (and had nothing to do with teaching). That hard and fast distinction between the teaching church (*ecclesia docens*) and the learning church (*ecclesia discens*) has only recently begun to disappear."

Personally, I'm certain that I learned as much or more about the living God I worship from a mother who never finished second grade than I learned from nearly all the Ph.D.'s who lectured to me about him. I am not ungrateful to them, but she knew both God and me person-to-person.

To my mind, it would be hard to overestimate how much that division of Christians into the Church-teaching and the Church-taught contributes to whatever dissatisfaction with the Church exists today: the anger/rejoicing/apathy aroused by Vatican II; the listlessness of liturgies which the faithful submissively tolerate; the relatively small number of lay people who seem to want to continue learning more about their faith or to commit at least some part of their week to direct (as opposed to financial) service of the less fortunate. In general, no matter what the official teachings about a return to full participation of the laity in the apostolic, teaching mission of the Church, far too many seem to be still saying, "That's the priests' job."

And yet, if as human beings we were made to know, to love, to grow, all the more should that be true if we profess to be even just "core Christians."

The Church Today
IS ≠ SEEMS

There are an enormous number of good things one can say about today's Church—though most Catholics get their news of it from the public press and, in general, good news doesn't sell newspapers; controversy and scandal do. However, in South and Central America, Church communities are not only being persecuted, often to the point of torture, imprisonment without trial, and assassination, but they are also giving a stirring example of Christian heroism—which somehow also eludes notice of the media. Although the liturgy is still too often closer to the propriety of the System than to the spontaneity of the counter-culture, the reforms of Vatican II are trickling down into common practice: the lay diaconate is beginning to grow, lay people have become lectors and ministers of the Eucharist, parish councils give the people some voice in local affairs, many churches have become less "rich." The Church *is* honestly trying to "de-Systematize." Marriage Encounter has re-enlivened many families; schools and colleges have inaugurated service programs and post-graduate volunteer programs to help the needy. And always, the Church—lay people as well as priests and religious—has served: in hospitals, prisons, soup kitchens, publications, clinics.

Too often, however, even when we hear good news about the Church's people, it is news about "somebody else." I find, too, that when students speak or write about the Church, it is "they" and not "we" who believe this or do that. There are other problems in and with the Church today, but that one I believe is the most critical. If even half of the members of a parish were to throw off their false humility, their apathy, their indifference, and say, "*I* am the Church!" there would never be a boring Mass in that parish again.

Weekend Mass is the only time in the week when the life of the Church and the lives of most individual Christians visibly intersect. I would be the first to grant that the "script" needs work; I loved "A Man for All Seasons" deeply, but I wouldn't want to see it every week (or day), with only minor variations, for the rest of my life. I would also be the first to admit that an uninspired celebrant could set people dozing or daydreaming even in the catacombs. But I have seen too many congregations where a celebrant with the combined talents of Walt Disney Enterprises couldn't get a response from them.

Alas, mere membership in the visible Church doesn't seem to make people more charitable, more concerned about the important things in life, not noticeably more like "the Man for Others" than many good atheists. As I look at my fellow Catholics I see precious little joy, not very much evidence of faith in the supernatural, and very little awareness of the presence of God among us, now.

In an age which turns all mysteries into problems there is a loss of a sense of awe—at anything, and therefore a loss of a sense of the super-natural. Whatever sensitivity is left in that regard is pacified by magic shows, horror movies, "The Force," and "The Wide World of Sports."

Part of this shyness, joylessness, and caution arises from an unde-niable confusion *within* the Church today. When it's almost common-place for priests to leave their vows behind and take marriage vows, it's rather difficult to feel too much guilt about petting. Many avowed Catholics do at least seem to give more time, effort, and concern to the material goods of the world than to the supernatural elements of their lives. It might be very incautious, for instance, to ask a high school or college student if his or her choice of career were in any way affected by the profession of Christianity, or whether the choice was based on ex-actly the same motives as those of a law-abiding pagan.

Concretely, too, there are problems and crises aplenty within the Church. Vocations to the priesthood and religious life have declined by almost two-thirds in a dozen years; more Catholics are being divorced and remarried; many Catholics have, with sincere consciences, rejected papal authority in the matter of birth control; many Catholics, both lay and clerical, take diametrically opposite positions on the haves and have-nots, on the exploiters and the exploited; women (and some men) are becoming increasingly more vocal about what they believe is a sec-ond-class citizenship in the Church for women.

In the face of such perceived apathy, joylessness, lack of individual involvement, and confusion, how does one have the gall to go to a young person and say, "Hi! Howdja like to be a Catholic?"

Easy. You constantly remind yourself that, at the root of it all, there is still that core, that Mustard Seed. And that is more important than *anything* else.

Effect on Ability To See the Truth

Crisis

Crisis has always been the call of Christ to the Christian; the para-ble of the Good Samaritan alone is evidence enough of that. As we've said before, if security were what Christ preached, he never would have been crucified, and the apostles could have lived out their lives among their fishing boats and their grandchildren. The Church has *always* been in or between crises: at the very outset, there was the controversy over whether non-Jewish male converts should be circumcised; then there was the argument over whether the Second Coming was just around the corner or indefinitely distant; there was the upheaval over defining the natures of Christ, the place of philosophy in theologizing, the relative power of Popes as compared to general councils. There was the enormous and scandalous rending of the Church into various sects at the Protestant Reformation, as well as the shameful corruption within the Church which in great part caused that division. In the seventeenth and eighteenth centuries, the philosophical movement known as "The Enlightenment" called in question the possibility of belief in anything that could not be proved beyond doubt, and in the nineteenth and twentieth centuries, the "Modernist" controversy threatened to split the Church into those who were unforgivably free-thinking and those who were unquestioningly obedient.

If you don't find the Gospel even a bit unsettling, then you haven't really heard it yet. No one with the slightest sense of the Church's history could say that the Church is static, unchanging, old-fashioned—unless "old" means anything that changed last week. Rather, the Church is always in evolution, growing—and as any adolescent can testify, growing is *not* easy. But it is what we were born to do . The fundamental question here, then, is whether one wants to be involved in that growing. If you honestly believe the core of Christianity, you have no other option.

The Solitary Christian

"Okay, I'll buy the core. It's important. But why can't I just go out in the woods alone and pray, confess my sins, worship?"

My first—facetious—response to that is usually, "Fine. *Do* you?" And the answer is usually a kind of blushing shrug, "Oh, well, I, uh . . . "

The reason is simple: the solitary Christian is a contradiction in terms. In the first place, part of the core of Christianity is that it is apostolic; it reaches out to others, to those in need of material and spiritual help. Second, Jesus said at the First Mass, "Do *this* in memory of me." Presumably, if he'd wanted worship to be a walk in the woods, he would have said that. Dealing alone with God is fine for other religions; it's even strongly recommended for Christians, but not exclusively. The Founder of Christianity didn't leave that option open. Third, as we have seen, just by the nature of human beings we don't learn alone, from scratch. The individual needs the support, the challenge, the pooling of talents he or she can find only in a group. It's the way we're made.

Even in solitary confinement the Christian is not alone. He or she is truly *with* God and *with* the others. Christian survivors of Nazi extermination camps maintained that that realization was the only thing that got them through.

The very core of Christianity is a direct challenge to isolation, alienation, and narcissism—which might be one reason that, if people "attend" Mass in cocoons, the Mass doesn't "say" what it was intended to say, nor does the Mass "do anything" for them.

To see the Church as a spectator, from the outside, is not to see the Church.

Facing the Real in Light of the Ideal

Only a few highly courageous people today can go back to the communes of the early Church. Even the saintly Dorothy Day failed at that, more than once. The rest of us must balance the real with the ideal, at times precariously, at times to our cost. Just as we have to infuse the aliveness of the counter-culture into the regimentation of the System, and the discipline of the System into the spontaneity of the counter-culture, we have to live with the real and imperfect embodiment of Christianity, but always challenge the Church—us—with our shortcomings and try to grow. In a sense, we are the loyal opposition to ourselves.

Chesterton, as always, said it well: can you hate something honestly enough to want it changed, and love it honestly enough to want to be part of the changing?

Who, if not you?

When, if not now?

Questions for the Notebook

Page 13. The "incautious" question: in what ways has or will your choice of career be affected by the core of your Christianity? If not, can you say why?

Page 14. Suppose you were trying in some ordinary, concrete ways to inject the core spirit of Christianity into your present school or office or neighborhood. What would some of those concrete things be?

A Prayer

God, help me to let down my defenses, at least a bit. Help me to stop protecting myself from other people, especially people in need. Help me to stop protecting myself from you. Amen.

The Un-Ideal School

My education was interrupted only by my schooling.
—Winston Churchill

Although it is a mere flicker of time compared to the hours we log in front of the Tube, most of us spend about ten thousand hours before we're eighteen sitting in rooms listening to other people talk at us about dangling participles, unknown factors, and Wheatstone bridges. Did you ever ask yourself *why?*

Well, for some reason it's the law. True, but why? Well, everybody says you have to have a good education to get a good job. But does anybody ever say—or try to find out—what "a good education" *means* and why everybody has to spend so much time getting it?

If we're trying to find out "how do I know?" then education would seem to have something to do with that

The Utilitarian Motive

The better your education, the better your job—or so the folk wisdom says. And "better" usually does not mean better chance to serve the community, but more money.

Is there any *logical* connection between the day-to-day content of one's schooling and a higher-paying job? On the one hand, other than corporation executives, for whom education would certainly make a difference, the highest paid people in America are entertainers and athletes. No need there, or on the way there, for calculus or even typing. On the other hand, if statistics hold true, most readers of these pages are or will be associated in some way with sales or housekeeping. No problem with that, except that you don't need trigonometry in order to balance a checkbook or French irregular verbs in order to make french fries.

If a Venusian examined our curricula, she might get the idea we were training young people for a lifetime of solving crossword puzzles and appearing profitably on quiz shows.

The bulk of the actual data we ingest and disgorge in the course of our schooling—in the sheerly utilitarian sense—will be absolutely useless to us in later life. We will never need to bring any of it to bear on a problem of daily living or working. Even the president of IBM need never have known that Shakespeare died in 1616, nor does it help a great criminal lawyer to be aware that the cosine of angle AOC is 1.0763. It is as meaningful, in a sense, as being asked for eight years to jump over a stick, varying in color from hour to hour, five hours a day. If you have been generally compliant in that process, you are then given a certificate which enables you to go on to four years of more complicated sticks, another certificate, and four or more years of jumping.

One catch: the longer you jump, the more expensive it gets. A cynic might be tempted to suggest that you ask your family instead to give you the forty or fifty grand and set you up in some nice business.

What effect does this have on one's ability to see the truth? Well, for one thing, it surely puts a damper on curiosity. For another, it insures contentment with mediocrity and passivity. "Is this gonna be on the *test?*" If not, let the teacher prattle away. It's her ballpark.

More deadeningly, considering school subjects only as "something to be gotten through" leads you to assess individual subjects not by their content, or by the insights they might offer into how human beings and the universe work, but by their ability to generate *certain* answers— so you won't be embarrassed on the test. Theology, for example, is thin to the point of invisibility, since all its answers are "up for grabs." Math, on the other hand, is the most comfortable subject: there is one answer, one acceptable way of getting it, and a fool-proof method of checking whether it is *the* answer. Science is often comfortable, too: there are definite formulas, procedures, objectives—and when the job is done, it's *done,* closed, sure. History is comfortable, provided the teacher limits it to memorized dates and names. And even grammar and spelling are reassuringly certain: it's either spelled rightly or wrongly, and it can be definitively checked in a dictionary. It may be boring, but at least you're certain. And cheating is easier.

However, that's really "cookbook" math and science; you are given only problems which are guaranteed to work out. *Real* mathematicians and scientists pick up questions that are mysterious, that may well have no discoverable answers. But that's another world. We're talking about school.

The truth is, ironically, that for *most* people, math and science will be the *least* useful studies for later life. Few are called upon ever again to factor a quadratic equation, nor will they feel frustrated by that lack of challenge. With an even heavier irony, there is no profession—no matter how technical or uncomplicated—in which people will not be called upon to use *words.* Therefore, the most utilitarian course in schools might indeed be Latin!

The Medium = The Message

Whatever the course *content*—physics, English, sociology—the *manner* of procedure is basically identical, and, for the unthinking, that manner *becomes* the message which is subconsciously internalized: this is the way the System works. You come in every day and I, as supervisor of this department, give you a certain amount of work; at the end of the week or month, I give you a "paycheck" which tells you—and your family—how satisfied I am with your performance. The work itself may be as meaningless as capping bottles in an assembly line, but it's the way "they" want it. Thus, no matter what the subject, the school is acting as a sorting mechanism to determine at which level of the System you can make the best contribution: mechanic, hairdresser, marine biologist, physician.

The trouble is that, after about ten years of that, even the dimmest wits have learned that lesson to the point of overkill. Recall your own first nervous days in high school: everybody had pencils (sharpened) and lots of (one's own) paper; everybody did all the homework and tried to impress teacher with carefully written essays. Within a year—at most—it's "Lemme borrow a pen, okay?" and "Anybody do the math?" You've learned which "bosses" can be conned, how often you can be late without too much hassle, when it's safe to fake another visit to the school nurse. You've learned that in ten minutes you can get enough swamp gas down on paper that a teacher has to give you at least a 70. In short, you've learned to get the maximum return for the minimum effort. Don't say, "When I get out into the *real* world." You're in it now, and have been since Day One.

The effect on ability to see? Mediocrity again. Learning becomes not a process of finding the truth but of finding ways to *avoid* it. Moreover, with all those bodies who stay around long after functional illiteracy has been achieved, educators must continuously search for undemanding programs of study. Teachers don't relish being despised and thus balk at demanding hard work and strict standards, thereby bestowing on the young the gift of spinelessness. The ignorant are consulted about what they need to learn. They are shielded from the fact that failure is a part of human life and thus march from the halls of academe convinced that being spoiled is an incurable disease. Lacking any underlying and unifying rationale, the university becomes a cafeteria of courses for people who can't think. And yet, if human nature is indeed still the same as it always was, and if only the fittest of the species "survive," the survivors will very likely be those who can think.

However, even without one's explicit awareness, every school subject does have something at its core which is common to all the others:

it at least tries to make you learn how to think. No matter what the course—English, math, history, biology—all of them teach the same fundamental process: (1) gathering data, (2) sifting out the most important elements, (3) grouping it under major headings, (4) arranging it in some logical sequence so that you can (5) draw a defensible conclusion.

The process is *precisely* the same, whether it's brought to bear on a history essay or a lab report. Why? Because *that's the way the human mind works.* It is, in fact, a slightly more technical development of the process of human perception we examined at the beginning of this book.

Perhaps the day's specific matter—Spanish culture, graphs of population growth, doing unspeakable things to pickled frogs—will never enter your consciousness again after the test. But it's sent you through that fundamental process once again: gathering, sifting, grouping, arranging in sequence, drawing conclusions. In a sense, the data itself is secondary, like the paper used to test experimental photocopiers. The paper ends up garbage, but the machine's effectiveness is improved.

The effect on one's ability to see is obvious, though avoidable. Whether the task at hand is how to unplug a sink, what career to choose, what plan to offer the boss, which person to marry, the process is exactly the same, the one all those teachers have been secretly teaching you all along: gathering, sifting, grouping, arranging in sequence, drawing conclusions.

The only part that puzzles me is *why* we keep that fact that we're all doing the same thing some kind of secret!

Making a Living/What Living Is For

But education should teach more than reading, writing, arithmetic, and socially acceptable behavior. It should even do more than give you a feeling and respect for logical relationship and balanced, fair-minded thinking. It should give you a realization of what being human is all about—what human beings are for. It should open up and give you some direction in pursuing the great questions of the physical universe and of the human spirit. It should make you face the mystery of human freedom: making responsible choices and accepting the consequences. It should teach you to cope courageously and creatively with "the unfairness of things"—like the suffering of the innocent, war, decay, and death. It should teach you the meanings of love. And, most of all, it should teach you that learning can never cease, that once one stops learning, he or she begins to die as a specifically human being.

A liberal education should be liberating. It should continue (even after the issuance of the last "certificate") to open up newer, wider, richer horizons. It should, in fact, be an endless series of *conversions.*

A liberal education should free you from the shackles of illusion, prejudice, and the superstitions and irrational taboos of this "tribe." It should free you from the tyranny of propaganda—whether from the System, the counter-culture, the Church, parents and peers, or even the school itself—and enable you to choose a life-view, opinions, and commitments for yourself, based not on uncritical conformity, nor on uncritical spontaneity, but on the examined truth, the real natures of things as they are.

That is not an unmixed blessing. The less you know, the more limited your choices, to be sure, but the more "certain" you can be. The more you learn, the more you begin to comprehend how much more there still is unlearned, more than any single life could dream of exhausting. At the bottom of every question is a little box with ten more questions inside it.

But that is the price of freedom. That is the price of being fully human. The piper must be paid but, oh, how beautiful the music!

Questions for the Notebook

Page 15. If you have a boring or ineffective teacher, what did/do you actually do about it? Go to the principal, chairman, guidance counselor? And if nothing is done even then, what do you honestly believe you should do?

Page 16. Report cards have been other people's ratings of you as a learner. On a scale of 1-100, how would you rate yourself? What are you proud about regarding your learning? What are you not so proud about?

A Prayer

God, without dreams, I become stagnant. But without a recognition of reality, my dreams and I are doomed to frustration. Help me to narrow the difference between reality and my dreams. Again, help me to see. Amen.

Peer (And Parent) Pressure

And when you are in heaven for following your conscience, Howard, and I am in hell for denying mine, will you come with me—for fellowship?

—*Thomas More in*
"A Man for All Seasons"

It should be fairly clear by now that most of our opinions are not personally and painstakingly researched but are more often taken "off the rack" from one or several of the agencies we've been considering till now. All of them affect us directly, over the TV set or radio or stereo, in the churches and classrooms. Even on points where they contradict one another, a little clever shunting allows us to keep the left hand side of the brain from knowing what the right hand side is doing. Thus, we plan to be very, very rich and famous, *and* at one and the same time very, very serene and generous; we can indulge ourselves sexually with the conviction that the Author of the Commandments is really after all just a big Pussy Cat; we can loll through school, ignoring the fact that our transcripts started filling up on that first day of the first year, secure that we'll get into the college we choose and live happily ever after.

The effects of the propaganda systems we've examined thus far are, in a sense, easier to separate from one another than are the influences on opinions to which we now turn: parents and peers. One reason is that they don't come at us at clearly defined times: commercial breaks, Mass time, class time. Opinions from our families and friends come more or less at unpredictable times, but the effect is so constant and consistent that we hardly realize we're being affected by them. Such influences come out when we say, "Well, everybody knows that," or "I've always believed that." Another reason is that many of our parents'/peers' opinions also have their roots in those conflicting voices of System/counter-culture/religion/education—filtered through the individuals, of course, and sometimes watered down below even the level of half-truths, but also remarkably strengthened by *loyalty* to two groups whom we know, live with, love, and above all whose approval and acceptance we all *need*.

Parents

The opinions of one's parents are not just ingested with the mashed potatoes over twenty-some years of dinner conversations. Very often we also live among and socialize with people of the same socio-economic backgrounds and interests, and few concerns can color opinions about the government's policies, the pastor's homilies, or the people you're allowed to associate with more than economic concerns. For instance, no matter on what other issues they may differ among themselves, ghetto families are solidly convinced that Welfare is too stingy and intrusive; upper-middle-class families are just as solidly convinced that Welfare is too bountiful and permissive. Where's the truth?

My parents were both uneducated people, but good and generous, with a wisdom that comes from dreams deferred and much pain reflected on. But my Dad and his friends, all registered Democrats, had been convinced by a tub-thumping radio priest named Father Coughlin that President Roosevelt (who was running for a third term) was a communist, so as little kids in the early 1930's we went around the neighborhood chanting "No man is good three times!" without the slightest notion what we were talking about. My mother always snapped the button to lock the car door if a black man crossed the street, and Father Coughlin had convinced her that all Jews were conniving shysters. And yet we had a black cleaning lady who came in once a week, and my mother and Althea poured out their miseries to one another over two-hour lunches, and when Al and Elizabeth Lebovitz moved next door, they became Mom's and Dad's best friends. Where's the truth?

Although, listening to some young people, I could be persuaded that both their parents wore swastika armbands, not all propaganda from parents is bad. I harbor no resentment toward my parents for toilet-training me, reading stories to me, or curbing my desires to brain my sister and enjoy the life of an only child. Nor do I begrudge the fact that they sacrificed to feed, clothe, and educate me. I do not even mind that they had me baptized a Catholic and trained me to believe as one, without consulting me. Their religion was precious to them, and had they *denied* it to me, I believe it would have been not an open-minded act of kindness but an act of selfishness. When I grew up, I could accept what I'd examined and found true and reject what I had examined and found false. Once I was independent of them, my parents would never have stopped my free choices—nor could they have, even if they'd wanted to.

One important point, however: even when I had left my parents' home and financial support, even when I had had fourteen years more formal education than they had had, put together, my parents—and my parents' opinions—still deserved my tactful *respect,* not because of the validity of the opinions but because of the people who held them. My Aunt Glad put it very well one time when I was getting a bit too uppity at nineteen. "Listen here, Mr. College Man," she said. "Don't you ever forget that, if it weren't for those two *dumb* people in there, you'd never *be* where you are now." I'm reminded, too, of a fine moment in Lorraine Hansberry's play, "A Raisin in the Sun." Beneatha, the hip college daughter, with a kind of patronizing tolerance has just told her mother, a cleaning lady, that believing in God is just a silly superstition. And Mama walks up to Beneatha, slaps her once and quite definitively across the face, and says, "Now. Repeat after me. 'In my mother's house, there is still God.' " And to that I say, "You *tell* it, Mama!"

I am beginning to focus for myself a kind of inadequate rule of thumb to determine what one accepts or questions about his or her parents' opinions and values. I find that, on the one hand, when adults speak from first-hand *experience,* for instance about behavior that's gotten *them* into trouble, I tend to be less willing to be critical. I listen the way I would to Lee Trevino about putting or to Colleen Dewhurst about acting. Their motive is not to rule the roost or spoil the fun; they don't want you hurt. Make mistakes (you can't avoid it), but for God's sake don't make the *same* ones *we* made. On the other hand, when adults speak their opinions on *ideas,* for example about politics or religion or careers, no matter how strongly they argue their views, the son or daughter not only can but must examine those opinions carefully, honestly, and without prejudice. How does one determine what to accept, and what to reject, and on what to reserve judgment? Evidence: personal experience, common sense, reason, and testimony—and not only from those who agree with me and against them.

There is one other way parents can too often misjudge the value which loyalty to them sometimes overweighs their opinions: their *expectations* of their children. A few concrete examples:

"Why don't you stop reading all those damn books and go out and play catch like the other kids?"

"What're you talking about? Take auto mechanics? A *girl?*"

"I'm gonna call that coach and let him have it. He hasn't played you in two weeks!"

"What do you mean you don't want to be an undertaker? An undertaker was good enough to put you through college."

"Social work? Now how the hell much can you make doing that?"

"Ninety-eight? What happened to the other two points?"

Kinda makes you want to crawl into a hole and pull it in after you, doesn't it?

Kids already have enough competition—quizzes, tryouts, the SAT's, the opposite sex, their own dubious self-images—without having to compete as well for their own parents' acceptance. In the delivery room, parents accepted not the children of their dreams but the children of their love.

On the other hand, however, the opposite extreme is just as corrosive: non-interference. Many parents don't want to cheat their children of those blissful, carefree teen years by demanding that they grow up before age twenty-two. Thus, one automatically cheats them of something rigid and flinty against which to hone their adulthood. Thus crippled, without the ability to think or stand alone, it is little wonder that they remain infantile prey to the siren songs of all the propaganda which promises ersatz fulfillment in exchange for freedom.

Another spectrum; another need for balance.

Peers

"Tell us, Dedalus, do you kiss your mother before you go to bed?"

Stephen answered, "I do."

Wells turned to the other fellows and said, "O, I say, here's a fellow says he kisses his mother every night before he goes to bed."

The other fellows stopped their game and turned round, laughing. Stephen blushed under their eyes and said: "I do not."

Wells said, "O, I say, here's a fellow says he doesn't kiss his mother before he goes to bed."

They all laughed again. Stephen tried to laugh with them. He felt his whole body hot and confused in a moment. What was the right answer to the question?

—*James Joyce, in Portrait of the Artist as a Young Man*

At times, the opinions of one's peers (most often second-hand and ill-considered) support the opinions of one's parents. If so, they deserve to be tested against the evidence and not swallowed whole. But there are other times when peers' opinions are in direct conflict with parents' opinions, and in areas which the parents consider far more important than the peers do. Then there is—or ought to be—a very real and sometimes long-standing and, one hopes, painful division of loyalties. I say "ought to be" simply because, if parents have very strong opinions on a subject, it is not only insulting but even arrogant and mean-spirited to treat those opinions, out of hand, as trash.

Of course it would be naive and unfair to argue that there are no times when parents are dead wrong: cases of bigotry, snobbishness, puritanism, injustice, and so on. A marriage license and any number of birth certificates do not immunize anyone from the truth blindnesses we saw extensively before. All the "victim" can hope for is to convince a priest or a wise older friend to argue his or her case. If that fails, each individual has to work out his or her own compromises—with the parent and, depending on the degree of the injustice, perhaps even with the truth. However, to make those choices without sound advice is foolishly risky.

The years have convinced me, though, that when opinions of parents and peers come into direct conflict, the parents are right far more often than not. That should be no surprise; they've got "the years" just as I have, and a lot of scar tissue of the soul on the side of their opinions.

But the need to belong—especially when the very nature of adolescence ("becom*ing* adult") is precisely to achieve gradual independence of parents—is a very strong and very deep need. So strong is it, in fact, that in some cases individuals will surrender just about any other opinion or conviction—or loyalty—simply to be accepted. There's no crystal ball to determine what causes that angry alienation. In some cases, it comes from the youngsters' convictions (right or wrong) that their parents don't accept them, or at least can't talk to them honestly and vulnerably, and they've got to be accepted by *some*body, no matter the price. At other times, it's just sheer damn hardheaded stupidity on the part of the youngster. After twenty years of working eyeball-to-eyeball with high school seniors, I still can't fathom why previously levelheaded young people will demean themselves and even crawl in order to secure the approval of an in-crowd which appears to be, in my not-inexperienced opinion, a pack of sneering sadists. And yet I've done it myself. Doubtless you have, too.

A hope of healing lies, of course, with the adults who are focal in the youngsters' lives. Unlike the teenagers, they've gone all the way *through* adolescence, although at times they seem to forget how painfully confusing it was. Presumably, they have more patience, and one would hope they trust their children—and more importantly themselves—to a degree that they can be *vulnerable* to their children's need to talk it all out again—and again. But if parents have any "hidden agendas," any convictions or concerns that override getting into their children's skins and walking around in them a while, there is little hope from that quarter.

The slavery to peer pressure is *in* the youngster. If he or she locks the door from the inside and smugly denies that any adult knows anything, then you need a professional. But reason and common sense aren't as powerless as too many parents believe. Eric Fromm writes of two different types of men and women: *productive persons*—who have a sense of their own integrity and therefore the courage of their own personally reasoned convictions—and *automaton conformists*—who yield to every signal from others and haven't a whisper of selfhood.

Adolescents do want to be accepted, but just as strongly they are searching for an independent *self.* That's what adolescence is about. They can see the illogic in trying to equate being a unique and independent individual with being exactly like everybody else. They can be led to suspect they are running away from family conformity straight into the chains of peer conformity. On the one hand, it's safer in the crowd, no need to think, develop a smiling mask for both parents and peers, adjust, adapt, roll with the punches. But it doesn't work, not for more than a year or so. Then the natural need to be a self emerges, undeniably. It *costs* to be a self, but for most kids I've known, it begins to look worth the price. (Meanwhile, their parents take options on rooms in mental hospitals.)

The question is, once again, how *much* is it going to cost? Can't I really shuffle back and forth between the parents' cocoon and the peers' cocoon indefinitely? Some few can pull it off, perhaps even for a lifetime, scuttling from bootlicking the boss' opinions, to bootlicking the pastor's opinions, to bootlicking the locker room opinions. But sooner or later it tears you apart; that's what causes the eventual midlife crisis: the person has no *center.*

The answer is in self-confidence, a stance somewhere in balance between arrogance and self-detestation. It doesn't come from looking lovingly in a mirror and singing, "I *believe* in *you!*" That's only one more false and therefore temporary mask. I can only tell you how it happened to me and hope that it can happen to you. I've written it before, but it's the core of what I have to offer anyone.

When I was a kid, I was bright, shy, and unathletic—any one of them enough to send a man to a monastery, but all three suggestive of remedial suicide. Gradually, a few people—sometimes purposefully, sometimes cruelly—challenged me to stand up and fight back. I risked more, but I was always the first to point out the shortcomings of anything I did accomplish *so that* I could short-circuit the power of the inevitable criticism. Finally, at the age of thirty-one, it was time to decide if *I* thought I was worthy of ordination as a priest. Of course! Of course *not!*

For six months in my ordination year, I taxed the epic patience of our spiritual father and most of my closest friends, unendurably. "Well, I'm not stupid. But I really *am* stupid." And so it went, from judging myself as not-so-bad to the certainty that I was a bucket of scum. Most significantly, it was not what *I* thought that mattered, but which of my friends could do the best job at convincing me that I wasn't totally valueless.

It came to an unavoidable head one Sunday in January 1963. At noon, I left the spiritual father's room after one more go-around: yes, no, maybe. Everybody else was going to lunch and then out to skate on a perfectly clear, ice-hard day. Not me. I hated them all. I was stupidly certain every one of the other seminarians was as sure of himself and his destiny as Jesus was, setting out from Nazareth. I was the only nobody.

So I went to my room and paced, and fussed, and fretted. Finally, I just couldn't stand it anymore; I had to escape. Obviously, there were no drugs or booze. I'd go to sleep; I'd shut it out for at least a while. I lay on my bed but I couldn't sleep. Then, suddenly, "it" came over me; it was—and I can put this only fumblingly—like "drowning in light." I was utterly certain that I was in the presence of God, without any need or ability to prove it. And, despite all the "evidence" of my worthlessness, I was *accepted.*

It lasted nearly two hours. At the end, I sat up and for the first time in my whole life I said, without the slightest fear, "I've got my faults, but I'm a good man. And I'll be a good priest, because I'm a good man." I grabbed my skates and went out to the skating lake; everybody was back in the house; and I skated around and around in huge circles, shouting, "I'm a good *man!* And I don't need *anybody* to tell me!" Because my Father had told me.

That realization has never left me. When I sin—and I do sin—I recognize its stupidity, but I know it was a good man who did it, someone *worth* picking up and starting over. And that's why I teach and write: so young people don't have to wait thirty years to understand that they have the approval of the only Person who truly counts.

That was real knowledge, first-hand, and as such it is communicable only in a notional way. Nor can one sit down saturated with his inadequacies, grind his teeth in some secret way, and rise inevitably armored in confidence.

Although it was powerless to make me see the truth, what sustained me *for* that moment of insight was the patience of our spiritual father and my friends. Like Annie Sullivan patiently drawing signs in Helen Keller's infuriatingly uncomprehending hands, they were giving me the tribute of being worth their time. Eventually, even someone as self-blinded as I had to see that.

There is only one answer: to be vulnerable to one another, to share not our strengths but our weaknesses. If the crucifix says nothing else, it says that.

Question for the Notebook

Page 17. In no particular order, list the things about yourself that you and other people genuinely like.

A Prayer

God, you called me from nothingness for some reason. They tell me it was because you love me. But, knowing how great you are and how riddled with faults I seem to be, that's hard to believe. I want to believe it. Help my unbelief. Amen.

The Meaning of You

I like to think of myself as a kind of "laid-back compulsive." I like to hedonize in the sun, but I also honestly get a genuine kick out of writing. So, for the last ten years I've taken my vacations in two-hour afternoon segments over the course of eight seven-day work weeks. Crazy, but it's too exhilarating for me not to guess that that's what I was made for.

For several of those years, every afternoon during hedonism time, a big black Labrador retriever used to come up to the chair where I was reading by the lake and nudge me with a stick. She was a really nice old dog, and from many previous afternoons she knew that, despite my pretended reluctance, she had me well trained. So I'd throw the stick, and she'd go gallumphin' into the water after it, come panting back, shake, and start the whole tease over, tail wagging lickety-split. Well, I threw the stick till my arm was linguine, and she was coughing and hacking like Camille on her deathbed. But that old tail was still thwapping away. Why? Because whatever joy an old black retriever could grasp came from fetching sticks. That was her *nature;* that's what she was born for.

What makes us wag *our* tails with joy—even when we're frazzled from doing it full-throttle? What is our nature? What were we born for?

One of the reasons we raise questions of God's *existence* is that, at least in part, we want to find out who *we* are. As we've seen, giving a "yes" or a "no" about God's existence is not sheerly an academic exercise. If the answer is "no," then our nature is—at least as far as we know—to be *the* masters of the universe; we are the minds who dictate the (temporary) purposes and values of things and people. However, by the mere accident of a birth over which we had no control, we are condemned to death—annihilation—after a life which seemed so tantalizingly beautiful. If the answer is "yes," then our nature is to be the sons and daughters of God; we are ransomed from final annihilation and meaninglessness. However, if we owe our lives, and all that is precious in our lives, *and* our immortality to that God, that is a debt so profound that one couldn't pay it off in ten lifetimes. How do you repay Someone for . . . everything?

Conversely, if man is indeed "made in the image of God," we can find out a great deal about the *nature* of God by examining his handiwork: us, and the universe which is our "context." Therefore, in the next three sections, I would like to help you examine at least in some beginning way who you are: what is the human nature you share with all of us and what will fulfill it; what is your own unique nature and what will fulfill that; and finally who are we together—with one another and with God?

Two warnings. First, one's life-view, one's philosophy of humanity and of oneself, has been strongly conditioned by all the factors we have pored over thus far in this book. It is well to recognize those influences, positive and negative, on our most basic beliefs and if possible "check them here at the door." Come at the study of humanity and yourself as an individual human being, with as few predispositions as possible, and not as a kind of sum-total of System/counter-culture/school/religion/parents and peers. Let this be *your* search.

Second, oversimple answers are generally false. Human beings and individuals are far too complex to be boxed in by half-truths, by answers that satisfy only the mind, or the libido, or even the spirit. Human beings are not merely heads, nor merely loins, nor merely hearts; divinize one over the others, and you will create zombies that are heartless, or gutless, or dis-spirited. Nor are human beings exclusively consumers, or exclusively patients, or exclusively worshipers. Ignore any aspect at your peril—and the peril of humankind. Human nature is too mercurial to fit snugly into any specialist's box.

What is the test? Evidence.

In the end, I believe the best test is the retriever test: what gives us joy—not just happiness, but the conviction and peace that, no matter what the fatigue, one is "right on." And its opposite is a good touchstone, too: what makes us miserable—not just temporarily irritable, but day-in, day-out hating our work, hating the people around us, hating ourselves. When you're in a state like that, it's pretty obvious you are being neither human nor yourself.

What Is Human Nature?
What Will Fulfill It?

We've seen a lot of answers to those two questions so far. We will see more presently: the answers of philosophy, biology, psychology. But there's no one reading these pages who hasn't *been* human for x-number of years. We're all more or less experts, with plenty of first-hand experience. And yet, why is it that we know just as little about "what being human means"—in the sense that we can put it into words—as we know about "what being Christian means" or "what being educated" means? Perhaps, again, it's cataloging all the trees and forgetting the forest.

A tree tells us what *it* is; therefore, when we compare it with all the objects in the scheme of things (the "context"), we can determine what it's *for*. Some purposes the tree had before we ever arrived on the scene: oxygenating the air and holding back erosion, for example. It took us a time even to realize those functions. But trees also have further purposes, i.e., anything our wits can tell them to do, within their limitations: turning into houses, spears, furniture, torches, books, PT-boats, salad bowls . . . whatever. The tree is held back only by its own properties and our ingenuity.

For centuries, philosophers used the tree also as a symbol: the Porphyrean tree, through which they tried to explain by analogy the quantum-leaps from inanimate, to vegetative, to animal, to human, to angelic, to divine beings. There really seemed almost a qualitative abyss separating the radical properties of each distinct level from those of its predecessor. No one denied that each succeeding level did, in fact, have all the properties of the lower level, but each new division seemed astonishingly advanced over what had gone before it on the evolutionary scale. Who expected a stone to get larger? Who expected a turnip to bleed? Who expected a sheep to write "Hamlet"? But as the race grew older and more learned, the "bins" seemed less comfortingly exclusive: stagnant mud puddles were teeming with life, we found; seaweed "learned" to adapt to new environments; dolphins and whales, we saw, could communicate quite cleverly over amazing distances. And then, my God, computers! The hard-and-fast divisions between the levels of

the Porphyrean tree were beginning to become a matter of not either/or but of more/less. Everything seemed up for grabs.

As we've seen, pendulums tend to swing too far, and here I think is one more case. The day a pig comes up to me and asks why he has to die, I'll revise my opinion. There are certain properties in the higher orders that don't seem even remotely accessible to the members of the lower orders:

A *stone* is located; it has weight, mass, electrical charge, length/breadth/height/depth.

A *tulip* has all the properties of a stone, but it can also grow, reproduce, radically adapt its properties to new environments at times. A stone can't do those things.

A *bear* has all the properties of a stone and a tulip, but it can move around freely, copulate with visible pleasure, feel pain, show mother love, even to the point of self-sacrifice. Neither a stone nor a tulip can do those things.

A *human* has all the properties of stone, tulip, and bear, but he or she can think and reflect back on his or her own experiences, anticipate the results of his or her actions, plan, hope, fear the not-yet existent future. We're the only animals who can do those things; we're a different breed of cat.

Our bodies share all the properties and potential of all the lower orders, but only human beings seem able to laugh—at least at their own stupidities. Only we are not prisoners of our genetic code or our environments—if we don't have wings, we'll make them; if we can't burrow under the ground or live under the sea, we'll devise ways; if our bodies don't have the means to cure our ills, we'll find means outside our bodies.

Animals have brains; we have wits.

But it is even more than that. The old philosophers also used to define human beings as "rational animals," that is, apes with wits. Not enough, I think. Unlike apes, our wits can design clocks which decree—with a tyranny more compelling than death—that until you have lived exactly 6,570 days you are not mature enough to drive a car, make a purchase at a bar, or tolerate an R-rated movie. Its instruments tell us when to get up, when to go to college, when to get married, when to have children. Material success is judged by these clocks; so is competition, so are expectations.

And there is even another "power" in us which, at least as far as we can determine, we don't share with beasts. After all, some "internal clock" in a stag also clicks on and tells him not only when but how to mate. The power we share only with God, if he exists, is a vehicle which takes us *outside* "clock time." It happens to me most often around water, or in fields empty of everything but sunshine and green and oneself. At least for that moment I have no promises to keep, no miles to go before I sleep. The woods are lovely, dark, and deep—and I can pause to share peace with them. In those moments we come nearer and nearer to the Kingdom of truth and joy, to who we really are, nearer to where God lives, if he lives, in a dimension of existence which is here, the quintessential *now,* and yet outside the competence of any measuring device but human receptivities. Here we encounter the immeasurable. Here we create, and find wisdom, and pray. Here we fall in love.

Call that receptive and creative power what you will; you and I have both felt it; its existence in us is undeniable. For lack of any other adequate word, I have called it "the human spirit." It is not a power strictly of the flesh—though especially in the imagination it seems to be rooted in the senses; nor is it a power strictly of the mind—though especially in works of the spirit, e.g., art, it seems to depend on order and control. It is as if two quite different power sources, flesh and intellect, were joined like the antagonistic positive and negative poles of a magnet to generate a third power: the force-field of the human spirit, which is neither of the two producing powers and yet could not exist without them, fused. (To get even heavier: Christian theologians could well use that same analogy for the Trinity: two powers "creating" a third entity who is their love.)

We are dogged by the weakness inherent in analogies. We can't get X-rays of the human or divine natures; we can explain them in terms of things we know more directly. Human beings don't *have* a mind and a body and a spirit; we *are* an organic fusion of all three. Nor does one element "beget" the other, and they in turn "beget" the third. All begin together, just as the magnet does. We become trapped in our own words. Nonetheless, it is at least the Christian contention that the spirit can literally survive without the other two.

Also, as our own experience evidences, we are a curious lot: why, why, why? What's more we don't like to be alone too long; we cling to one another in the dark. And there's also an itch inside all our powers which is discontented with what we have: we want more.

Human beings are therefore, by nature, *rational:* we want to do more than just react to stimuli like the lower orders; we want to *know* why we react that way. And we are *social:* we want more than just the comforting warmth of the herd; we want to *love,* even people who are not "our own." And we are also *self-transcending:* we want more than to be "stuck" as the other orders are where a capricious evolution has left them; we want to *grow.*

Moreover, each aspect of the human fusion has those three properties or urges. I'm not content just to know and love with my hands and my genitals like an animal; I want to know also with my mind and my "heart," too. I'm not content to grow only automatically in my physical stature; my mind and spirit are hungry, too. Further, just as junk food takes its toll on my body, the "junk food" of *The National Enquirer* and the ballscores and soap operas are not enough for my mind and my soul. Finally, although my need for more can be perverted to mere material acquisitiveness, my mind and soul warn me by their restlessness that I was made for more than that.

It would follow, then, that the more one transcends himself or herself, the more he or she grows in knowing and loving, the more human he or she is.

What is human nature? A fusion of mind and body and spirit. What will fulfill it? What will make us wag our tails for joy? Growing—in mind and body and spirit.

The key, then, seems to be in growth.

Self-Transcendence and Perfectionism

The misery caused by solitary confinement and sensory-deprivation experiments is evidence enough that human nature was not meant to be static. Human individuals may not be on an unvaryingly upward graph, moving from one glittering success to the next; we do have our ups and downs. But even worse than the risk of "downs" is no risk at all: stagnation, boredom, inertia. Stones sit, stolidly; flowers grow, unquestioningly; animals graze, warily. We itch.

There is one more interesting insight into what being human means: only human beings screw up. We're not perfect; only human beings need erasers. Only human beings can be called on the carpet for doing stupid things. If a puppy wets the rug or a sheep gets caught in barbed wire, we may irrationally beat the animal, but it had no idea what it was doing. If normal adult humans wet the rug or get caught in barbed wire, however, they feel embarrassed. They should have known better; they should have anticipated the consequences. Nor can they simply shrug and say, "Oh, well. It's only human!" Ordinarily when we say that, what we're actually saying is that what we've done is not human but childish or animal.

The members of every other lower order perfectly fulfill their purposes, their natures. *Only* we are free to screw up, to go *against* our natures: to be *ir*rational, *anti*-social, self-*impoverishing.* Only we are "unfinished"; only we are imperfect. That imperfection is the inescapable and paradoxical corollary of our need to grow; you can't be perfectly complete—and also still have more learning and loving and growing to do.

Only human nature, then, is free to fulfill itself or not. Only human nature is an invitation, not a command.

"Aha!" says the fundamentalist Christian, "but it says with absolute clarity in Matthew 5:48, 'Be *perfect,* as your heavenly Father is perfect.'" I always cringe when fundamentalists cry "Aha!" and use so many exclamation points, as if finding the truth, especially in Scripture, were a matter of who can score the most debating points. Jesus simply couldn't have meant that God intended us to be "perfect" in the sense of "flawless." In the first place, it's demonstrably impossible. Second, that would make us equal to God—a temptation God has made it pretty clear, since the day of Adam and Eve, that we were not to succumb to. Third, as the results of that temptation show, being perfect is in defiance of our own human nature, which is to grow. Fourth, even Jesus was imperfect as a man, since "he grew in wisdom and age and grace." Fifth, my fundamentalist seems to be unaware that when a Jew like Jesus used the word "perfect" (which is also a synonym for "holy"), he meant "whole" or "integrated," or, as we would say, "He has all his (beep) together," or "She knows who she is and where she's going." Finally, Jesus seemed to accept—even love deeply—people who were consistently *im*perfect, like Peter. One isolated verse doth not a theology make.

Therefore, when Jesus told us to be "perfect," he was not equating Christianity with perfectionism. When he used the word about his Father, "The One Perfect," he spoke of a person who was complete and flawless; when he used the word about us, it was a call to be whole, integrated, all-together, at peace *but* in process.

Human beings are *not perfectible.* But we are indefinitely *improvable.*

That is not merely a handy verbal distinction. Failure to comprehend that stark difference is, I believe, at the root of most—if not all—the problems good people have ever brought to me as a priest or as a friend. They are not what they "ought" to be—or what the System/counter-culture/etc. tell them they "ought" to be. What they ought to be, they feel, is without sin, like Our Lady—or better. Moreover, I believe perfectionism is also the root, ironically, of the mediocrity to which so many people too quickly resign themselves: "Hell, it didn't take me too long to find out I wasn't one of those 'brains.' "—"Oh, I hardly ever speak up; I'm nobody."—"If you can't be the best, be the worst!" Even further, it is the root of the gullibility we have before the siren songs of propaganda—eat this, buy this, drive this, and you'll become like a god. We can't become like God; we can only become more like God today than we were yesterday.

A coach once told us that, if you couldn't throw from home plate to second base, aim for center field. All well and good, but when we could at last hit second base we forgot that's what we were aiming for, and we hated ourselves because we still couldn't throw to center field.

Of course we must excel ourselves; that's our nature. But I find a perversion of that natural urge in a kid coming off a field after a losing game and saying, "If only I'd tried *harder!*" Understandable, but stupid. He'd tried his *best.* What was he to do, try his best-*er?* Worse, I've heard reputedly intelligent adults say in the same situation, "If only they'd given that extra little effort!" God!

If the growth our nature calls us to implies incompleteness, then all our enterprises will fall short of perfection. I have never put "100" on a paper that couldn't be surpassed; every Gold Medalist is going to be excelled, if not in four years, then in eight; we may be "Number One!" for the moment, but not forever. As a race and as individuals we are, by our nature, unfinished.

Perfectionism is disheartening because it is anti-human, the virtue of growth perverted into the vice of self-hatred.

Uncertainty

There is another by-product of being human: uncertainty. If we enjoyed the powers of God, we would know the future; we would see with utter clarity the consequences of our choices before we were forced to make them and live with them; there'd be no temptations, no need for

108 / Meeting the Living God

calculated risks, no need for faith. It'd be great. But we are not God. If there is any truth about which we have far too much evidence, it is that one.

However, the same perverseness in us that craves perfection also craves certainty: "I don't *want* to believe; I want to *know!*" Sorry, Charlie.

We know we were not made to be certain by using the "retriever test": there is no joy in absolute certitude *because* there is no risk. What joy is there in a game one can't possibly lose? Even God (if such there is) took a risk in making us free and improvable, able to fulfill our nature—or not, as *we* chose. (If he does exist, there's a real insight into his personality.)

What's more, we can tell from people who do act as if they have complete certitude, as if they had no need to deepen or broaden or enrich their ideas further, that smugness and arrogance are in defiance of who we are.

If you can feel fulfilled only when you are perfect or totally certain, better start shopping around for another universe.

What Being Human Means

We live in "context"—a spectrum of entities which runs the gamut from the infinitesimal *pas de deux* of the hydrogen atom to the nearly infinite Great Dance of the Universe—and perhaps beyond. But, having examined that context for thousands of years, we find that we are the only entities (we know of at this point) that can know and love and grow in the specifically different way in which we do. The love of a human mother, for instance, is similar to but far different from the love of an animal mother—simply because her child has a whole range of potential which the animal cub does not.

Until we discover otherwise, there is a certain truth to the assertion that we are the masters—or at least the overseers—of creation. Our need to transcend ourselves is a clear indicator that, like the tree, we are limited only by our own properties and our own ingenuity. It seems clear that human beings were made to use anything in the universe insofar as it makes us grow as knowing, loving beings, and to reject the use of anything in the universe which makes us less able and open to know and to love. Such use of things to dehumanize or degrade ourselves or one another would be a "sin" against our human nature.

However, there is another clue to our meaning in our "context." Unlike our less sophisticated and therefore more parochial predecessors on this planet, we now know that the earth is not the center of everything; it is not even the center of its own solar system. We are, in fact, the inhabitants of a planet which—if seen even from the relatively nearby vantage point of our galaxy—would be invisible. It could disappear in a wink, and the overwhelming bulk of the universe would be utterly unaffected. If even the whole earth is not the focal center of "everything," then surely we, its temporary inhabitants, are not. Unless the center of reality is judged by some norm other than a material, spatial norm? That question should give us pause.

Finally, human beings are not unique in having brains and bodies; all animals have both, in a whole host of varying shapes and sizes and capacities. But at least as far as we can judge, *only* humans have the experience of capacities we associate with the human "spirit." What will fulfill—"make whole"—that power? The best answer I know to that is given by St. Paul when he discusses the ways we can see *the* Spirit visibly manifest in the Christian: "love, joy, peace, patience, kindness, goodness, trustfulness, gentleness, self-control" (Gal 5:22).

This is the ultimate touchstone by which to judge the claims of the System, the counter-culture, the school, parents and peers—yes, even the claims of the Church. *Do* they challenge us to increase our ability to know honestly and love unselfishly? Do they appeal to what is human in us, or to what is less than human?

In the end, it is the touchstone by which we judge our very lives.

Question for the Notebook

Page 18.   We can use the words "he or she is a good person" about very widely different individuals. What do you mean, basically, by "a good person"—concretely, specifically, day-by-day?

A Prayer

Oh, God, for all that has been—Thanks! To all that shall be—Yes! Amen.

(Dag Hammarskjöld)

Who Are You? What Will Fulfill You?

We grow too soon old, too late smart.
—*Jewish proverb*

This is, I fear, one more of those intimidating "who do you *really* think you *really* are" sections with which well-intentioned teachers routinely plague people's lives. It is, in a sense, one more mirror, and mirrors can become addictive. On the one hand, as we've said, if you keep pulling up the carrot to examine it, it will never grow. On the other, as Aristotle said, the unexamined life is not worth living. Extremes; balance.

The major reason for inserting this meditation here is not to feed juicy tidbits to a teacher's insatiable curiosity. It's for you, with or without a teacher, a kind of annual (or even first) spiritual retreat to reassess your individual self, especially in the light of the chapters we've done so far about seeing the truth—not only negative but positive—without self-blindness, without warping by false propaganda, without perfectionism or a demand for certainty. Do you really believe the things you say you believe, about human life and about yourself?

Some elements of yourself you can meditate on again and again till you die, and there's no hope of changing them. Other aspects of your personality and the way you handle the invitation of your humanity *can* be changed, but it'll cost. Count on it. That's why we don't like these little excursions into "who do you think you are?" It's why we'd prefer not to go to confession more often than we can avoid. Things may be kind of "blah" but they'll get better, like the TV selections of an evening. Let sleeping dogs lie. As Hamlet says, "it makes us rather bear the ills we have, than fly to others that we know not of."

What Cannot Be Changed

The Limits of Your Humanity

You're a human being—not a rock, not a vegetable, not a stud. You're free to *act* non-human, but you're not free to *be* non-human. If you balk at the considerable effort and risk it takes to learn and love, your body and mind and spirit will let you know. When you're going in the wrong direction, you will have what old black people wisely call "the miseries." No need to spell them out; we've all been there.

There are limits to being human. Whether there is or is not a God, it's pretty sure we're not "it." Only in a limited (though nonetheless significant) way can we change "the way things are," and the one thing we certainly can't control is death. We're also forever imperfect and uncertain, two shortcomings with which no god could hold his or her job too long. We die without food, and therefore we must work. Our mental and spiritual circuits melt if we don't take time off, and therefore even the most irreligious need a "sabbath." We need love; we need other people; we need to keep our minds occupied—no matter with what. We need some assurance that, if we wade through all the crap, there *must* be a pony. Those are "givens."

At first it seems there are no limits. Babies want to try everything, such as sticking their hands on the stove, because for a baby everything is new, everything is possible. But as we grow up, the infinite number of our possible choices is narrowed down. Some are eliminated by recognizing brute facts; for instance, the law of gravity kills the dream of flying by jumping off the garage. Experience of consequences teaches you that your belly rejects a wide range of objects like pins, mud, and under-ripe apples. The range of possible—and desirable—choices narrows down.

Other possibilities are eliminated (at least temporarily) by other people. For instance, your options were limited by your parents as regards letting your room get as grungy as a pigsty, staying up till midnight, missing school and Mass and dentist appointments, even picking your own nose. Your brothers and sisters and friends taught you that you didn't have the freedom to possess anything you wanted, like their toys or piggy banks or membership in their gangs.

Face it: you will never be free until you give up the hope of total freedom; you will always be improvable. If you "if-only" your way through life, you will die without having lived. Accept "the rules of the game," and get on with it.

The Limits of Your You-ness

You're a *unique* human being. Until we start cloning, your DNA code is absolutely one-of-a-kind. Even then, even with your exact skin tone and body configuration and IQ, your clone could never reduplicate the influences of your unduplicable parents, your neighborhood, your past experiences. They're yours alone, assimilated by a unique receiver. You can straighten your hair, mask your skin, pump iron, get psychoanalyzed, but inside it's still the same basic you. No hope? Oh, yes. Your talents are indeed limited, but so, you must realize, are your shortcomings.

Education is to the individual in you what the growing-up experience is to the human being in you: you learn where the sharp edges are. If you're educated by wise, watchful, caring people, they open up the whole general store to you: "Please touch; please feel free to make mistakes; walk on the grass; fiddle with this even if it breaks." You handle all the possibilities, and get a "touch" for them. You find out, for example, that you like poetry but not math; you like individual sports but not contact sports; you like biology but can't stand blood. In the ideal order, you find out who *you* are. It sounds good in the brochure, but ideals are hard to concretize, using imperfect people on both sides. Often you quit too soon, not because of a lack in yourself or the inability of the subject to grab you, but because of "bad chemistry" with the teacher. It happened to me again and again. I still literally shudder when I pick up a set of trig tables. And for years, as I've said, I was convinced (by what?) that I was stupid.

That situation seems to be one of those things that can't be changed. At least until you're age twenty-two, it's "their" ballgame. But it's not. "Oh, they won't do anything!" Sez who? And who is to say, once again, that *your* complaint might not be the last straw? Teachers don't get into that business, surely, because of the prestige, or because it's so easy, or because they couldn't get five times as much repairing toilets. They want to help young people grow. But at times they're scared, too, and react defensively; at times, they've been at the job and unchallenged too long. By guess who? It takes courage to be a self.

There is one other matter in this regard from which you can also liberate yourself: from the paralyzing tyranny of "if only." "If only I'd been born white ... if only I were 6'6" ... if only I were a boy ... if only my parents were rich ... if only I were a knockout ...." If wishes were horses, beggars would ride. Face the truth, and set yourself free. "If only" is the most useless pairing of words in the language, because they automatically say that anything that comes after them is absolutely *impossible.* Go ahead; keep trying to throw from center field to home plate; keep trying. But don't blame anyone else for your miseries after a lifetime of trying and failing at it. Set yourself free, not from dreams, but from utterly impossible dreams. Make peace with who you are; forgive yourself—and God—for your untalents; then take the talents you have, and make a somebody out of them.

What Can Be Changed

Our human purpose is to grow, to change—ourselves and our environments, even when it means leaving behind something good, comfortable, and well-smelt, for something better. We can never deny our pasts, but we are not *prisoners* of our pasts. Even Freud maintained strongly that we can go *against* everything that was untrue or warping in our training, our socialization, our habits, our hang-ups. If that were not the case, what purpose would psychotherapy have?

There's a second awakening in later adolescence: you find you can reassess most of the old possibilities that you thought were closed. The law of gravity and the laws of your stomach are still pretty well unchanged, but you realize that a great many of the doors that propaganda "closed" while you were younger can really be reopened if you want.

You know, for instance, that short of physical violence no one can force you to accept anything—Mass, school, work, athletics, morals. Even when they can blackmail you into *acting* as they want you to, they can no longer make you *believe* what they want you to.

There's a catch: you're not free to choose what you don't know about, what you're afraid to know.

The only chance is to challenge yourself to new horizons; they're open to you. Try on a few new masks; who knows, they may not be masks at all, but the true face you never knew was you. Tell yourself, "T'hell with what they all think, I'm going to try out for a play." Try working your tail off for a month or so; you might find you love it. You'll surely be less bored. Actively try to meet a whole host of new people and be as open as you can with them. Who knows where a really beautiful friendship lies hiding? After all, all your present good friends were once strangers. Don't expect an instant soul-mate; don't try for center field. Just try reaching further than you'd planned.

It's always smart, however, to have someone older and wiser with whom you are completely open, so that he or she can throw you a few question marks about your new discoveries. I've known more than a handful of painfully shy people, for instance, who at seventeen suddenly took hold of their courage and discovered the exhilaration of going to beer parties with other people. They were accepted! They were drunk! The problem was that they couldn't see the two were separable.

Other than wise advice, there is another simple test: does this new person, or crowd, or idea, or activity make me more genuinely human, or less? Is the joy that it generates authentic? Does it open me up to a wider horizon—or does it, really, detour me into a narrower and very dead-end street?

Values/Obedience/Freedom

Do you really believe the things you say you believe, about human life and about yourself?

We all like to think we are the kind of persons who want to be honest, to care for others more than for ourselves, to grow in our scope of knowing and loving, to be truly free. But is it true? Let me offer a little test.

For those not knowledgeable about true art, that picture is a little girl. In one hand, she has a stuffed rabbit; in the other, she has a real $50 bill. If in some preposterous twisting of events, you were told by a wicked witch with a wart on her nose to throw *one* of those objects into a furnace or be thrown in yourself, which would you choose?

In the sixty or so times I've done this in class, it has never failed that at least one wantwit sniggers "the girl!" to an answering chorus of sniggers. If it *didn't* happen, I'd be almost disappointed.

Then, just as predictably, people say the rabbit, because it is objectively the least valuable of the three. Then, the more sensitive realize that, to the little girl, the rabbit is terribly important and the bill is, by comparison, meaningless.

How high would the number of the bill have to get before you'd seriously consider throwing the little girl into the furnace? No one would ever know. It's only one little girl. Think of all the *other* little girls' lives you could enrich with, say, $1,000,000.

Nor is this just a silly, dreamt-up exercise. In the early 40's of this century, men and women were faced with just such a choice, literally: throw little children into ovens, or go to the Russian front. They were forced to weigh the possibility of their own deaths (and what that would mean to their families) against the certainty of the children's deaths. At the Nuremburg trials after the war, the defense was, almost without exception: "I was only a soldier following orders."

No need to tell anyone else, but what do you honestly believe you would have done?

They tell a story, too good to have happened, about George Bernard Shaw sitting at a dinner next to a voluptuous woman, dripping diamonds. "I say," he said, "would you sleep with me for 100,000 pounds?" She blushed, demurely, and replied, "Why, I rather think I would." He harrumphed, "Would you sleep with me for *five* pounds?" In horror, the lady glared back, "What do you think I *am?*" And he responded, affably, "We've already settled that. We're only haggling over prices."

The man we saw before who couldn't give up the $15,000 and go back to the happiness of his previous job at least seemed to have had a price. We'd all like to believe no one could buy us. But is it true?

Not too long ago, a psychologist named Stanley Milgram advertised for assistants in a memory experiment at Yale. The assistant's job was easy. The "subject" was strapped in a chair in the next room behind a two-way mirror; electrodes were strapped to his arms so that, if he made a memory mistake, the assistant at a console triggered a minor jolt of shock to the subject. Moreover, there was a calibrated dial by which, after each memory mistake, the dosage was increased. It went all the way to "Danger: brain damage."

Actually, the subject was an actor who got the same tiny tingle of electricity each time, but increased his reactive struggles more and more, to the point of screaming panic. The true purpose of the experiment was to study not memory, but obedience—susceptibility to brainwashing, if you will. The real subject was not the actor in the chair, but the assistant at the console.

Before the experiments, psychologists polled agreed that probably twenty percent of the assistants might go all the way to "Danger: brain damage." In fact, almost ninety percent of them did—especially when Milgram assured them that he was a Ph.D. from Yale in psychology, that he certainly ought to know what he was doing, and that he would sign a paper taking full legal responsibility.

Again, no need to tell anyone else, but could anyone assume responsibility for *your* actions? Would that be enough to quiet your conscience, at least after a while. Or do you ever "lay off" responsibility for your actions—as Adam did on Eve—onto "Society" or the "the System" or "I had no choice"?

In 1968, a group of American soldiers under Lieutenant William Calley were ordered into a village called My Lai in South Vietnam. They were told to "kill anything that moved," although Lieutenant Calley later testified that he preferred the word "waste," since the word "kill" set up negative responses in men brought up on "thou shalt not kill." When the soldiers had rounded up hundreds of villagers at a ditch, Calley gathered his sergeants and said, "All right, tell them to waste 'em." Perhaps the rest of the story is as apocryphal as the Shaw story above, but it was reported that one of the sergeants said to Calley, "What? They're only little kids and old people!" Calley reminded him they were under orders. But the sergeant, reportedly, said "—— you," and walked away.

I ask myself at times, "Could you have done that?" According to military law, Calley had every right to shoot the sergeant then and there. Was it even worth the risk? It wasn't going to stop anything. Still, what did the sergeant remain in possession of, which the others surrendered?

Why do men and women in armed services on both sides of the Iron Curtain wear uniforms? To lessen their sense of independent individuality. It's a trivial matter, but quite effective. Why do they spend mind-numbing months marching, marching, marching in tight, well-ordered columns? Surely not to prepare them to march into battle that way; packed up like that, they'd be slaughtered by a single round of mortar fire. No, it is to *condition* them to respond to orders *without thinking.*

Suppose, in a battle, the captain says, "All right, men. We'll probably have seventy percent casualties, but we *must* take Porkchop Hill. Move out!" Suppose one of the men were to say, "Uh, excuse me, sir, but there are only, uh, *ten* of us. Could you explain to me, please, why that piece of rock is more important than seven human lives—just-beginning lives? I mean, I'm not a coward. If you can make me understand it, I'll go. And it's not really for myself. Could you tell me why that little hill is important enough to deprive my two children of their father?"

He'd be shot. Or at least branded forever as a coward. For thinking, for asking . . . "why?"—for doing the one thing that makes us human and not beasts.

The Cost of Freedom

The first sentence in these pages was: "This is a book about freedom." We've already seen how many strings are attached to being free. Ironically, to be free *costs.*

In the first place, true freedom requires the often considerable—and sometimes dangerous—effort of asking "why?" and a sometimes unnerving delay, till you have a reasonably satisfactory reason, before committing yourself to a choice. Freedom requires seeing—and thinking—for yourself.

In the second place, true freedom requires responsibility. Again ironically, freedom ties you down: to accepting personal accountability for the consequences, right or wrong, of your own choices. If you are "only following orders," you could console yourself that you have no personal blame for the ovens or the electrodes or the ditch at My Lai. But can you absolve yourself as casually for surrendering your freedom, your self, your soul, to someone else?

The difference between a child and an adult (as opposed to a "grown-up") is that adults take *full* responsibility for who they are, what they say, and what they do. A child—no matter at what age—is eager to lay off blame on the handiest scapegoat: "The *dog* did it!. . . She *pushed* me!. . . I did *too* come in at 1:00; ask Ellen; she was *with* me!. . . How do you *expect* me to act any different with the background *I* came from?. . . When are they gonna do something about Mass?. . . It was the woman *you* put me with; *she* gave me the fruit, and I ate it."

The adult says, "No matter what my 'socialization,' I made the choice. If I chose wrongly, I apologize."

Dostoevsky's Grand Inquisitor says, perhaps too cynically, perhaps not, that there is no gift a human being will surrender more willingly than his or her freedom. If that is true, then there is no gift a human being will surrender more willingly than his or her humanity.

Questions for the Notebook

Page 19. Below are listed various qualities and values by which (and over which) individuals differ. They are extremes, but circle the one in each case which *most* closely describes you or appeals to you, and write a profile of yourself. It will be inadequate, of course, but a start.

extrovert ....introvert	athletic............unathletic
intellectual ....anti-intellectual	clumsy ....skillful
careless ....careful	cheerful...........discouraged
inquisitive .....indifferent	handsome ....ghastly
trusting ....wary	resentful..........forgiving
decisive ....fluctuating	spiritual ....worldly
creative ....plodding	dull ....interesting
self-giving .....self-protective	leader.............follower

A Prayer

God, give me the serenity to accept what cannot be changed; give me the courage to change what can be changed; give me the wisdom to know the difference. Amen.

The Scope of Your Meaning

This section is pivotal, not only in the sense of "crucial," at the core of what this book is saying, but also as a "shifting," an attempt to focus all that has gone before and then open out to what will come—examining the two other questions: does God exist and, if so, what is he like?

Up to this point, we have seen that the real truth is outside ourselves, in the real natures of things and people. But there is a secondary truth inside our minds, our perceptions of that primary truth and the opinions which come from those perceptions. That opinion—that secondary truth—is really quite trustworthy, provided it's buttressed with sufficient evidence to validate it. However, there are obstacles within us which can hinder us from accepting evidence even when it's right under our noses: blinders like prejudice, protective indifference, and especially false humility. And there are obstacles outside us—propaganda systems—which try, each for its own reasons, to sway our perceptions and opinions to their views.

You can't be free to answer the "you" questions unless you *see* evidence as clearly, honestly, and vulnerably as you are able to. And what you believe of yourself and the world around you will have a profound influence on how you approach and answer the God questions.

The primary truth of who you are is in your human nature, with all its potential and limitations, and in your unique embodiment of that human nature with its further, specific potential and limitations. It is difficult for me, at such a long and too-objective distance, to suggest any more possible avenues to insights into your individuality than I already have. I can hope in the rest of this chapter only to sum up what seems true of us all, no matter what the surface differences. What is the scope—the outer limits—of our human urge to know and love and grow?

It seems beyond argument that the more things and people we know and love, the more fulfilled our lives will be, the more human we will be. But is there a point at which we have "enough"? Is there even a point after which we risk having all our rational, social, and spiritual circuits blown?

Trust

Very likely all of us have played the game of "Trust": one person stands behind another, pats him or her reassuringly on the back, then lets the person fall back a few inches, then a foot, then all the way to just short of the floor.

The results are pretty predictable. There's a lot of nervous laughter, overly hearty guffaws, the rollicking denial of fear you also encounter in locker rooms before a game or soldiers' bars before a battle. But the last thing everybody does is give one last wide-eyed look over the shoulder: "Now, you're *there,* right? No messin' around, *right?*" Then you fall, eyes clenched, body as stiff as a crowbar, and for an instant that seems like an hour, you say, "Oh, my God, nobody's there! It's a trick!"

Even when we've done it in a thickly carpeted room, even when I've shouted that I'd make life miserable for anybody who fooled around, I've seen hockey players—who can skate down-ice at 90 mph and check a man into the boards, without blinking—fall back as serenely as if I'd asked them to fall back into a pit full of rattlesnakes.

Why the overreaction? Because you have no control; you're being asked to put yourself, in however trivial and temporary a way, *into* the hands of someone else. Even if you've known everybody in the room for years, you've still been warned always to keep the doors locked, avoid hitchhikers, ignore strangers, especially with candy bars. Everybody's got an angle; it's a dog-eat-dog world out there, kid. What's more, your own first-hand experience supports those warnings: you've trusted friends and been betrayed; you've tried to make friends and been rebuffed; you've reached out to someone lonely and he or she turned out to be a leech.

Thus, *nobody*—except the *most* carefully tested few—can really be trusted. Psychologists have a name for that attitude; it's called paranoia.

Consider it from another viewpoint. Look around your classroom or office sometime and count how many people about whom you can say for sure: where they live, what color their eyes are, what jobs their parents or spouses have. Trivial questions, of course, but perhaps the seed of an insight. More significantly, how many have you never eaten lunch with or had even a ten-minute conversation with? In how many years? The insight begins to grow a bit disconcerting.

We have *great* power, power to give life to others and to enrich our own lives. But that enormous power is stoppered up by a tiny fear: the fear of being "taken."

What if somebody in the group (perhaps even you) were to make it his or her business to find ways to convince the rest that we *all* are holding back, and all for the *same* reason? What if one or two could find ways to assure that, within three months or so, just about everybody knew everybody else a little better? Let's say, for example, that when anybody in the group gave a party, everybody else in this class or office would be invited—even the nerds, wimps, and dips? What would happen if, after those three months, just about everybody in that small group could say, *"They care* about *me."* Gasp! You'd have to run up banners and shoot off cannons every morning, there'd be so much joy!

Of course, we all want that; it's what we were made for, after all. And it's within our power to *have* it, anytime we're ready. When, if not now?

But I'm gonna get hurt.

Yep, true enough, but not all the time. Most people—by far—are trustworthy: they willingly pay their bills; they stop at red lights; they don't beat their children or their dogs; they want, as we all do, to live good, peaceful, productive lives. Maybe *once* out of ten times your trust will get you hurt. You know that—so to avoid that one pain, you give up those nine friends. Crazy, huh? But we all do it: settle for the small cocoon of tested friends, and let the rest of the world go by—lost. It's safer to be "cool," invulnerable. And yet "vulnerability" and "trust" and "love" are all words for the same thing. Don't say you want love unless you also want to be vulnerable. You can't have one without the other; that's the nature of love.

You're not alone; nor do you particularly *feel* lonely, most of the time. You have a family and probably a small circle of good friends, plus a bit wider circle of people you "sort of know." Considering the five billion people now alive on the earth, of course, that's pretty paltry. Considering the number of people within arms' reach, though, people you *could* know, people who could enrich your life and people whose lives you could enrich, it becomes a bit incriminating. It is your defenses that protect you *from* being loved; your secure aloofness immobilizes most people's power to share your life. All that aliveness stoppered up by childish, baseless, stupid fear.

In a sense, no matter how enlivening your family and friends are, they, too, can be one more form of self-protective truth blindness, keeping you from seeing the host of friends—the richer life—you could have. Again, we fear conversion, even to something immeasurably better than what we have. To try to show you what you're missing, let me ask you to imagine that you truly are alone—without even that very small but reassuring defense of family and friends. Then, very, very slowly meditate on this true story.

The Moment at the Pump

Once upon a time, there was a little girl. And she was a very bad girl. In fact she was downright vicious. She blundered through the house like someone crazy, knocking into tables and china and people. No one made much effort to control her. After all, what good would it do? Because she was deaf and dumb and blind. And her name was Helen Keller.

Try to imagine what her life was like—without color, without tone, without distractions. The only things she could contact were surfaces and vibrations with her hands. She knew by the smells and textures when she was in the house—but she didn't know it *was* a house. Somehow, she'd worked out a safe path through the house, a dark little world where she could remember where the harmful objects were, like stairs and doorways. But outside it was different. The outside was too big to plot a safe path through it. When she felt the soft thing under her feet (that was grass), every step she took was taken in fear, because the next step could be the edge of everything.

She was the only *person* in her safe, dark, little world. All the others were just bodies. There was one with a lot of cloth around its legs that pampered her. Helen didn't know it was her mother. She didn't know what a mother *was*. She was utterly alone, and everything else was enemy—banging unexpectedly into her shins, disappearing in steps beneath her feet, taking her hand out of her plate—dark, unseen, always threatening.

And then one day there came smashing into her little world the enemy of enemies, a teacher named Annie Sullivan, herself half-blind and Irish and damned if she was going to content herself with just teaching this little beast table manners. She was going to crack open that safe little self-centered world and let the great world come flooding in.

For weeks they wrestled and fought and punched and clawed, until finally Helen relented a little. She found that it was more pleasant to be clean rather than dirty. She found that when she was willing to eat with a knife and fork, Annie would let her eat. And always there was the funny game in the palm of her hand. Whenever her doll was put into her arms, four funny signs in her hand. Whenever she got a glass of water, five funny signs in her hand. Whenever the one with all the cloth around its legs came near, six funny signs in her hand. That's all it was. Just a game.

And then one day it happened. Helen was out in the yard and her shoulder brushed against the handle of the pump. She felt vibrations somewhere nearby and she was curious. She hit the pump handle again and reached out her hands. They were wet. Something inside her was beginning to connect; something choked up into her throat. And from her twisted mouth came the only word she could remember from her babyhood, before the darkness: "Wa-wa."

She ran to the one with all the cloth around its legs, and in her hand she spelled "mother." And then she ran to Annie, and in her hand she spelled "teacher."

It had happened. It was the invasion. Helen Keller had discovered that things have names. That there was a world beyond her darkness, that—even though she couldn't see them—there were other *persons,* like her, people who could communicate to her through the strange game in the palm of her hand. Poor frightened girl. She'd made the most liberating of all human discoveries: she'd discovered that she wasn't alone.

Rest there; let Annie Sullivan and Helen Keller "talk" to you. Put the book aside for a while, and mull it over for yourself before I intrude any further. Come back when you're ready, and don't come back too soon. Don't let me do your thinking for you.

The Scope of Our Meaning: With One Another

Before that shattering moment of realization at the pump—that conversion—Helen Keller was more or less "content," a bit restless and unruly, perhaps, simply because if it is human nature to know and love, Helen's human powers were tragically constricted. Like ourselves and our small circle of supportive people, she was "satisfied" only because she hadn't the slightest notion what she was missing, although (like us) her unrest was an irritating hint that she must be missing *some*thing.

Annie did indeed "crack open her safe little self-centered world and let the great world come flooding in." However, after the first days of wild exhilaration, as with all of us, Helen must have been just a touch apprehensive. How could she take it all in? How much was it going to cost?

In a sense, even without an inspired teacher like Annie, we are *free* to crack open our own worlds, but that fear of being drowned by it all makes us dig in our heels and hang on to what we've got. If you think of all the people—just the ones within reach—that, with a little courage, you *could* know and befriend and perhaps even love; if you go into a library and look at the spines of all those books that, with a little courage, you *could* read and find in them even wider horizons—well, it just gets too breathtaking. Better to zip up the cocoon and be content to sit by one's cozy little fire, undisturbed. And wait for the death of curiosity to bring "peace."

There is only one handle on the door into and out of yourself. It's on the *in*side.

To quote Roz Russell again: "Life's a banquet and most poor bastards are starving to death."

The Scope of Our Meaning: With God

Since human life began, men and women have suspected that we are not alone in the darkness of space. At first their apprehensions were primitive: there was an aliveness in everything about them, an aliveness we now have demythologized into the force of gravity on the waterfall and the power of electricity in the thunderbolt. Later, tribes set up idols to remind them of the mysterious "power" around them, and often the physical symbol—the stone—replaced the non-physical reality it was merely standing for. And yet in the most polytheistic societies, there seems to be a suspicion in their ritual chants and creation stories of a single Power behind all the other powers, the root of aliveness from which all the other alivenesses spring. Even now, even the most sophisticated among us wonder if sheer accident could give rise to a world which is, in great part, so predictable; could we have the Periodic Table and the immutable "laws" of physics if there were not a Mind behind them?

Thus far, the God questions are still "open." What the theist asks you to do is to entertain the possibility that those questions are worth pursuing, that there *might* be Someone "out there" who is worth seeking. The theist claims that just as Annie Sullivan drew signs in Helen Keller's hands about a whole world which Helen couldn't see but which was real and rich beyond her dreams, and just as all the people and books you brush up against every day are "drawing signs in your hands" about real and enriching worlds you may not yet have allowed yourself to acknowledge—just so, everything in the universe from the hydrogen atom to the Great Dance of the Universe is also "drawing signs," whispering that "there is an even richer Reality beyond us."

In the safe darkness, content with the small pleasures we have, that sounds too good to be true.

But what if it *were* true?

Question for the Notebook

Page 20. What does the story of Annie Sullivan and Helen Keller say to you about the scope of your "world"?

Page 21. Slowly, meditatively, list the names of the people who love you and whom you truly love—even though you may at times take them for granted. (If you write only five or six names, either you are underselling the people who love you, or it is not worth the effort to find out how much you are really loved.)

A Prayer

God, I admit my limitations; perhaps I even harp on them too much. But am I safe in admitting my potential? Is it possible that I've set my sights too comfortably low, so that there is less chance of my failing? Help me at least to try to trust—myself, and them, and you. Amen.

The Meaning of Faith

Here we will be probing more deeply into areas we touched on only sketchily before. In fact, everything we have said so far about perception, obstacles to seeing truth, and the process of forming opinions has been leading to this question: what does faith mean?

On the one hand, there are geniuses who are atheists, convinced (sometimes passionately) that God is an illusion, that there is no entity outside our minds which validates the idea of deity we have in our minds. On the other hand, there are geniuses who are theists, convinced (sometimes passionately) that God is a reality, the Mind behind the universe to whom we owe everything.

But even atheism, ironically, is an act of *faith*—an *opinion* based on evidence and a life-commitment based on that opinion. No atheist has *seen* the nothingness that he or she believes "occurs" at death, any more than any theist (with the exception of Jesus, if he was telling the truth) has seen the face of God.

Nor is faith restricted only to one's position on the God questions. Since our first-hand experiences and our time and ability to reason out everything from scratch are severely limited, it is beyond denial that most of the things we accept as true are accepted, to one degree or another, on faith in the experiences and reasonings of others. Even our own personal reasoning, as we have seen, rests on a trust that our minds are indeed capable of finding the truth.

Some of our opinions, to be sure, are evidenced by *real,* first-hand knowledge; most of what we know, however, is evidenced by *notional* knowledge—made at least to some degree precarious, questionable, subject to doubt or revision, by the fact that it rests on fallible reasoning or on second-hand (at best) testimony about the experiences and reasoning of others. With any kind of notional knowledge, there are varying degrees of probability that the knowledge is indeed validated outside the mind.

Also, we act on these opinions—sometimes quite irrationally, or at least without any reasoning at all. For instance, on the one hand we commit our very lives into the hands of individual airline pilots, cooks, and doctors without the slightest direct evidence of their competence. On the other hand, we refuse to commit even a half hour of our lives into the hands of people with whom we've been in the same school or office or neighborhood all our lives.

Faith, then, is worth some serious study, in regard to not only theological questions, but all questions.

There is no such thing as "blind faith." When we use those words, as in a situation like: "Look, I can't explain all the reasons; you'll just have to trust me," the faith asked for is not blind—except when asked for by a total stranger, in which case there is question not of faith but of idiocy. But when a friend asks for trust in this particular situation and is unable to give reasons right now for your giving the trust, your faith *is* based on evidence—not evidence about this case, but evidence of your friend's trustworthiness on all previous occasions. Even in the cases mentioned above of the pilots, cooks, and doctors, there is at least some ground for trusting *this* individual, namely, your knowledge (however remote) and trust in the Civil Aeronautics Board, the American Medical Association, and the general assumption that this individual would have been caught by now. (Unless it's his or her first time!)

Faith is a *calculated risk.* The important question is how much calculation does this particular risk require if one is to be prudent. On the one hand, if an acquaintance asks for a quarter, you risk losing it, but it's not worth taking a half hour to assess the pros and cons. On the other hand, if someone asks you to invest all your savings, or to become your spouse for life, or to base all your life-choices on a commitment to a God you can't see, it's worth more than a half hour to assess the pros and cons.

In the next two sections we will be dealing once again with two complete extremes and a balance between them. At opposite ends of the spectrum are those who require total certitude before committing themselves (the tyranny of logic) and those who commit themselves sheerly on whim, with hardly a whisper of solid evidence (the abdication of logic). Between the two is faith, which is neither extreme—neither pure calculation nor pure risk—but a balance of both: a calculated risk.

One perhaps unnecessary note: although other authors for justifiable reasons distinguish among them, for our purposes "faith" = "be-lief" = "trust" = "opinion." I make this point only because over the years I've heard too often, "I don't have faith in it; I just *believe* it." My unvarying response is: "*based* on *what?*" We are back to square one here: faith/belief/trust/opinion are only as trustworthy as the evidence that backs them up. And we *act* on them. My sole purpose is to keep you from getting hurt—by acting on opinions which are unsubstantial, dangerous, or even inevitably deadly.

The purpose of this whole book is to cut down the distance be-tween you and the evidence. A great deal of the evidence will always remain notional—although many testify with their very lives that first-hand evidence of God is possible. What I hope to do is lessen the pre-cariousness of your own faith-commitment—whether it be to atheism or to theism—by lessening the "second-handedness" of your evidence on the God questions. Many of the believers I know (on both sides) base their faith not on their own study of the evidence, pro and con, but rather on their parents' act of faith, or on some friend's act of faith, or—worst of all—on "everybody sez."

This time, one way or the other, let it be "I believe because *I've* studied the alternatives and *I've* made a choice."

The Limits of Logic

The essential is always invisible.
                    —*Antoine de Saint Exupéry*

We keep thinking how easy it would have been to believe if *we* could have been there to witness the miracles of Jesus. Or if he'd just show up right now and walk across our swimming pools, then belief would be easy.

Highly doubtful.

One could at least argue that it was *harder* to believe for people who had hands-on experience on Jesus than it is for us. In fact, the further away one gets from the physical, historical entity who was Jesus Christ—and thus the more strictly theoretical the question becomes—the easier it is to believe.

Imagine being right next to Jesus when he raised Lazarus from the dead or turned water into wine. Honestly, what would be the first question that popped into your mouth? I know what mine would be: "How the hell did you *do* that?" And if he'd say, "Why it's quite simple really; you see, I'm God," I'd have bolted right out of there, muttering, "Either he's crazy, or I'm crazy, or both." That memory would have bothered me for the rest of my life, but I'd never have gone back for more.

All right, the miracle was astonishing. But surely it was some kind of gimmick, right?—like a magician making a girl disappear from a box and instantly reappear at the back of the theatre. Things like that don't really happen; they defy reason, the laws of physics, common sense.

How could those people standing next to Jesus deny the evidence of their *senses* that told them, beyond argument, that this was just another man? They could smell Jesus' sweat, see the dust caked in the creases of his skin, sense his unquestionable humanity in the very act of doing something utterly beyond human capacity. There *had* to be some other explanation. "Isn't he the carpenter's son? Don't we know all his relatives?" It would have been easier to believe it was black magic, that he'd made a pact with the devil—to tempt us to believe that a man was God, when there is obviously only one God.

No, it's far easier, at this long distance, to deal with Jesus as a head-trip question, poking around for loopholes in the Scriptures, sniffing out contradictions, debating the night away with those who still cling to their beliefs with stubborn tenacity and very few solid, persuasive arguments. It's just too unthinkable. No one has ever seen God, and no one's ever likely to. And if one did, it'd probably be a hallucination, auto-suggestion. There'd obviously be some scientific explanation for the delusion.

Ah, if someone could give me *scientific* proof of the existence of God, then surely I'd believe.

The problem is that no one has ever seen God. Of course, no one has ever seen an atom, either. Oddly, though, the same people who demand absolute proof for the existence of God can accept the existence of atoms without a flicker of doubt or questioning. Even though no one has ever seen an atom—or a neutrino, or a gluon, or a quark. And we never will see any of them. Our eyes simply aren't fast enough. The invisibility is not the fault of the atom, of course (or of God); the fault is with our receptivities. Still, anybody with intelligence would surely deny the palpable evidence of his own senses and say the rock that just cracked open his knee was *not* rock-solid but rather aswarm with galaxy upon galaxy of moving particles—and most of the rock is really empty space.

Right.

No one has seen an atom, only its effects. But the effects of an atomic bomb are so stupefying that it would be foolish not to accept what experts claim to be the cause of that effect—even if it means denying one's own personal experience. The rock only *seems* solid, because of my limited point of view.

If we pause to think about it, the universe is a pretty stupefying effect, too. Compared to the seemingly illimitable universe, any atomic explosion—or even the disintegration of the entire earth—would be a mere burp in a hurricane, But if splitting an atom triggers an atomic explosion, who or what triggered the universe? It's surely the effect of something. Of what? The universe is either the result of some Mind that planned it this way, or the result of an endless series of mindless, unplanned accidents. It had to be one or the other: planned or unplanned. How does one determine which? No one saw it happen. The answer is simple: reasoning about the evidence we do have. Whether the problem is the existence of God—or of atoms, or love, or the Big Bang—we can argue only from the effects to their most probable causes.

It is a paradox, as we have seen: we accept, sheerly on the word of experts, with no direct and very little indirect study of our own, the "preposterous" fact that rocks are not solid. And yet, perversely, we have to probe and probe—without ever reaching unquestionable certainty—the questions of whether we are loved or not, or whether there is a God or not. No matter how many experts assert that we have nothing to worry about, those questions still hunger insatiably for more "proof."

Why? Because, like the flutterings of my eyelids and the rivers of my blood, atoms can go their merry way without too frequently intruding on my consciousness or my way of living. But love? And God? They could change one's whole life. There is not just calculation involved in those questions. There is also a great deal of personal risk.

Here we arrive smack dab against the third of the questions which have pursued us since page one: *how can one be sure*—especially when the choice affects one's whole life down to its very roots?

Again, to be sure that we cover all possible positions on that question, let us consider the two most extreme positions: at the one end, there is the demand for absolute certitude which some require about the existence of love and of God; at the other, there is a kind of what-the-hell blind "faith" we have about the existence of atoms and China. To give those extremes a slightly more academic tone, let me speak about the *tyranny of logic*—demand for exhaustive proof sufficient to compel assent or denial—and the *abdication of logic*—an assent or denial based on only the slightest (or no) consideration of the evidence. The first stance is completely *objective;* the second is completely *subjective.* All other positions lie somewhere between those two.

In an age of skepticism and paranoia, it does not take much to show the weaknesses of subjectivism. We have become very wary of being hoaxed, of being caught with our pants down. But for that very reason, it is not so easy to attack Cartesianism and the need for unbreakable proof.

Objectivism: The Tyranny of Logic

One man usually credited with exalting the demand for absolute certainty is René Descartes (1596–1650). He was a mathematician, philosopher, and father of what is called *Cartesianism.* This man has had an enormous effect on all our expectations of truth, even though you may never have heard of him before, except in connection with algebraic graphs. Descartes' first principle reads as follows: "In order to arrive at the knowledge of all things . . . never to accept anything as true unless I know from evidence that it is so . . . and to comprehend in my judgments *only that which presents itself so clearly and distinctly in my mind that I can have no occasion to doubt it.*" (Emphasis added.)

I can agree without hesitation with the first, unitalicized part. In fact, if I have done anything so far it is to flog to death the assertion that knowledge and judgments are only as good as the evidence that backs them up. However, I do have difficulty at least with what I read is *acceptable* as evidence in order to achieve Cartesian certitude. How many things do we know "so clearly and so distinctly" that we have "*no* occasion to doubt" them?

I'll grant that there are few, but not too many—compared to the things about which we have at least some slight doubt. What do we know that we don't have to hedge with something like, "if my calculations are correct," or "unless some as yet unknown factor exists"?

If I held a brick out the window and offered to bet that, if I released it, it would go down, no takers. Cartesian certitude. The laws of physics seem to have Cartesian certitude. There is one other: we will all die. It's hard to think of more. Give it a try if you like.

Of which of the following statements can we have anything near Cartesian certitude:

There is intelligent life in outer space.

The sun will rise tomorrow.

I will see the sun rise tomorrow.

This stock is the best buy on the market at the moment.

This defendant is guilty and should be executed.

This is the right college for me.

I will love you and honor you till death do us part.

I am a good person.

None of them. And yet only a few of them are unimportant.

Science vs. Scientism

Scientism is the belief that the research methods of the physical sciences are equally appropriate and essential to all other academic disciplines such as theology, humanities, and social studies. If that were to mean nothing more than the gathering and sifting of data, inter-relating groups of data to form a hypothesis, drawing a conclusion and testing it—no problem. Theologians, humanists, and social scientists have been doing that for generations. For any kind of honest study, one must be governed by the objective nature of the data and leave all subjective hopes, pre-conceptions and (especially) pre-judgments aside. To be sure, every physicist and every theologian hopes his or her hypothesis proves trustworthy, but he or she doesn't start the process prepared to ignore any data contrary to the hypothesis. (There are many otherwise quite brilliant people who believe theologians *do* precisely that: purposely ignore any truth, however undeniable, which threatens their "case." There are also believers who would *like* theologians to do precisely that, as if the truth could somehow harm the faith.)

The fatal flaw in this extreme scientism (as opposed to science) is in its cramping narrow-mindedness. Its adherents claim that the scientific *method* is not enough; the norms of truth must also be established with scientific *instruments*. Unless an entity can register on a Geiger counter or photometer, it cannot be said to be "present"; to all serious intents and purposes, it does not exist. Since God, and the human soul, and love cannot be detected by such instruments, God must be a delusion to help us face imperfection and death, the human soul must be a misnomer for the complex entity resulting from years of socialization, and love must be the result of certain electro-chemical impulses in the nerves and brain.

None of us can help but be tempted by scientism, to want proof so clear and distinct that we can have no reason to doubt it. (I suspect that is one reason for fascination with the Shroud of Turin.) The difficulty is not only that scientism doesn't work for theology and the humanities; it doesn't even work for science.

We get the erroneous idea that physics, chemistry, and biology are "hard" studies, whereas theology, humanities, and the social sciences are "soft" studies. Science has rock-hard proof for all its assertions; theology is a product of wishful thinking. Part of the reason is that most high school and early college science courses are "cookbook science": the students are assigned *only* experiments guaranteed to work out every time, provided they follow the directions. Thus, to the relative beginner, science seems totally certain in all its conclusions. Very much to the contrary, real scientists don't work that way. When a biologist walks into her lab at a cancer institute, she doesn't know if she'll find an answer, even after a lifetime of experiments—or even if there *is* an answer. She works not on certitudes but on faith: in her intelligence and skill, in her schooling, in the established conclusion and formulas of her discipline, in her instruments, etc.

I said a few paragraphs back that there are really only two things we can know with Cartesian certitude: the inevitability of death and the laws of physics. Now I begin to be uncertain even about the laws of physics—not about their existence, but certainly about their human formulations. We have to remember that Copernicus upset all the certitudes of Ptolemy, and that Einstein made most of the calculations, at least, of physics not absolute but relative to the place from which they were being made. But no one skewered the legend of scientific infallibility more thoroughly than Werner Heisenberg.

The Principle of Uncertainty

Most of us are comfortable with the familiar pictorial model of the atom: a nice stable nucleus with its proper number of electrons whirring around it, predictably, each in its own regulated and unswerving orbit—like moons around a planet. That's solid; it's certain.

But that's not the way it is.

Sixty years ago, experiments too complex to detail here convinced scientists of three unnerving facts. First, on the microscopic level, the very intrusion of measuring devices changes the very data the devices are introduced to measure, thus causing an element of uncertainty. For instance, if in the everyday world a tiny thermometer is put into your 98.6-degree mouth, it is small enough that it itself will not absorb enough of your mouth's heat to change the very temperature it is trying to measure. But if you were to put an industrial thermometer into a cup of coffee, it would absorb so much heat itself that it would measure the coffee as cold. Similarly, devices to measure subatomic activity skew the evidence by their very presence.

A second corollary discovery was that, when dealing with the measurement of two related, observable quantities (such as the relation of an electron's position to its momentum), it is impossible to determine *both* variables accurately. The conditions needed for accuracy in determining the electron's momentum are in direct conflict with those needed for accuracy in determining its position. The more accurately the observer determines one, the less accurately he can know the other. He may be certain of the electron's position *or* its momentum, but not of both at the same time. Thus enters another element of uncertainty.

A third disquieting discovery was that the electron—which we had always thought of as a little pellet moving, moon-like, around the nucleus—was doing some very un-pellet-like things. It was in fact acting at times like a wave. But how do you *picture* something that acts like both a pellet and a wave—and yet is neither? The answer is disconcertingly simple: you don't.

Finally, in the late 1920's, Werner Heisenberg resolved the difficulties with his revolutionary formulation of quantum mechanics and the principle of indeterminacy. What he asserted was that Newtonian mechanics which serve us quite well in the everyday world (as in determining where the moon will be at a particular time) simply do not apply on the subatomic level! The electron does not go around the nucleus in an inescapable iron ring of "permissible" orbits like a pellet; it also moves with the properties of a wave, whose position and speed one can only make educated guesses about at any particular moment. The electron is, in fact, not a pellet or a wave, but both. If, he hypothesized, you could fire an electron from a gun at a barrier with two holes, it would as likely go through either of the holes. If not both at the same time.

What Heisenberg had done was throw out all mechanical models of the atom, thus rejecting a method which had led physicists to triumph after triumph for two hundred years. In its place he substituted a concept of the atom which was instead a matrix of mathematical relationships; thus, science cannot tell what is really going on in the atom at any given moment, but can give only a statistical *probability* of what it is doing. Therefore, statements about subatomic particles are not "laws," in the sense that we use the word about the mechanics of our everyday world—like the laws of gravity and motion which give us the iron certitude that, if you hit a cue ball with a certain amount of force from a certain angle, you can predict where it will end up. Such predictions made about the movements of subatomic particles are rather *educated guesses*—reliable, to be sure, but only as reliable as the actuarial tables which predict the probability of a particular person's death at a particular age.

For establishing "The Principle of Uncertainty," Heisenberg was awarded the Nobel Prize in Physics in 1932.

Thus, real scientists are far more humble and hesitant about their findings than many of us believe them to be. They speak not of certitudes but of hypotheses. "Scientific proof" of God's existence would mean far less than the people who use those words might want. An eminent scientist trying to explain the relationships among the muons and gluons and quarks in the atom is as tentative—and mystifying—as an eminent theologian trying to explain the relationships among the Persons of the Trinity.

The Limitations of Cartesianism

Basically, Cartesianism and Scientism are limited when used exclusively simply because they leave out too much of the pertinent data.

Let me take one specific, non-theological case to show the limits of Cartesian expectations in solving any question. Much blood, sweat, tears, and ink have been spilled over the Scholastic Aptitude Tests (SAT's) as valid predictors of an individual's success in college—and later. They are and probably will continue to be about as scientific as such tests can be. And yet to use them exclusively would be a terrible misapplication of science. Every college knows that; even the Educational Testing Service knows that. Many students and their parents do not. But there are at least two very crucial aspects of a prospective candidate which objective tests simply cannot measure: insight and motivation.

In over twenty years of teaching students who were National Merit Scholars, I've found them all brilliant, highly verbal and logical, excellent at taking objective tests and quizzes. They were superlative in solving problems. They were not without insight, but they were almost never the students with the best insight, nor were they always the students with the best motivation or the students with the best high school grades.

The ones with the best insight were the creative ones, the ones who had hunches, smelled rats, got below the surfaces of the data, were hypersensitive to nuance. I suspect one of the reasons they performed less well on the SAT's is precisely their uncertainty over many answers which, properly nuanced, appeared better or as good as the "correct" answer.

Let me not be read as condemning the powers and tools of the intellect. However, I do believe that "intelligence"—while including the powers of the intellect—goes *beyond* intellect. Intell*ect,* logic, and brain are tools of all knowledge, whether scientific, theological, or humanistic, and they are tools that serve us well. They reduce unknown situations to problems and, step-by-step, these mental powers *solve* them. Once the solution has been reached and checked, the problem ceases for the moment to exist. Intelli*gence,* reason, and mind are the tools of the total human being. They serve us well, too. They face far less tangible and far more mysteriously complex situations which cannot be resolved into problems. When you are faced with choosing a career or a spouse or with judging whether to entrust some shaming confidence to a friend—or whether to believe in God—there is no one answer which can give you certitude before you move. Your brain and logic are only a part of the knowing powers which contribute to your decision. There is always an element of risk. And a decision is not *the* answer; it is *an* answer which you choose. Love, for instance, is often illogical, but it is not always unreasonable.

Thus, SAT's can quite validly give an indication of a prospective student's intellect, but not necessarily of his or her intelligence. Nor are they an indicator of motivation, which is a quite significant variable in one's success in higher education. At best, even grades from a teacher who sees the student every day for a year are a quite fallible assessment of a student's achievement—not of his or her potential, spine, or willingness to work. Grades are not always a reliable judgment even of what the student knows. After all, Hitler never graduated from high school and Einstein never graduated from college, yet each in his quite different way was a genius whom the deservedly famous Austrian and German school systems failed to recognize. There is no ammeter or litmus paper which would give an admissions officer certitude. All he or she can do is gather and sift all the data, organize it, and come to a quite fallible, prudential conclusion. And then hope.

Finally, the scientific method cannot deal with an element of our lives on which we depend constantly: testimony. Taking something as fact *solely* on the word of another is highly "unscientific," and yet we do it all day long, every day of our lives. We accept the testimony of teachers, news commentators, statesmen, friends—and scientists—without the slightest felt need to check out the information. We accept the sworn testimony of witnesses in a law court, even though we know men and women lie very easily and have often been known to put self-interest ahead of truth. The whole fabric of human society is built not on irresistible scientific fact but on fallible human trust, not on Descartes' certitude but on Heisenberg's uncertain probabilities.

What I say about scientism is not meant to degrade science. Scientific studies provide us with valuable information, but they don't answer our deepest questions. A baby's first question and a dying person's last question is still: why? We don't know the reason, at least not a scientific one. Yet we *trust* that there is a reason. If we didn't, we wouldn't bother to ask the question: why?

Subjectivism: The Abdication of Logic

The precisely opposite extreme from objectivism or Cartesianism is subjectivism or Relativism. Where Cartesianism and scientism throw out individual differences in favor of the least common denominator, Relativism drops the LCD in favor of the unique differences. Edmund Husserl (1859–1938) and a long line of philosophers all the way back to Heraclitus felt that life was so dynamic, people and objects so different even from members of their own "class," so unique, that there could be no real categories or labels. We must school ourselves, they say, to see only separate phenomena, each a privileged moment. As Heraclitus put it, twenty-five centuries ago, you never step into the *same* river twice.

The relativists had become sick unto death with the strangling philosophical "systems" which were so logically perfect and so humanly deadening. In a sense, they believed, scientism had crept in and taken over the study of human nature, and it had turned human beings into objects rather than persons. And, as we have seen from the beginning, you can *never* get a *perfectly* objective reading of the human data; distortion is *bound* to creep in, no matter how carefully we perceive, categorize, evaluate, etc. And the "object" under investigation—the human person—is too mercurial, too changeable, too contradictory to lock into any absolute statements about humanity, much less about individuals.

Therefore, to make absolute statements about human morality—or in fact about any aspect of human life over the centuries—is not only impossible but paralyzing. Even without reading Husserl or Heraclitus, street-corner moralists who say, "It's up t' th' individual, man," are perfectly articulating the relativist position. Statements about human beings made even ten years ago are interesting only as history; we're stepping into a different river today.

The Limitations of Relativism

Basically, Relativism (pure whim) is limited in solving *human* questions because, like Cartesianism, used exclusively, it is anti-human.

Need for Categories

Relativism denies the undeniable power and urge of the human mind to organize and classify things, to make connections and see relationships. If Husserl were right, life would be nothing more than a series of incoherent, disconnected events, and we would be nothing more than movie cameras dumbly recording one-damn-thing-after-another. Thinking *means* connecting things; but if nothing *can* be connected, thinking is a cruel deception indeed.

Need for Words

Despite the fact that Relativism says "nothing is constant," its adherents *do* use common words. But common words are (again more-or-less) constant, unchanging. That constant factor is the reason we can communicate. Therefore, as soon as you talk with words, you expect others to understand in more or less the *same* sense you do; you are in the realm of at least some temporary absolutes. And as soon as a relativist says "all things are relative," he's cut his own throat. That's an absolute statement.

Democracy Run Wild

If nothing is constant, if everything must be spontaneous or else "phony," then something strange has happened to the word "democracy." All men and women are indeed created equal—as human beings, as persons deserving of respect, concern, food, clothing, shelter. But all men and women are *not* equally talented, equally smart, equally experienced, equally worthy of having their opinions taken seriously. Your opinion on "Hamlet," for instance, is more than likely *not* as good as mine. On the other hand, my opinion on contemporary music is most certainly inferior to yours, no matter how little you know about it.

We have already seen the unthinking statement, "My opinion is as good as anyone else's." Like most witless assertions, it has a way of backfiring. If you have a right to say anything your feelings tell you to say, everyone else has the same right. So don't be too angry if someone goes around telling people you are a thief. It's his or her opinion.

Perhaps you personally feel everybody ought to do his own thing about rape. But if you rape my sister, don't be surprised if I am somewhat disquieted, nor should you be too disquieted if I rape *your* sister. It is the same with all moral strictures, which is the reason why every ethical and religious system is based on: do unto others as you would have others do unto you.

You have a right to your opinions, but that does not mean they are as good as anyone else's. Are they as well-founded on a full view of the evidence, as well-tested over a long range of experiences, as free from dangerous or even self-destructive consequences? Those questions have no meaning to the man or woman who has abdicated reason. But because some people are color-blind, must we all see only gray?

If the meaning of words varies from individual to individual, then communication is futile. If opinions are a judgment about reality, then their validity has to be *governed* by objective reality. When each individual can spontaneously decide what words or things or people mean, words and things and people cease to have any meaning whatever.

Logic and the God Questions

We've spoken here of extreme positions probably inhabited by no one but the deranged. Still, there are people who are perilously close to one or other extreme on the God questions: on the one hand, they will wait forever if they expect unassailable proof or, as Darwin did, leave the whole question behind since absolute objective proof is—truly—impossible; or, on the other hand, they will say, "Oh, what the hell," and jump one way or the other.

Relativism alone (sheer hunch) won't work with the God questions, and the decisions on the God questions should affect your whole life and its values, even more than choosing a spouse. But nobody walks blindfolded into a roomful of strangers, taps the first person who smells nice, and says, "Hi, honey. We're getting married."

Nor will Cartesianism alone (sheer logic) work with the God questions, because you'd spend your whole life gathering arguments on both sides and die with an unfinished list. What would be *enough* time to decide whether or not to jump off a bridge? Similarly, what would be *enough* proof of the existence of God? Suppose you're alone in your room tonight reading, and you become vaguely aware that a beautiful silver cloud is forming on your ceiling. The cloud quivers with light and, suddenly, out of the cloud comes a deep, majestic, authoritative voice: "Hi! I want to make one thing perfectly clear. . . ."

You'd run screaming for a psychiatrist.

What's *enough* evidence?

Question for the Notebook

Page 22. The data on your IBM cards, SAT cards, etc., are presumably correct. Are they true? Do they "capture" you?

A Prayer

God, my Father, help me to understand both the powers and the limitations of my mind. Help me to see what is really "out there," not blinding myself to unpleasant facts nor fooling myself by pretending things are different from what they really are. Lord, that I may see. Amen.

Faith: A Calculated Risk

Finally, Margaret, in the end, it is not a matter of reason; it's a matter of love.
—*Thomas More in*
"A Man for All Seasons"

At this point, it is important to distinguish "faith" from what many speak of as "*the* Faith." That latter term refers to a whole body of notional knowledge—doctrines—held by a particular religion. We are not (yet) that ambitious nor that particularized; we are not talking about any specific religion yet. In fact, in the first half of this chapter, we will not yet even be speaking about faith in God. Before we tackle that more difficult relationship, we can examine what faith itself means.

We can do that rather easily by considering an act of faith which each of us has experienced and, even though we may never have analyzed it explicitly and sequentially, we've certainly mulled it over a great deal. *Friendship* is an act of trust, which can deepen in intensity all the way from vague interest down to a profound interpersonal intimacy. At each stage, friendship is an act of faith, not in something theoretical and personally uninvolving, like the atomic theory, nor in something seemingly distant and non-concrete, like God. It is an act of faith in a person, tangibly present, whose moods, habits, quirks, talents, and shortcomings I have direct experience of. Therefore, I want to analyze how an act of faith—friendship—starts and grows. We've all experienced that act of faith; here, I am only explicitating what you already know.

Friendship

Acquaintances

Imagine that the whole room that surrounds you while you sit there reading this page stands for all the five billion people who presently are ambling around this planet, going to work, falling in love, eating their breakfasts. Conservatively, 99.999% of them are—and always will be—completely *anonymous* to you. Only in the most notional sense are you even in the slightest aware of the nearly one billion human beings in the streets and fields of China, or the people in Alaska, or the people you brush past on the street or in a supermarket, or even the old lady down the street or the freshman you stumbled over in the corridor this morning. They do exist, of course; they are real, but, given that habit we have of limiting reality to where *we* are, they are not and will never be real-to-you.

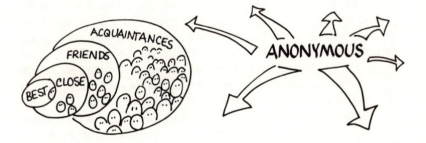

So if the whole room you're in stands for the people you don't know, then the little series of concentric circles above stands for the people you are at least aware of. As the circles narrow down to yourself at the focus, they symbolize the deepening of the intensity of your relationships with them: from mere vague acquaintance, through a general kind of friendship, to your close pals, and finally to your most precious friends.

All of us were told as children never to talk to strangers. But think for a second of your *best* friend, the person to whom you could tell anything. At one time, he or she was a stranger, one of the faceless mob; you didn't even know he or she existed. Other than your own family, how did that one person get from out there in "non-existence" all the way into your innermost heart? What was the *very* first step—without which that person would have remained a stranger forever?

When I ask that, the answers usually tumble over one another: you have the same interests . . . you say hello . . . you're introduced, and so on. But there is a step even before those: you have to *notice* the body; you have to focus the face out of the blur of the crowd so that it is *this* face and no other. Some jump right out at you, because they are so gorgeous, or so different, or so bizarre. There are some people who like to sit in airports or hotel lobbies just studying the faces. Most "sightings," though, are by chance: by accident of the alphabet you're seated together; you bump into one another at a party or a dance; you're hired for the same department. Nobody planned it; the two of you just "converged."

It's worth noting that, as we saw at the beginning of this book, we put up barriers to filter out most of the skatey-eight zillion stimuli that bombard us at every moment. But if you use that protective disinterest on people, the circle even of your vague acquaintances is going to be pitiably small and, as a result, the number of your friends is going to be severely impoverished. It starts right there: noticing or refusing to notice. Not too many friendships are going to begin in elevators, for example. We both clamp our eyes on the floor numbers, with the concentration of Buddhist monks, so that, a minute later, we couldn't even tell a policeman how tall the other person was.

Also, most potential friendships dead-end right there: noticing. It remains bits and pieces of surface impressions, notional knowledge. You may find out the person's label—his or her name; you may even exchange "the time of day" occasionally and say a less-than-sincere "Good to see you again," but the whole thing stays pretty distant: acquaintance. You can say, "Oh, yeah, I've seen her around," or "I know him." But not really. We know them less than Helen Keller knew Annie Sullivan.

How are the people you really call your "friends" precipitated out of that group of acquaintances?

Friends

We're not speaking of bosom buddies here, just someone who is not so negligible as an acquaintance is. The trigger is time/talk, mostly chit-chat, pretty surface stuff, but nonetheless a step without which nothing further can happen. You're thrown together, again most often by accident, and have to be together for more extensive periods, and you have to "pass the time" together: sitting together by chance in the stands at a game, sharing a bus seat, waiting for the dentist. The more often that happens, the less reluctant you are to ask, "Hey, can I bum a quarter?" or "Do you have any extra fabric softener?" You're not likely to ask him or her home to dinner or to blurt forth the revelation that at the moment you have diarrhea. You're more or less comfortable together—but at a bit of a distance still.

In the process, you begin to be at least vaguely aware of the other person's seriousness or playfulness, how he or she treats bullies or outcasts, how bright she is, how moody he can become. We size one another up. We take in a million disconnected bits of perception and, sometimes randomly, sometimes intensively, we try to figure one another out, to categorize and evaluate one another, and try to come to some conclusion from studying those effects what kind of personality is their cause.

Right there is the possibility of an opening down into the next level.

Close Friends

These are friends that don't just accidentally "happen"; you choose them, or at least they attach themselves to you and you don't brush them off. These are the people you automatically call up to play cards or go to a game or a movie; they're the people you gravitate to in a cafeteria; they're people you just . . . presume. At least to some degree, you confide in them. Why? Because you've discovered reasons—evidence—to support *confidence* in them.

Often through the accident of being with the same team or play or club, you find yourselves spending much more time talking about that enterprise, with a far greater intensity than mere chit-chat. It's important—because it has required *sacrifice* from both of you, *for* one another. This is nowhere more true than in the armed services, especially during a war. Men and women usually hate that time: the fear, the loss, the painful separation from home. And yet for many, it is the only time in their lives—before or after—when they felt so alive. Why? Because the barriers we use to defend ourselves from intrusion are—literally—blasted away. There is simply no alternative to reaching out in the dark and saying, "Take my hand. I'm a coward, too."

Here we are no longer talking just of friendship. Whether you are free enough to use the word or not—and men are more perversely reluctant to use it than women—we are talking about love.

Giving and receiving love involves much more than merely hanging around together. It implies a responsibility for one another. It is not loving only up to a point where it becomes inconvenient. It is handing the other a blank check and signing it with your word, your name, your self. It is accepting the possibility of being deceived. It is a risk, no matter how careful and calculated it is.

Best Friends

I might be over-simplifying if I said the difference between close friends and best friends is that you cry together. But that is not too far from the truth. In my own life, my best friends didn't become so precious because we'd gone to the circus together, but because we'd gone through hell together—and remained friends. I can't think of a single person in my own innermost circle—and I'm blessed with more of them than a man deserves—whom I haven't hurt terribly and who hasn't hurt me terribly.

We've opened ourselves to rock bottom, exposed all the knots and twists, invited one another in to walk around our deepest fears. We've seen one another at our "worst," and yet kept on saying, "So? We're still friends."

The best friends have peeled away the outer layers of resistance which guard themselves. The more open-heartedly one uses one's self to discover and share, the stronger will be the commitment.

The more *real* knowledge we have of one another, the stronger is our *faith* in one another.

Here, to me, is one of the most pervasive tragedies in a life which is a banquet, but at which most poor bastards are starving to death. We stay inflexibly secure on the safe level of chit-chat, gossip, and the ball-scores. We engage in mutual monologues; we debate. We erect ramparts of "cool" invulnerability. If instead we could share not our pretended strengths but our real weaknesses—our own doubts and fears—we would begin to recognize a bond. We would cease to be mere facts, mere bodies, to one another. We would be edging toward that moment of enlightenment and conversion at the pump. We would be in danger of loving one another.

Trust

At the end of every stage, the key into the next stage is trust—an act of faith in oneself and in the other. Even saying hello to a stranger is an act of faith: will she become a leech, will he start an argument, how do I know they aren't afflicted with something devastating like dandruff or bad breath? It's easier to "blur" them all back into anonymity. And yet, ironically, you will never get to know him or her unless you trust, *before* you know that person, that he or she *might* be worth knowing.

Further, the deeper the relationship becomes the more intense the demand for trust becomes. As we've seen (far too often) you can "cap it off" right there, settle for what you have rather than risk you know not what. Even the deepest personal relationship—between husband and wife—can grind slowly to a dead halt. Once he's got her "all figured out," once he becomes a problem solved and not a mystery to be probed still further, the love stops growing, and by that very fact starts to die. In one sense, I'm not overly worried by that. "The way things are" has a habit of throwing unexpected curves—sickness, the kids in trouble, money problems—that ask the two people to go deeper than they'd planned, to trust one another more profoundly than they ever thought they'd be asked to. The curves are guaranteed. However, the growing acceptability of an "easy" divorce threatens to undercut my hope. Too many couples have not had "the wisdom to know the difference" between the things that truly can't be changed and the things that—with a great deal of renewed trust and sacrifice—can be changed.

Remember, too, that friendships have "relapses." Of course, the best of friends can remain just as devoted to one another even though they don't see one another for years. In some cases, though, we "fall out of touch," literally and figuratively. I had a best friend in high school; for four years we were just about inseparable. But we went to different colleges, made new very deep friendships, developed new interests the other didn't share, began to write less frequently till finally it got down to a Christmas card. Seven years later we happened to meet again for dinner; halfway through, we were both pretty sure we didn't know one another anymore. Neither of us, I think, wanted to face the very likely fact that we didn't even like one another anymore.

When we speak of faith—friendship—love, we confront two of the most basic and most antagonistic drives within us: on the one hand, the *animal* drive for self-preservation, which wants to exclude, to cut down risks, to narrow the number of friends to a few; on the other hand, the *human* drive for self-transcendence, for growth, which wants to reach out for more, to take the risk and enrich one another, to open up the self unreservedly to other selves.

It's that simple: how much humanity are you willing to risk?

God

This book will spend a great deal of time from now on examining the reasons for and against the existence of God. But that question of existence is in part tied up with the nature of God. As we saw earlier, we are looking at first only for the entity about *whom* atheists and theists differ: the Mind behind it all. We are, then, looking for a *person*—not a *physical* person, the way we tend to define "person" from our limited, parochial viewpoint, but an intelligent being, who therefore can see alternatives and choose among them. If he/she does make choices, then he/she has not only a nature but a *personality* (no matter which religion has the closer picture). There are things he/she likes and doesn't like—again, no matter what they specifically are.

Therefore, if you want to know God, notional knowledge is not enough. The best arguments for God's existence will never make a conversion irresistible. You will never discover God at the end of a series of second-hand reports or classes or homilies or debates. Even the Scriptures are the record of *other* people's encounters with God.

Right now, if you've come to a level of religious education where you're ready to read this book, you undoubtedly know "enough" *about* God. The question is whether you know *God.*

If God is a Person—a Mind (and there is no other sense in which the question is meaningful), then God can "prove" himself only the way any other person can "prove" himself or herself to you: by *precisely* the same process as the one described above.

Faith in God—or in anyone—is based not just on notional knowledge, but also on *experience* with a *person.*

For some, God remains as *anonymous* and distant and "unreal" as some old man who is just now bending over planting in a Chinese rice paddy. I don't need him or God (for the moment). If God is to be found, it is only by those who have an educated hunch that he *is* there and then go looking for him. As with anyone else, we have to trust God *before* we can know him. We have to begin by giving him at least the tribute of noticing, perceiving disconnected pieces of surface impression.

We have as much or as little chance of meeting God as we have of knowing those anonymous figures that bump us daily in corridors, cafeterias, and buses. Unless we feel instinctively drawn to find him behind the words and propositions, God will remain as academic as Napoleon. One begins the search for God not with the catechism, which stops with the head (if it ever even arrives there), but by being-with, which starts with the heart and may or may not work up to the head later.

What are the triggers that start the process? Sometimes the search for God is triggered by suffering or fear or helplessness. Sometimes it's a realization of gratitude for, literally, everything. Stars on a clear summer night do it for me every time! Sometimes, as I hope we'll see, it is the sudden realization of some other person or idea, like death. But it starts with a needful realization. Otherwise, he will remain like the undiscovered friend, like sex to a small child, like light to the young Helen Keller.

Others become *friends* with God, but still at a sort of distance. There isn't much time for (or interest in) sizing him up. Such people "cap it off" right there. I go to him when he's important (i.e., when *I* am in need). To put it cynically, our relationship is a straight business deal; he gets his hour a week.

Still others become *good friends* with God; he's right there with them "in the trenches." But such a relationship cannot exist if you are only vaguely aware of his presence. The search for God is meaningless without the attempt to pray. Take a chance on *that* commitment and you risk its being a monologue, that there is really no one listening. (Of course you risk that in any conversation; I certainly risk it in every class I teach!) It is a sacrifice which is particularly humbling for a mind that demands clarity. It is an admission that one has *not* found all the answers.

This is the moment of risk the wise men and the shepherds faced when they were sent to find a king and found only a baby. It is the moment of danger when an ordinary stranger walked by the apostles and said, "Come." It is the point of faith when you have it in your power to change comfortable facts into never-to-be-solved mysteries. Or to stay comfortable, in the dark.

When, as in a marriage dying of fatigue, you have God "all figured out," there is another possibility of "capping God off." Many people—sometimes even in their late teens or thirties or even sixties—are still dealing with a God, sadly, who is frozen in the simplistic images and insights available to grade-school children. Once they get out of religious education classes, case closed. The friendship has "relapsed"; God is my old best pal from childhood but, well, we just don't really see much of one another anymore.

Finally, there are some people for whom God is one of their *best friends*. They have broken through the surface of chit-chatty prayers (nothing wrong with them for a start!) to a relationship where, as in the best of marriages, merely being together is enough—no need to impress one another, or to test one another, or even to communicate in a lot of words. The friendship is "right," though they can't *prove* why it's right any more than a woman can say "*This* is why she's my best friend," or "*That's* the reason I chose him as my husband." It's not logical, but it makes sense.

With God, as with my other friends, the deeper the relationship, the more the demand for trust. And, God! Does he sometimes ask for trust, almost beyond one's ability to give it! On the one hand, for three years I begged God to free my mother from her pain and terror and mental imbalance; I pleaded, I bargained, I even tried to call in his "debts" to me for all *I'd* done for *him* in a half-century. I even cried. Often. And my mother's pain savaged on. On the other hand, I've preached at far too many funerals for teenagers—wonderful, alive kids with their whole lives ahead of them, we thought, and I've seen their families' anguish, fighting to understand what reasons a good God could have for this.

At those many times I've been angrier at God than I have ever been at any of my other friends, angry enough to forget who he was and all he'd given me and meant to me. And I've told him so. I've berated him. I've bawled him out. And then I had to forgive him—for being God, for having reasons I couldn't comprehend. Because he is my friend.

God and I aren't friends because we've gone to the circus together, but because we've gone through hell together—and, no matter what the pain and the demand for trust, we have remained friends.

Conclusions

Faith, then—belief in our friends and God—is not an intellectual assent to a series of debatable propositions. It is a commitment of one's entire *person*. A gamble. A calculated risk. I take the leap on a hunch, a hunch based on the testimony of other people and on my own experience—first of meeting, then of knowing. There is the initial attraction, the preliminary sparring, the sense of risk and then the commitment, the gradual learning and perhaps, much later, even logic, definitions, erudition. Without the initial intrigue and the hunch that this is "right," though, there is nothing but notional knowledge.

To try to exhaust this new discovery is both futile and deadly. The poet knows far better than the scientist or philosopher what to do in these early stages of discovery. Chesterton sums it up: "Poetry is sane because it floats easily on the infinite sea; reason seeks to cross the infinite sea, thus making it finite."

Oh, there will be doubts. But doubt is no sin. Sometimes certitudes are.

Question for the Notebook

Page 23. Considering the whole process described in the chapter of moving from *notional* knowledge to *real* knowledge, describe an actual situation in your own life when you yourself have gone through this same process with a stranger who became a friend.

A Prayer

God, give me the curiosity and the caring to look before I leap. But help me find the courage not to be afraid to leap without an absolute guarantee. Don't allow me to let life just happen to me. Amen.

Does God Exist?

Death: The Crucial Mystery

> If Cinderella says, "How is it that I must leave the ball at twelve?" her godmother might answer, "How is it that you are *going* there till twelve?"
>
> —*G. K. Chesterton*

From the outset we've spoken of expectations, how faulty perceptions and propaganda can warp the realities of our lives out of focus—and with them our expectations. Even with as honest a view as possible of the world around us, and no matter what our real limitations, we still look into the future with hope. We can't help it; that's the way we're made. Sometimes we long for a crystal ball ("if only") that will let us peer into that future so that the certainty would motivate us to prepare for it. Will I marry well? (Well, *I* won't, but will you?) Will I have a job I'll find fulfilling even after forty? Will I have children I can be proud of, or will they be proud of me? Certainly there are some quite obvious things one can do to make those outcomes *less un*likely, but in the future, *nothing* is that predictable.

Except one thing. You will die.

Your death is not an unpleasant possibility. Your death is an unpleasant fact. Some find it so morbid or even grisly that they refuse to acknowledge it even as a possibility worth considering.

Death is as obscene in our day as sex was in the days of Queen Victoria. It is too vulgar, too dangerous to talk about in front of the children. The aged are hustled off to be hidden away in nursing homes, and dying is usually done "properly" in a hospital. The mere image of oneself growing old, invalided, lonely, and senile is more repulsive than the most pornographic magazine. Oddly, now that sex is above-ground and clean, death is underground and dirty. One has only to see how sadistically and violently death is handled in the media. There, death is so blatantly and relentlessly flaunted that it is trivialized. Who could count the number of real and staged deaths we see in one week on TV? Either way, hide death away or hide it in plain sight, death still does not cease to be real—just comfortingly unreal-to-me.

All along, we have said that only by seeing the truth is one set *free* to live the truth. Conversely, refusing to see the truth, denying that it is true, will backlash on one as inevitably as the fourth martini. This holds for no truth so much as it holds for the truth of death.

You can deny the fact of your death; most people do. On the one hand, *over*-awareness of death can be paralyzing, as any hypochondriac proves. It can make us fearful, sullen, morbid. No people in their right mind keep a skull on their desk just in case, for a moment, they might forget. On the other hand, many people (most?) use that very morbidity as an alibi for never considering death at all—just as some students alibi their lack of work by pointing to "all those four-eyed bookworms who never have any fun." Again, the truth is closer to the pivot than to the extremes.

In the first place, ignoring the truth of death *altogether* allows you to live in a world of *illusion.* Like prisoners condemned to death by the mere accident of birth, we cling to the foredoomed hope of a reprieve at the last minute. (We are not talking of an after-life here, but of death itself. Even the most ardent theists have to face the end of life *here* and the separation from loved ones.) Death is like an algebra problem, isn't it? You can always turn to the answer key or ask a teacher. But no matter what does or does not lie beyond it, there is no "solution" to death.

And yet we keep on secretly hoping that someone will invent a way to freeze us and bring us back, that we will be reincarnated, that there will be pills when we get to be seventy that will allow us to keep going till we're a hundred and twenty.

If only.

In the second place, no matter how constant or how complete our denials, death is inexorably going to intrude into our lives sooner or later and shatter our illusions. Long before we have to face the infuriating "injustice" of our own deaths, we will in all likelihood have faced the unanswerable and unchangeable deaths of people we love. Curves from "the way things are" are guaranteed.

Facing the Truth of Death

The capital thing about death is that it renders everything that preceded it unchangeable.

—*André Malraux*

When you ask the meaning of death, you ask the meaning—and value—of life. Conversely, when you avoid facing the meaning of death, you avoid facing the meaning—and value—of life.

There are three facts about death which no atheist or theist would—or could—dispute: (1) death is inevitable; (2) with the exception of suicides, death is unpredictable; and (3) death is the ultimate test by which you gauge the value of your life.

Death is inevitable; that is one of the few Cartestian certitudes. *No one* in the history of humankind has managed to avoid it—with the possible exception of Elijah and Our Lady, only two out of uncountable human beings who have lived here over 300,000 years. Whether you accept or dispute even those two cases, either way, you and I are not prophets nor the mother of one. Not much realistic hope there. It is going to happen. The question is when.

Death is also unpredictable. But we can't spend all our days looking apprehensively over our shoulders for a dark-cowled figure with a scythe. Life is about life, not about death. There are some "constants," backed up by hard statistics, to keep us going. According to the National Center for Health, most American males can expect to live to age 68.7, and most American females to age 76.5.

But not all.

In 1978, about nine percent of Americans died: 1,924,000 people. Not all of them were old: 45,000 of them were infants under five; 103,000 died in accidents "before their time"—30,000 of those involving automobiles. Only about sixty-seven percent of any age group will reach seventy, which means one out of three Americans in your age group will not; one out of ten in your age group will not reach even fifty. "But it's *not* going to be *me!*" I truly, honestly, hope not. But as I have said, I am only one priest and yet I have still been at too many funerals for teenagers.

There is a difference, on the one hand, between acknowledging death, adapting your values and expectations to its truth, and moving on and, on the other hand, kidding yourself with the false assurance that "I'm young; I've got a long, long time before I even have to *think* about that." That latter stance says, in effect, "I *can't* die 'before my time.' " An interesting irony there. It is, I am certain, in the back of the minds of most kids I know who in winter put their cars into skids for the thrill of it all, or who drive cars even when they've had so much to drink that they couldn't even write their own names legibly. It is also, beyond doubt, the major reason I have been to too many tragic teenage funerals.

Put it at its grimmest: we are all walking time bombs. The timer is set, and no one knows the setting. Grim, but true.

Finally, death is the ultimate test by which you gauge the value of your life. No matter what does or does not come after, death is the boundary and limit of human experience *here*. Without a realization of it, one has no sense of responsibility—much less urgency—for the quality of his or her life. Realizing death, however, we come to know the very real possibilities and limitations and values open to us on *this* side of death.

It is true, as we will see extensively in the next section, that death leads *either* to nothing *or* to something further. No other alternatives. That outcome will surely have an effect as well on how one deals with the choices he or she has *before* death. If death is a dead end, we are only marking time; therefore, anything goes; the so-called "saint" and "sinner" (meaningless terms) will get exactly the same reward/punishment: annihilation. If death is a bridge, then it is the ultimate in self-transcendence; we will see clearly a Fifth Dimension of our lives in which we have *been* since the moment of our births; there is a Mind who gave us purpose, and we can truly judge ourselves "saints" or "sinners" by whether we fulfill that purpose or not.

In this chapter, however, I want to consider what effect the fact of death has on your life and how it ought to affect the way you go about living the one life you have—whether there is a God or not, whether there is an after-life or not.

Perspective

By facing the unavoidable and ultimate anxiety, at least we do not sleep our lives out, or waste our days in running from that inevitable moment of loneliness on our deathbeds. And, painful as that awareness may be, it at least does open up for us the choice of what we shall do with the hours between now and then. Thus we can take steps to bring some meaning, some love, some pleasure—some creativity into the time which we do have.

—Rollo May

The Romans were wisely wary of triumphant generals getting fatheaded and convincing themselves that there was no limit to their power to command. Thus, whenever a successful commander returned in pomp from the field, preceded through the city by the spectacular cavalcade of his booty, his thousands of prisoner-slaves, his exultant troops, the city went wild screaming his praises. But the senate decreed that, each time, the slave boy, who stood behind the general holding the golden laurel wreath of victory over the great man's head, must keep whispering into the general's ear: "*Memento mori!* Remember: you're going to die." As Dr. Johnson said of hanging, death tends to put things into their true perspective.

Time

Death limits life. Our days are a finite number. Therefore, by that very fact, each one of our days is incredibly precious—whether we realize that or not. Diamonds are precious; dirt is not, because diamonds are scarce and dirt generally is not. Just by the way our body/mind/spirit is made, we do have a genuine need to "waste" time. There's nothing wrong with games or music or just lazing around shooting the breeze, just as there is nothing wrong with alcohol or sex. They all make excellent servants but deadly masters. The balancing fact is that because our days are a limited number, they are too precious to squander too *many* of them.

Understanding the negative fact of death can also have a remarkably positive effect on one's attitudes. I, for one, never get up grouchy; in fact, the people I live with would probably be far happier, fumbling for their Wheaties, if I were a bit less eager in the morning to challenge the day. But I know that a lot of people far more worthy—and far younger—than I did *not* wake up this morning. Therefore, having this one more day is not something I merited, much less one more burden laid on me. It's a *present* that I needn't have been given. It would be mean-spirited, I think, to grouch at having to accept it. And there will be a day which will *be* my last, but I probably won't be aware of how irretrievably precious it is. Therefore, all days are precious. Similarly, whenever somebody asks me "How're ya doin'?" I always answer, quite cheerfully, "Better than I deserve!" For the same reason, I always sent my mother a present on *my* birthday. After all, she did all the work, and if she'd decided it wasn't worth that much effort, I would never have had all those days and their precious burdens. I go to Mass for the same reason.

Seeing each day for what it is—a gift—also has an effect on what you do with the day, on the quality and intensity of your work—no matter what the work is. When you have an unpleasant—and unavoidable—job, you might as well do it to the hilt, with pride. God forbid I should "go out" after a day of shoddy work, half-hearted effort, unrelieved bitching. Life's also too short to spend what little time I have being afraid that, if I stand up for the truth as I see it, "they" will laugh. "Life's too short" became a cliché because it is so invigoratingly true.

What's Important

A felt awareness of the inevitable reality of death shows you what is really important—and it is an infallible touchstone with which to test the truth of the claims from the propaganda all around you. In the face of death, your acceptance by the family you take for granted looks far more truly important than the acceptance you crave and never get from the sneering in-crowd.

In the face of death, assaults on one's own easily-bruised ego shrink to their true triviality. Thus, I can never go to bed with a grudge; I have to call up before I go to bed and heal things—even when I'm *certain* "they" were wrong. At one of those too-many teenage funerals, a boy came up to me, near tears, and said, "What can I *do?* The last thing I ever said to him was, 'Get lost, you asshole!' " There was nothing he could do, not for the boy we were burying. He could only promise himself that if he ever did it again, he'd apologize, soon.

In the face of death, other people's opinions of what is "acceptable" yield to the truth. One time, just as my parents were ready to leave after a visit to the seminary, my Dad said to me, alone, "Pray for us, Bill. This last year's been hell." It was the first time, ever, he'd shared his weakness with me; he'd had to be the "man," more reassuring and unbreakable than a man can be. And I had bought the same "unwritten rules": for the last ten years it had been "unmanly" or worse to kiss your father. But that day I kissed *my* father, and I didn't give a tinker's dam if everybody in the seminary had his eyes glued to the windows watching. God, I'm so *glad* I said t'hell with what "they" think. It was the last time I saw my Dad alive.

Salvation

I do not mean to get ahead of myself, to deal with the claims of Christianity, but I do think this is the place to consider at least very briefly one of the major reasons Christianity can seem unattractive—or at least irrelevant. The Gospel says Jesus is our "Savior." From what? Surely not from sin. I've been baptized, confirmed, and ordained; I've confessed and been forgiven of my past sins. But none of it has "saved" me from sinning again.

What the resurrection of Jesus—if it is the truth—saves us from is the permanence, the dead-endedness of death. But if death is not *real*-to-you, if you shield yourself even from admitting that your death is a truth, how can you see a *salvation* from that death as a gift? Even a thinking atheist who had come to terms with the reality of death would see such a salvation as a mind-boggling gift—if it were only true. Perhaps, once again, born-Christians are too spoiled.

Some Conclusions

In his book *Man's Search for Meaning,* Viktor Frankl shows how in the Nazi extermination camps the only ones who faced death with dignity were the ones who had faced the *fact* long before they had to face the *act.* Your death is not a question; your death is a fact. As we have seen, accepting the truth can enliven your life. As we will see in the next section, the *nature* of death itself hinges critically on the answers to the God questions. If life is a gift, death will be a meeting with the Gift-Giver. If life is an accident, death will be a sudden death-rattle in the throat and then silence. And then nothing.

Question for the Notebook

Page 24. An epitaph is a brief statement on a monument to sum up in a few words the way the one buried believes he or she has a right to be remembered. Here are a few of them:

> He hopes to appear once more in a new and more beautiful edition, corrected and amended by the Author. (*Benjamin Franklin*)

> Life is a jest and all things show it. I thought that once and now I know it. (*John Gay*)

> He was sometimes in error, but never dishonest. (*V. Steele*)

> Try in a few words to sum up the way you honestly would *like* your life to be remembered.

A Prayer

God, let me understand how my days are numbered and how precious they and the people who fill them are. Help me be unafraid to tell them. Help me not to be dead before I die. Amen.

No

If that's all there is, my friends, let's keep on dancing. Let's break out the booze and have . . . a ball.

—*Peggy Lee*

One question underlay the earlier sections of this book, and it is still with us: what are you worth?

The question of your worth can be reduced to its simplest terms: either you have *eternal* value or merely *temporary* value. Eternal or temporary: there is no other alternative. Death brings either of two absolute opposites: *infinity* or *nothingness*. Each of these notions is nearly impossible to imagine, but in order to find who you really are, we have to try.

In this section, as honestly as I can, I will try to set forth the atheists' position, why they hold that belief, and the effects on human meaning which, with unavoidable logic, follow from that act of faith in the non-existence of God.

The basic premise of atheism is Cartesian, but not simplistic. The atheist is not waiting for a thunderbolt to compel his or her acquiescence. Rather, the question is decided by the strict evidential principles of the scientific method. [Note: I do not equate science and atheism; many scientists are theists. They are such, however, because they approach the God questions with investigative tools *not* restricted to the scientific method.]

We can see neither atoms nor God. Yet atheists accept the one and not the other because, even though they can't see an atom and must argue to its existence (with fallible reasoning), they can act on the atomic supposition and get *results.* They can bombard heavy nuclei like uranium with neutrons and split them, producing a titanic explosion of atomic energy—which is somewhat difficult to argue against. They can manipulate invisible entities which they have strong, educated suspicions are there, and it *works.* Therefore, even if direct perception of the atom is impossible, they know it's "there."

Although others would disagree, atheists maintain that you can't set up similar experiments and make contact with God. Therefore, although you can't prove the non-existence of God, you cannot prove his existence. Furthermore, you can get along just as well without a "god"; whether you are atheist or theist, you both put your socks on one at a time. And, to speak truth, the act of atheist faith is a kind of forthright liberation from the uncritical superstitions and taboos of our unsophisticated ancestors, and from the intrusions into our lives by manipulative priests, whose only claim to authority is "we know something that *you* don't know. (Most atheists I have read or read about have come from very conservative—even strictly orthodox—Catholic or Jewish backgrounds.)

For someone brought up a theist, it is difficult to comprehend the *effects* of a denial of the existence of God, i.e., the reluctant admission that there is no primary entity outside our minds which validates the secondary idea of God, an idea which surely does "exist" even in atheists' minds, just as unicorns do.

Clicking God "off" doesn't snuff out the sun; it doesn't send us all scuttling back from civilization to the jungle; the planets stay pretty much where they've always been. What it affects is *the human position in the order of things.* At least as far as we can know scientifically, we're *the* top of the Porphyrean tree. There may be other intelligences roaming the universe, perhaps even meddling in our affairs, but we have no more ways of proving that or manipulating them than we have of proving or manipulating a God.

We're out here alone, and we might as well get on with it. How do we find meaning *for ourselves* in the godless universe in which (1) there is no single "director" or "script": we are all improvising, and (2) at least for oneself, death ends everything; the "play" goes on perhaps, but I do not.

In the very first sentence of *Cosmos,* Carl Sagan says "the cosmos [the three-dimensional universe and time] is all there is and all there ever was and all there ever will be." Therefore, with God out of the picture, we must find our meaning in the more severely limited, four-dimensional "context" of space and time. The *only* answers must be found *within* that system. In a sense, in eliminating a nebulous God and afterlife from the question of human meaning, we have made the "yard-stick" more concrete and quantifiable, but smaller.

Add to the two norms of time (how long you live) and space (the goods and property you can accumulate) another less quantifiable yardstick of human fulfillment: your own accomplishments. This is less firm than the other two simply because, lacking some over-all God to set standards for all humans, each human determines his or her own personal idea of "accomplishment" or "fulfillment" or "success." If humans are "the top," if we have "replaced" God, you are no more human than I; each decides for himself; to each his own. Therefore, you may define "accomplishment," by which you determine the success or failure of your life, as building Eiffel Towers with toothpicks or as conquering the world, as saving all the lepers of Calcutta or as eliminating all the Jews of Europe. You set a goal for your life, and judge yourself by how well you achieve it or not. No one else can set it for you, although as we saw in studying propaganda systems, others will certainly try (not always disinterestedly) to influence your choice of goals. Generally, however, atheists (and a great many theists) would agree on money, fame, sex, and power as at least some of the norms by which to judge human accomplishment and fulfillment.

What do these three norms—time, space, and accomplishments—say of the ultimate meaning of your individual life in a godless universe?

Time

About sixty-seven percent of us can expect to live to about seventy. But that's it. At the end of your seventy years, you cease to be real, like the wake of a ship. What does that mean against the background of "time" as we know it from scientific research? At least as far as we can determine at present, our particular solar system in its present form is about 4,500,000,000 years old.

SOLAR AGE (1″ = 1 billion years)

Solar System Formed	Oldest Fossils	Oldest Fossil Flowers	Signif. Oxygen Atmosphere	
4 ½ bil	3 ½ bil	2 ½ bil	1 ½ bil	½ bil

300,000: homo sapiens
3,000: recorded history
70: your life

The final three lines at the right are, of course, laughably inaccurate.

Against the objective background just of the age of our relatively recent solar system, your seventy years are utterly negligible.

Important-to-you, but not really important.

Expand the view even further: to the universe. [For the data here, I am indebted to Carl Sagan's *The Dragons of Eden*.]

If you compress the age of the universe to the dimensions of a single year, the Big Bang would occur the first second of January 1, and today would be within the last second of December 31. A few other significant dates:

Jan 1		Big Bang
Sep 14		Formation of Earth
Dec 16		First worms
Dec 24		First dinosaurs
Dec 28		First flowers; dinosaurs extinct
Dec 31,	11:00 P.M.	First humans
	11:59 P.M.	Cave paintings in Europe
	11:59:51 P.M.	Invention of the alphabet
	11:59:59 P.M.	Renaissance in Europe (14th-16th cc.)

From that very objective and very scientific perspective we see four hundred years as $\frac{1}{60}$ of a second; then your seventy years (if you have that many) is from 11:59:59:56 to midnight. Then the ball is over.

If "the cosmos is all there is or ever was or ever will be," your seventy years aren't a hiccup in a hurricane.

REAL $\neq$ REAL-TO-ME

Space

Some of us are six feet tall; some are 7'6" or taller; some are 5'2" or smaller. Inside a small room, that's pretty noticeable and significant. Standing next to the World Trade Center, it's not. The Ponderosa Ranch looks mighty big when you ride its perimeter for days without lapping yourself. But when you look at a map of all Texas, the Ponderosa isn't as impressive. When you get up in a space capsule, even Texas doesn't look as overwhelming as it did when you had your face pressed right up against the map.

Imagine you could get even further out. Say you were coming through the Milky Way galaxy (about a 920-quintillion-mile journey) on your way to someplace else, and you spot this little solar system with only one sun and nine (or maybe ten) tiny planets orbiting around it.

Solar Space—Mean diameter: 7 billion miles ($\frac{1}{16}$" = 62,500,000 miles)

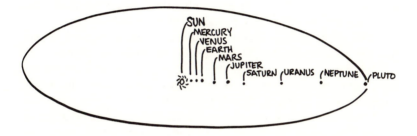

Again, on such a cramped scale, the dots representing each planet—and even the sun—are laughably too large.

Ignore the following chart, if you wish, but some will find it interesting (distances in miles).

Body	*Mean Distance from Sun*	*Distance on this map*	*Diameter*
Sun	———	———	864,000
Mercury	36,000,000	ca. $\frac{1}{32}$"	3,000
Venus	67,000,000	$\frac{1}{16}$"	7,600
Earth	96,000,000	$\frac{3}{32}$"	7,918
Mars	141,000,000	$\frac{1}{8}$"	4,200
Jupiter	483,000,000	$\frac{1}{2}$"	87,000
Saturn	886,000,000	$\frac{7}{8}$"	72,000
Uranus	1,800,000,000	2"	31,000
Neptune	2,793,000,000	3"	33,000
Pluto	3,680,000,000	3 $\frac{1}{2}$"	4,000 ?

It is also interesting to note that the nearest star is seven times the distance to Pluto (about twenty-five billion miles, or 2,500 times farther away from us than the sun is). Such stars move at tremendous speeds, but they are so far away that their motion doesn't change their "apparent" (to us) positions in the heavens sufficiently for anyone to perceive that change in a single lifetime.

The fifty United States cover about three and a half million square miles. That's a *lot* of territory, but it would be impossible even to locate them on that ludicrously enlarged pinpoint third from the sun on that solar map. And we are talking about this one tiny solar system, not the universe. You yourself take up about, oh, fifteen square feet of all space, give or take a few inches here or there. The point is obvious.

The whole earth could disintegrate in an instant, and most of reality—the cosmos—would be utterly unaffected. And what of you?

All this is very interesting, but—as more than one student has said over the years—"Who *cares* about all that stuff?" My only answer, sometimes too acerbic, is: "People who *think!*"

"All that stuff" is just a bit too intimidating; it threatens the importance we would like to attach to our presence, to our very lives. And, to be sure, you can zip up your cocoon and forget you ever heard about how objectively trivial your presence is in the godless universe. But if there really is no God, then that's the truth—whether you care to face it or not.

Human Accomplishments

In your seventy years, you will love a lot of people. You will perhaps give life to several children. You will achieve a certain temporary social status and contribute perhaps significantly to your community. You may invest something, build something, have your name in the newspapers a few times. The accumulated value of these accomplishments is non-material, but try to imagine all you can accomplish in seventy years as some kind of physical quantity—like the tons of water behind a dam.

Now compare the whole weight of your human accomplishments with the accumulated accomplishments of human history—the harnessing of fire, the invention of the wheel, the *Dialogues* of Plato, Caesar's conquests, Michelangelo's art, Shakespeare's plays, all the wars waged and the peaces achieved, the harnessing of the atom and the exploration of space. Compared to that background, your personal achievements look pitifully puny. And against the unfolding power of the universe, they come as close as one can get to nothing.

And there is death. You may kid yourself that you "live on" in your children or in your work. That's fine for them, but *you* have ceased to be real. You will not be aware of any continuing value, because you will not *be*.

The Atheists' Need for a Redeemer

If God does not exist, I am God.
—*Fyodor Dostoevsky*

What we have seen so far in this section has been, to put it mildly, somewhat depressing. It is, nonetheless, what the thinking atheist accepts as the truth. Godlessness logically imposes on the individual a radically new stand toward the world and himself or herself. We are alone and—against the objective background of time and space—negligible.

What do we do while we're waiting around for death to show up? In "clicking off" God, we also automatically negate all God-based, religious value-systems, all scriptures, all so-called "norms of morality" which "ought to" govern human living, in no matter what era or what country. A thinking person, liberated from a Creator who rewards and punishes, is thus an accident of mindless fate and evolution; therefore, there are no objective "oughts." It's every man or woman for himself or herself, from scratch.

But most of us can't handle starting from scratch. That's why the lure of propaganda is so tempting; let one or other of those value-systems do all that for you. But we left "cocktail-party atheism" behind us long ago in this book. Since what differentiates human beings from sheep is the ability to think, we are talking about *thinking* atheists.

Against that disheartening background of negligibility, even the atheist needs a "redeemer," something or some philosophy to give the individual's life a direction, something to stave off the conviction that we are ultimately valueless—except to our negligible selves. The atheist has to find some value in going on. Easy enough when you're young and riding high and the future looks like an endless series of "ups." But when everything collapses around you—when people you love die, when you're starving, when a war or a hurricane or fire sweeps into your life and destroys everything precious to you—in short, when you live the life most people have sooner or later to face, you have to find some *meaning,* some *why,* to justify the suffering you are forced by the mindless accidents of fate to undergo. If everything you do and everything you suffer is ultimately obliterated and made meaningless by death, you have to discover some reason to come back for more. As Camus said, in such a world, without a God, the *only* question is: why not commit suicide?

Nietzsche, the grandfather of modern atheists, gave the answer to that one hundred years ago: "He who has a *why* to live for can bear almost any *how.*"

Here are three atheists' "why's."

Three Atheisms

Meaning from Power

Friedrich Nietzsche (1844–1900) realized that, in the godless universe, the individual is dependent on no one, indebted to no one, and directed by no one. All answers are from *within* this system; there are no externally imposed values. Nor is meaning "out there," waiting to be perceived and digested; it is something we have to manufacture for ourselves. Individuals must produce out of themselves—out of nothingness—something which will (at least to their minds) transcend their own sufferings and death. Therefore, the individual who realizes his own freedom, autonomy, and will to power—the Superman—*creates* and *legislates* meaning. "There is no truth but *my* truth." And the origin of this individual's "truth" arises not out of the disposition of some God, or even out of the objective natures of things, but from the *will* of the individual Superman.

This doctrine is something like the child's game "King of the Hill."

It is quite literally the doctrine of might *makes* right. As long as I'm king of the hill, I call the shots; I say what's right and what's wrong, what's to be sought and what's to be avoided. If your will legislates some "counter-truth" you'd just better be stronger than I am. Till then, *I* am "the measure of all things."

There is, of course, a price to this solution. With this doctrine there is nothing to keep the self-legislating superman from using other human beings, their productivity and their deaths, as material for some future society, as men like Stalin and Hitler did—giving due credit to Nietzsche. If there is no one above humankind to whom each individual is answerable, then individuals are answerable to themselves alone. There is the great possibility—no, actuality—that, in murdering God, Nietzsche has created an endless line of self-justified Hitlers.

Meaning from the State/Society

The philosophy of Karl Marx (1818–1883) claims explicitly to be a doctrine of atheist "salvation" or "redemption"; it is nothing less than a plan to eliminate the problem of evil and suffering from human history by purely material, this-world means.

At the root of all human suffering, Marx sees greed. By nature, men and women "find themselves" in their work. But with the rise of capitalism—based on individual greed and the increase of one's own *private* property—the world was divided between the exploiters and the exploited. For the benefit of the few, the many must surrender finding themselves in their work and work instead on things they do not and cannot own. Thus, they are not only effectively enslaved but *alienated* from fulfilling their true natures.

Since, according to Marx, the evolution of humanity follows necessary laws, this unnatural state of affairs *cannot* last; it carries within itself the seeds of its own destruction. Therefore, the only way to "salvation" is actively to *force* things to get worse, until life is so intolerable that the workers will finally have the courage to revolt. Then, under the "dictatorship of the workers," a society will be formed which will be, literally, paradise on earth.

Thus, an individual finds value to his or her life insofar as he or she contributes to the revolution and to lessening the days before that paradise is attained. *That* is what gives meaning to a human life in a godless universe.

Again, there is a price to this "salvation." In it, the individual is a pawn of a mindless "history" working its way inevitably to fulfillment. Fine for history, but no person alive today will be around to enjoy it; along the way, the individual may have some minimal value, but only the value of a sacrificeable pawn in a game "played" by a blind force.

The human race of the future may, in effect, be as deprived of freedom by the Marxist as preceding generations were by the so-called God. One need only read Orwell's *1984* or Huxley's *Brave New World* to have a vision of the Marxist paradise. The problem of evil is the problem of human freedom; take away human freedom and a great many of the evils we know will disappear. It is a heavy price.

As Ivan Karamazov puts it: "I don't want my body, with its sufferings and its shortcomings, to serve as nothing more than manure for the Future Harmony."

Meaning from Sheer Bitchery

Albert Camus (1913–1960) has been, to my mind, the noblest, the most fair-minded and balanced, and for two painful years the most appealing of all atheists.

He, too, sees the recurrence of human misery but, unlike Marx, he will not attempt to kid himself or anyone else that, ultimately, some stranger, somewhere, will profit all unknowingly from my anonymous contribution to the Workers' Paradise. Camus is scrupulously honest and clear-sighted. He knows that there is no God and therefore human beings can never be divine. They can never be truly meaningful except to themselves. To give them hope would be a betrayal, and yet to offer them nothing but despair would undermine their courage to cope with life.

To Camus, of all the evils which came out of Pandora's box, *hope* is "the most dreadful evil of all." And the cruelest burden a human being has to carry is his own intelligence. The intelligence, by its very nature, demands meaning in a world where there is no meaning. Better to be a pig. No pig knows he must eventually die.

The core of the absurdist doctrine can be found in *The Myth of Sis-*

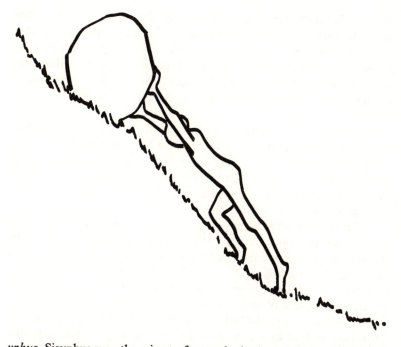

yphus. Sisyphus was the wisest of mortals; he had stolen the secrets of the gods. As punishment for that knowledge, "the gods had condemned Sisyphus to ceaselessly rolling a rock to the top of a mountain, whence the stone would fall back of its own weight. They had thought, with some reason, that there is no more dreadful punishment than futile and hopeless labor."

Sisyphus is Camus's metaphor for each human being: ceaselessly struggling to succeed, only to fail, succeed a little, and fail—and finally to die. Why not cheat the non-existent "gods" of their sport, then? Why not commit suicide? Because suicide is ignoble; it is quitting.

It is when Sisyphus trudges back down the mountain that he finds his reason for going on: sheer bitchery. He will *not* be beaten by faceless fate! He fires the arm at fate and suicide. He *wills* this absurd life to be meaningful. Therefore, he assumes single and total obligation for his own existence, to-be-for-himself, in *scorn* of fate.

Salvation is thus *within* the individual. Each must become in his or her own eyes "authentic," taking on individual responsibility rather than leaving it to any collective like family, Church, school, or government. If everyone is condemned to death at birth, each new day when we awake still alive is a *reprieve*. Only the "existent now" is sure (thus the term "existentialism"), so we must become indifferent to the future and the irresistible "plague" which is death. We must have a passion for earthly life, no matter how ugly fate might make it, and milk every moment dry.

There is a price, however. In the end we are still really only kidding ourselves. As Camus says, "The whole being is exerted toward accomplishing nothing." He is only acting "as if." Still, even if impersonal fate can't understand that I am standing up to it, *I* can. Revolt gives life the only value it is ever going to have. It is a noble stance—dignified, honorable, but so terribly lonely.

If there is no ultimate answer in society, or work, or education, or sex, if death eradicates them all, then I'm out here all by myself. With the apparent disappearance of all transcendent norms of human fulfillment, then Nietzsche is right: we are God. The expectations of the race dwindle down to what we can achieve on this bit of cinder floating in the vast indifference of space. We are not Cinderellas singing our peaceful Magnificats in a God-filled cosmos. We are freed from guilt, but we know that the handsome prince will never come, and hell began the day one was born.

Question for the Notebook

Page 25. If Camus is right, why are hope and intelligence "a cruel burden" in a godless universe?

A Prayer

What I ask for is absurd: that life shall have meaning. What I strive for is impossible: that my life shall acquire a meaning. I dare not believe, I do not see how I shall ever be able to believe: that I am not alone. Did You give me this inescapable loneliness so that it would be easier for me to give You all?

(Dag Hammarskjöld)

Yes

No one can see God without dying.
—*Exodus 33:20*

Does God really exist?
If he does, what is he like?
How can I know whether I'm right?

Before I begin with my own answers to these three questions, I should warn you that there are several presuppositions which run through all I will say. I "presuppose" simply because we've spent a lot of time so far establishing them.

Real/Notional. First, remember that these are *my* answers. I no longer believe they are true simply *because* the Church tells me to believe them. I believe because *I* have found these answers for myself. And, oddly enough, when I put the finishing touches to them, they turned out to be the same ones Christianity had been telling me all along.

For me, these pages are a combination of notional and real knowledge. For you, they are all notional, second-hand, because the real evidence detailed here happened to me and not to you. Nevertheless, I hope it will be provocation enough to justify for you, not an act of faith in God, but at least evidence enough for you to make a calculated risk at least on the *search* for reasons to justify your own act of faith, either way.

Whatever philosophy you discover, it must be—before anything—true to the evidence and it must be your *own.*

Probability. There is absolutely no chance that you will get a Cartesian conclusion about God, a conclusion so certain that you have "no occasion to doubt it." Nor can you hope—though we all do—that God will suddenly appear in your room and say, "Okay, here's *proof.* Here I am." He already tried that two thousand years ago, with mixed success. "Even if one should come back from the dead, you still will not believe."

The best we can hope for is what any jury must content itself with: a strong *convergence of probabilities* so that, once you've balanced the evidence fairly, you have a conclusion with such a high degree of probability that you can safely base your life on it. That may not be Cartesian and exhaustive, but it's pretty damn good!

God Is a Mind. No matter what his *nature,* if God does exist, that entity must be greater than *I* am. Anything less is not God. Since I have intelligence to see alternatives and choose among them, God must have at *least* that. If what we search for is an "It," nothing but a mindless "Force," then there is no God. Even when an atheist says God *doesn't* exist, that is precisely the entity he or she denies: the Mind behind it all.

Existentialism. For me, these are not three nice academic questions—like did King Arthur really exist and what kind of man was he, really? For me the three questions are existential questions. My whole life and value depend on the answers. If God doesn't exist, there is no need for any worship, whether as a Catholic or Jew or Moslem. In my own particular case, being a priest and a religious would be utterly moronic. But if he does exist, my whole life and all I do with that life shifts into a whole new key.

Furthermore, the existential question is not just does some Mind exist but does God exist HERE . . . NOW . . . FOR ME? If he's only an aloof "Prime Mover" or "Uncaused First Cause" or a God "out there" beyond space—if he just started the whole thing and then turned his almighty back on it to busy himself with other things—okay. That's a nice academic question again; it doesn't touch my life.

I'm talking about my *life.*

If I'm not right, then Camus is most definitely right, and I'll try to pattern my life on his, as the only legitimate and honest way for a man to live. If God isn't someone who *gives* a damn about me here and now, someone energizing me and my world, then I quit not only the Catholic Church but any other slightest hint of religion.

For me, that's what the stakes are. It's not a kid's game.

Why I Believe God Exists

What tells me there is some kind of God—some kind of being greater than all creation and responsible for it?

Let me lay out my evidence schematically first, according to the rules of evidence we saw earlier, and then develop it. If it serves no other purpose, it might be easier to remember later, when you get into the unavoidable discussion of the existence of God, across bunks in a college dorm or across barstools at one in the morning. The inevitability of God arguments is only a whisper away from a Cartesian certitude.

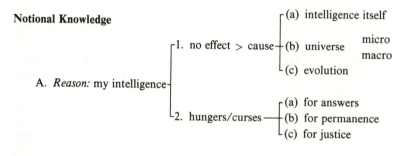

Notional Knowledge

A. *Reason:* my intelligence

1. no effect > cause
   (a) intelligence itself
   (b) universe — micro / macro
   (c) evolution

2. hungers/curses
   (a) for answers
   (b) for permanence
   (c) for justice

B. *Expert testimony:* verbal/example

Real Knowledge

C. *First-Hand Experience:* ordination
D. *Testing the Conclusion:* a lifetime
E. *Common Sense:* Pascal's "Wager"

Notional Knowledge

Reason: My Intelligence

1. *No Effect > Cause.* I want to start with something *un*deniable: I do most certainly have intelligence. Furthermore, that intelligence tells me, again undeniably, that *no effect can be greater than its cause or complex of causes.* Therefore, I apply that law of causality to three once more undeniable facts: (a) my intelligence itself, (b) the universe, and (c) evolution.

(a) My *intelligence* is an effect which came from some cause, and yet none of the lower "orders" at least seem to have it. Therefore, I can't understand how intelligence simply "boiled up" into me from any or all of them; I can't find sufficient cause for intelligence *within* this four-dimensional system.

I see power in chemicals and electricity, but I don't see in them the ability to change their minds, to rebel against their own natures; I don't expect water to change course uphill nor bricks to fly upward when dropped. And yet, human beings change course quite profoundly, and they have learned how to cheat gravity.

I see adaptability in plant cells, but I don't see in them a *choice* to change; they are bound to the iron laws of physics and chemistry; I don't expect a violet to survive long unwatered in a dark and stifling place. And yet human beings who are just as needful of light and air and water can.

I see a kind of "intelligence," shrewdness, trainability in other animals, but I don't see any attempts in them to wrestle with such puzzles as the God questions; I don't expect a cow to write "Hamlet." And yet people do both.

It would be foolish to deny that there could not *be* some hitherto undiscovered power in matter or vegetation or animality to account for my speculative intelligence. If there weren't some possibility of some other answer, I would not be stuck with a calculated risk; I would have Cartesian certitude. Till I get some clear evidence of that other possible cause, I am left with the conclusion that human beings must have gotten intelligence from some other Intelligence.

The effect eludes a mindless cause. To deny God, I have to deny the evidence of my own intelligence.

(b) The *universe* looks remarkably ordered. I don't "impose" the Periodic Table on the physical cosmos; bits and pieces come *to* me, and I just slip them in the proper slots. Men and women who ought to know tell me that the laws of physics are everywhere the same. If at one extreme I look beyond the limits even of an electron microscope, what do I find? Each body turning on itself, two bodies flirt in attraction and repulsion about one another, and that pair moves about others, and that whole system moves about and through others in an infinitesimal but predictable dance. Fascinating. But then, if I go to the completely other extreme, beyond the limits of the most powerful radiotelescope, what do I find? The *same* dance! Bodies turning on themselves, revolving around others, and others, and so on. That's pretty damned impressive if there is no Choreographer!

Yet it is more intricate still. There is order; the rules of the dance are everywhere the same: the laws of physics. But there is also surprise. No two dancers are exactly alike: spirals and rings, raging hot and rigidly glacial, smooth and pocked, positive and negative and neutral. This is not the dead movement of machine-tooled spheres but an endlessly varied carouse. Order and surprise.

My intelligence boggles at such unvarying order and such capricious surprise resulting from an accident: getting *order* out of *chaos* without a Mind. Variety, yes, but not the immutable laws of physics, not the Periodic Table.

The effect eludes a mindless cause. To deny God, I have to deny the evidence of my own intelligence.

(c) The theory of *evolution,* at least in its major outlines, is so well-evidenced that one would be a fool to deny it. What's more, unlike the stricter fundamentalists, I find in science in general and evolution in particular not only no threat to religion but a massive *support* to religion.

If you look at the progress of evolution, it appears to be an intricate *plan* working with infinite patience from one Porphyrean level to another and "finally" to us, to human beings. But to call it a "plan," you have already ruled out accident; there can't *be* a plan without a mind. To say that "natural selection" accounts for the survival of those varieties better suited for survival is at the very least an inaccurate use of the word "selection." If evolution is a series of mindless accidents, there can be no "selection." Only a mind can see alternatives and select among them.

Suppose by way of some time warp, you could be wafted back four billion years to a time when the earth was still cooling. There are no mountains yet, no trees, no animals, no people. Just a rich laval soup. Could even the most brilliant physicist look at that molten sea and, with a straight face, say, "Ah! Given enough time and good luck, I can see finally emerging from this soup Albert Einstein dreaming e = mc²!" My intelligence chokes on that one.

In *Cosmos,* Carl Sagan says, "One day, quite by accident, a molecule arose that was able to make crude copies of itself." Now that was *one* helluva shrewd molecule! In speaking of the herds of trilobites which teemed in the oceans five hundred million years ago, he says, "They stored crystals in their eyes to detect polarized light." How did those trilobites "know" there was any light there to be detected, I asked myself. Later he asserts, "Eyes and ears evolved, and now the cosmos could see and hear." I found myself scrawling in the margin, "Just like that!" Dr. Sagan seems to imply that, because there is light, someone must see it. The logic escapes me, especially since there is much light (X-rays, gamma rays) we don't see, and since most occupants of this planet can't see at all. For me, the existence of the human eye alone is sufficient evidence of the existence of God.

I am stuck with a choice between two (and only two) mind-smashers: *either* there is an invisible Mind overwhelmingly more powerful than I, *or,* for "reasons" we can't fathom, order came out of chaos and entities achieved abilities (like sight) without any discernible cause—by sheer *chance.*

Sagan writes: "It is only by the most extraordinary coincidence that the cosmic slot machine has this time come up with a universe consistent with us." And with no one to insert the silver dollar and pull the lever! "Extraordinary" is far too puny a word!

To change the metaphor: picture the pieces of a clock all spread out helter-skelter on a bedsheet. Four people, one at each corner, throw the pieces up in the air an *infinite* number of times. What the atheist is expecting me to accept is that, given enough throws, part A will sooner or later attach itself to part B, and part A/B will attach itself to part C, and so on, till eventually you will have a clock in perfect working order. And it never needs rewinding. And the universe—or just the human eye alone—is immeasurably more complex than a clock. Perhaps that is possible, but it sure makes a God look like a far more likely answer.

The effect eludes a mindless cause. To deny God, I have to deny the evidence of my own intelligence.

2. *Hungers/Curses.* Besides the chemical and electronic juices in me, there are also hungers which I have discovered that every other human being seems to have: (a) the hunger for answers, (b) the hunger for permanence, and (c) the hunger for justice—at least for oneself. These hungers are so invariant that it seems undeniable that they are essential components of human *nature.*

(a) *The Hunger for Answers.* More than any other question, I ask: *Why* should my cousin Judy be twisted by cerebral palsy when she's so beautiful inside? *Why* was my mother in the hospital two or three times every year for thirty years? *Why* did I have to spend every Christmas for three decades sitting next to a sickbed watching other people's Christmases on soap operas?

Why must *anyone* suffer? Why must anyone live so few years and then die?

If there is no God, the only answer to those questions is, very simply: "That's the way things *are,* Buster." There are *no* answers. There are *no* reasons. Everything that happens is an accidental result of a mindless evolution. The intelligence that *drives* me to ask "why" is a curse, a lifelong frustration. It is very like being born hungry in a world where food did not exist. As John Hoeffel, one of the brightest and least lauded students I have known, wrote: "If there is no God, life is an invitation to an Easter egg hunt. But there are no Easter eggs."

To deny God, I have to accept that—alone among all the other natures on earth—the very intelligence that makes me human is a curse. I know no other entity in the universe so cursed by its very *nature.*

(b) *The Hunger for Permanence.* I don't want to die. I have known *no one,* even potential suicides, who didn't want to survive death. Something inside craves a place where everything is permanent—where friends do not move away and forget me, where love does not grow stale and die, where joy does not always fade slowly into boring routine or crash dramatically into pain.

I'm absolutely certain that such a state of permanence will not come in this world. People are too free and contrary to allow it. But even if the Marxist dream were possible, it can't possibly come in my lifetime—or yours.

People say that that hunger *creates* the illusion of an afterlife. Perhaps. But if there is no one who can give me an afterlife, my hunger for permanence—like my hunger for answers—is a "natural" curse. The normal state of human life is an absurdity: hungering for answers that don't exist and a permanence which is impossible. According to the law of the survival of the fittest, any entity with such hungers for "food" that doesn't exist would long since have died out. Such unfulfillable hungers violate every other nature in the universe.

(c) *The Hunger for Justice.* You don't have to *teach* a little girl that, if her brother swipes her candy bar, she's got a right to bop him. Maybe it takes more time to teach her that her brother also has rights, but even a dog will let you know that you don't mess with *his* bone. Children and animals have an inborn conviction about possessions. But no lioness, at least that I know of, recognizes that the right of a doe to feed her young is at least comparable to the right of the lioness to bring the doe home to feed *her* young.

I have an inner conviction that every human being has rights. My intelligence tells me that a child—any child, in any society, at any time in human history—is more important than a fifty dollar bill, more important than placating an angry idol, more important than holding back communism.

Obviously, this is not a morality *imposed* on me by my society, since the American society has long tolerated, at least, the killing of children for "a higher purpose." Yet my intelligence tells me that the child's right to life is higher than my personal whim, higher than the temporary morals agreed on by this or that society, higher even than "the way societies have felt through most of history."

But who can be above all that? Who can have made human beings in such a way that even a child has inborn human rights? Accident?

If it is not a God who arbitrates between our contradictory philosophies, if it isn't a Mind greater than all mankind put together, then *anything* goes. Hitler and I only have a legitimate difference of opinions.

To summarize briefly: my natural powers are either sources of frustration or sources of growth. The first alternative flies in the face of all the evidence—including the very power with which I judge the evidence: my own intelligence. My intelligence can't accept an answer that says that very intelligence is a worse-than-useless curse.

All this is enough to convince me that God must exist. Note that I didn't say "prove"; I said "convince." It is a calculated risk, with evidence enough at least for me sufficient to bet my life on it. I have bet not only my life but my poverty, celibacy, and obedience on it. I'm not into hedging my bets.

Expert Testimony

I've read the atheists and, however noble, they seem to be an unhappy lot. No wonder, when you realize that even happiness is futile! Don't get me wrong. I've read "godly" people, too, and some of them are stupefyingly dull: Puritans, mostly; small-minded people who quote Scripture chapter-and-verse and haven't the slightest touch of "give" or forgiving; even lots of long-faced certified saints whose God is rigidly judgmental—even after they've apologized and been forgiven. If those people have a fix on the *real* God, then I don't stand a chance. Nor would I want to. My Aunt Glad, who as I said called 'em as she saw 'em, was one of the most self-sacrificing women I've ever known, but one of the few times she ever re-entered a Catholic church was for my first Mass. If ol' Glad is not good enough for God, then I sincerely do not want to go where he is.

Perhaps I'm "choosing my experts," but I have no time for those "experts" who say, "I know *lots* of people who go to church every week and are rotten the rest of the week." Perhaps. But such critics seem deftly to omit the people who go to church weekly and are wonderful people. They have apparently refused to acknowledge the apostle Peter, who denied his faith three times in one night, with plenty of time to know what he was doing, and was still made Pope—because he loved deeply. They seem to know nothing of the great St. Teresa, a woman of prodigious mortification and good sense and wit. Have they heard nothing of Thomas More, that sly and merry man? Or Thomas Becket, or even Tom Dooley—feisty men who stood up to the Establishment in the name of God? Surely they have heard of Dorothy Day and Archbishop Oscar Romero and Mother Teresa of Calcutta. Just seeing *pictures* of them reveals a radiance and peace that all but the most iron-souled must envy. I say nothing here of the believers who have touched my own life—my mother and father, my cousin Judy, my friend Bill Jenks.

All I know is that, if all those joyful and beautiful human beings are stupid to believe, I want to be stupid with them.

Real Knowledge

First-Hand Experience

Earlier, when I spoke of the source of my own "self"-confidence, I spoke at length about my fear of ordination and about the most intense meeting I ever had with the living God. I could describe it only clumsily as "like drowning in light." It has happened at other times, never so profoundly, but just as real. Perhaps those two hours were our "honeymoon," and the last twenty years God and I have gotten used to growing old together. All I know is that our love affair, although it has grown far less highly dramatic, has grown far more deeply satisfying.

Could that moment before ordination have been self-delusion—some psychological "knot" inside me suddenly snapping from so much unnatural pressure and yielding up to me precisely the impossible answer I *wanted* to be true? Of *course!* But then you weren't there, were you?

Testing the Conclusion

It's been twenty years—and a lot of miles—since that meeting with the living God, 7,300+ days of work, love, loss, trust, confusion, joy, sin, success, failure—even a brush with fame on the old silver screen. And the conviction that he is with me has never left me.

What's more, when I look at my life *before* that moment, I could almost laugh, if it hadn't been such a tragic waste of thirty years. Then, I was hag-ridden by my stupidity, my ugliness, my joylessness, my unprofitability as a servant. Since then, I know I'll never win a Nobel Prize; no one will ask to immortalize my face and form in stone. But by *God*—and the words are well chosen—I am the world's luckiest man!

If you can find a better offer, *take* it!

Common Sense

Blaise Pascal (1623–1662) was, like Descartes, a French mathematician and philosopher—but a wit of a very different wisdom. Like every man or woman of intelligence, Pascal knew that belief in God was asking a great deal: the surrender of autonomy as a self-legislating Superman. Not only was the price high, but the guarantees were more than a trifle flimsy at times: no one has *seen* God. Neither the atheist nor the theist has a sure thing; both are left with acts of faith.

However, long before Nietzsche or Marx or Camus, Pascal realized that in the godless universe, with death always ready to annihilate you and all you had accomplished, you had to *pretend* that your life had some permanent value. Well, even if the atheist *is* right, why trudge through the few days you have before annihilation, kidding yourself that your for-the-moment Supermanship, your toil for the Workers' Paradise, or your firing the arm at faceless fate is important? It's so grim. Why not go all the way? Why not kid yourself that *Christianity* is the truth? Why not go out expecting a party!

No one *knows* what's beyond the door of death. It could be annihilation, or it could be a party. But one thing is sure: if Nietzsche is right, he's not going to be on the other side of the door, thumb to his nose, sneering, "I *told* ya so; I *told* ya so!" If Nietzsche was right, Nietzsche isn't real anymore. On the other hand, if I'm right, I'm gonna buy old Fred a beer!

We keep thinking that, if God and an afterlife are a hoax, we're going to wake up in the coffin, find out we've been had, and then cork off again. No. If God and the afterlife were only comforting illusions, once you have a flat EKG, there's no you anymore.

Pascal's "Wager" isn't the core of my faith by any means. All that went before it is far more important. But there are times, times when I say "Hey, what about *me?*" or "Why the *hell* did you let that kid die?" when the "Wager" sees me through for a while till I can remember my real reasons.

Oh, yes, there's another clue, too: loving. Try that on your Geiger counter.

Question for the Notebook

Page 26. What is the evidence behind your own belief—or disbelief—in God?

A Prayer

Oh, God! You sell all good things to us at the price of effort.

(Leonardo da Vinci)

What Is God Like?

Notional Knowledge

The God of the Philosophers

You have an altar inscribed: To An Unknown God. Well the God whom I proclaim
is in fact the one whom you already worship
without knowing it.
                    —*St. Paul at Athens, Acts 17:23*

Where do we get our information about God? Only from the priests and
scriptures of the world's religions? No, at least not exclusively.

We've already seen, from reason alone—without much intrusion
from any strictly religious revelation—a great deal about God. He is a
Mind, capable of seeing alternatives and choosing among them; what's
more, he is the Mind behind it *all:* the Creator. He made up "the
Game," and we can tell a great deal about him—without recourse to
any religious system yet—from his *creation.*

For reasons known only to himself, he chose *this* universe; he made
it *this* way, with each component having *its* nature. From what we can
understand from what they "tell" us about themselves, he made rocks
to sit and await the uses of human ingenuity. He made plants to give
oxygen and food and beauty. He made animals to challenge, to give
food and clothing, and at times even companionship. He made human
beings to know and to love. From plants, animals, and humans we get
the idea that he's "into" growing and evolving. And yet, paradoxically,
he also chose a universe in which all things that grow eventually die—

even the rocks erode. Of all the universes open to him, he chose one in which there could be suffering and death. If he is the Mind behind it all, he must have had a reason, and yet he is often unmercifully silent about his reasons. He is a God who hides in plain sight, and yet he is not obvious.

The Great Dance—from the tiny tryst of the hydrogen atom to the stunning carousel of the heavens, too teeming at either extreme for our minds to cope with it all—speaks, again paradoxically, of his delight *both* in order *and* in variety. Who could have created both the giraffe and sex without a sense of humor? Every year the seasons follow one another, predictably, and yet each one is uniquely different, even in something as trivial as snowflakes: each crystal is cut from exactly the same pattern, but even in all of Antarctica no two of them are the same. Every human being has the same heart, the same set of limbs, the same facial components, and yet even in the same racial strain—even with twins—each is individual.

The paradoxes mount. In the search for truth to which our nature impels us, we long for simple, uncomplex answers at either extreme, and yet we find the truth most often only at the critically precarious balancing point which fuses the power of each extreme. He made *only* humans free but limited, self-transcending but rubbery-willed, hungry for love but fearful of vulnerability. Only human nature is an invitation, not a command. Only we can elude the shackles of our genetic codes and our environments. Only we are tempted to play God. It seems he has special plans for us.

The paradoxes of God are puzzling, but once we have accepted the necessity of his existence, we have to deal not with the God we'd fashion for ourselves but with the God we find. Anyone who says that fearful humans make up an illusory God to suit their own needs seems to forget that any fool could fabricate a God who threw far fewer curves than the present Incumbent.

Somewhat in line with this reaction to God's elusiveness, his "Other-ness," we experience the obscure and essentially unsearchable movements of the human spirit in response to stimuli from the world around us which we can't easily explain. Just as one can only in the remotest sense "analyze" love, those who have felt moved by the nearby presence of God can explain those moments to others only clumsily in inadequate metaphors. I could say only "like drowning in light." It is this sense of the "holy"—not merely the "otherness" of the distant Creator, but the awed sense of a more than natural aliveness right at our elbows—that gave rise to the primitive religions which found the god encased in the waterfall or the lightning bolt.

Still, even after centuries of science, demythologizing, and sophisticated education have peeled away the layers of superstition, even the most erudite among us still confess to feeling the awe which gave rise to those superstitions. We feel it in spring when everything is renewed; we feel it in summer when the skies are clear and ablaze with stars; we feel it before the immensity of the sea and great canyons and vast savannahs of grass; we feel it in newborn children. We feel it in all those moments when the hugeness of it all seems too great for us to hold without bursting. Even Carl Sagan felt it, visibly, in his television series when he looked out at the heavens. Awe.

It is our human response to what Hopkins called "the freshness deep-down things," to what Bonhoeffer called "the beyond in our midst."

One suspects that too many today are now carefully shielded against feeling awe. It is not merely that we are boxed into cities enrapt with our TV sets, nor that we so rarely encounter the immensities of sea and sky, nor that we go shod and unable to feel awe even at the simplicities of earth and seed and bread. We are carefully brainwashed to crave *inner* security as well; it is our guardians' greatest hope that we not be hurt, that we not take risks, that we not be vulnerable.

But the invulnerable can never know awe. They can never know love. They can never know the God who coruscates beneath the surfaces of everything and everyone we see. Their mirrors get in the way.

Here is the ultimate paradox of the God who emerges from the testimony of reason, of creation, of people who claim to have been touched by him: he is incredibly distant, and he is incredibly close. Like any other friend.

Immanence/Transcendence

"Immanent" means within, indwelling, in a sense "locked" in this four-dimensional system of space and time. It is "natural," "physical." At its most obvious, the immanent view of God is captured by primitive religions which show him (or some facet of him) somehow "trapped" within the waterfall. He is a very neighborly God.

"Transcendent" means beyond, apart, in no way boxed in within this four-dimensional system of space and time. It is "super-natural," "meta-physical." At its most obvious, the transcendent view of God is captured by the more "enlightened" theisms which show him sitting serene and unsullied amid the clouds on a throne the very purity of which would scorch our hands off. He is a very stand-offish God.

From our point of view, depending on one's mood, God can look different at different times: an old pal when things are going well, an old ogre when we've messed up. But that's our point of view. God is both. At once.

Little imaginational problem there, like trying to picture a saintly sinner or an angel made of mud—which some religions claim humans are. And yet human experience of God—no matter what the religion (except for the purest and dirtiest extremes)—seems to testify that God *is* both immanent and transcendent. Far easier, of course, to go one way or the other—as we will see in the next section—but the testimony seems to boil down, unsatisfactorily, to both. But how do you *imagine* someone who is both "the wholly other" *and* "the beyond in our midst"?

My own difficulties with the out-there/in-here God came to a head one time when I had to write a homily on the ascension. And the solution came when I tried to picture what actually happened on that hill in Palestine on an afternoon two thousand years ago. According to the report, he said goodbye and then just rose up out of sight into the heavens. Well, I find it a bit difficult to picture Jesus moving slowly up through the sky, like a missile in slow gear. I mean, I can picture it for the first few hundred yards, but then it begins to look kind of silly. I find it impossible to picture him shooting head-first up through the stratosphere, through the Van Allen belt (did he become radioactive?), nodding gravely to the moon as he passes by, and then out past the galaxies and planets and endless, endless space. Out, out, out until finally he comes to the very, very thin membrane that separates the material universe from "where God lives." Then—zooooop! pop!—he's through the membrane and into heaven where God is. Sorry.

In the Einsteinian universe "up" has meaning only in reference to the place *you* are rising from, and you're not the center of it all. Even the whole earth isn't. If Jesus went "up" from Palestine, where does the old Chinese lady rise when her soul goes "up" to heaven? Maybe it means orbiting for a while till you find the right "window." Back to the drawing board on that one.

The trouble with "rising" is that it depends on the knowledge of the cosmos available to first-century witnesses—not just for the fishermen who were there, but for the wisest minds of Greece and Rome and Alexandria—except for a few very perceptive men and women who were laughed to scorn, not only by the priests but by their own scientific colleagues. The earth was flat, they believed, and covered by an immense crystal bowl through which the stars shone and the rains fell. Beyond the bowl was God. One can't blame them for not having a more sophisticated view of the universe. In fact, it wasn't until about fifteen hundred years later—only four hundred years ago—that *anyone* had proof that the round-earth people weren't crazy after all. Even today, we who know better still talk about the sun "rising," as if we didn't remember that—even though it seems motionless to *us*—the earth is a carousel.

The trouble with the apostles' attempt to explain the "ascension" is that matter *divides* the immanent God *from* the transcendent God—and yet we are stuck with explanations in terms of matter. The explanation says that earth is earth, and heaven is heaven, and never the twain shall meet. This is pretty insulting to the earth which God created (and apparently inhabits or at least visits) and pretty limiting to a God who, according to the explanation, daren't sneak out of the confines of "heaven"—lest perhaps he sully himself with his own creation.

This is the radical problem: trying to "keep God in his place," like locking him in a church building so he can't find out what we're doing in the marketplace. If God existed before space and time, before the laws of astrophysics and aerodynamics switched on—if he created them *all,* he is not *subject* to any of them.

I just boxed myself into a corner, didn't I? How (in God's name) do you deal with a *person* who can't be *located?* How do you pray to a God who is everywhere—at once?

Certainly the answer is not in walling him off conveniently behind the pearly gates of the heavenly Jerusalem. Christ didn't go to some new *place;* he went into a new way of *existing.* And yet we are trapped by our need to physicalize, just as Helen Keller was trapped into the limits of understanding without eyes and ears. We can explain things we barely understand only in terms of things we do know: physical things. Therefore, let me try a few different ways of coping with the paradox of the God who is unbearably distant and yet dwells in our very souls, ways of explaining which were not available to those disciples standing befuddled on a hill in Palestine two thousand years ago. Jesus was gone, but not *really* gone; he was very far away, but he was still very close; he was once again both immanent and transcendent.

The distinction and fusion of "immanent" and "transcendent" may seem to be merely one more theological game, but I am convinced that unless one understands those terms, he or she will either find all religious questions a bunch of irrelevant mumbo-jumbo, or will deal with God on the same terms that he or she dealt with him in grammar school. Such believers deal all week long with the complexities of business, education, engineering, raising children, and yet on Sunday have to check their brains at the church door and deal with The One of Great Age who sits on a throne immeasurably far away in "heaven."

To my mind, there is no more critical question in this book than to establish the fact that the transcendent—the supernatural—the metaphysical realities actually *exist,* outside our minds, validating the ideas we have of them.

1. *Science.* As we've seen, the explanations of phenomena by modern science sometimes seem indistinguishable—with its muons and gluons and quarks—from science fiction. I have no problem with that; fiction is sometimes our only way of dealing with some truths. Anyone who understands, even remotely, Einstein's theory of relativity should find it easier to imagine how, to God, there is no past or future, and how our view of reality is limited by our *self*-centeredness or even by our delusion that earth is "the center." For instance, astronauts traveling near the speed of light to Alpha Centauri would spend about a year of *their* lives on the journey out and back, but when they returned to earth, eighty years would have elapsed, and everyone they'd known would be dead. Or consider the intriguing "black holes." From the *outside,* anything sucked into one would take, by our clocks, an infinite amount of time to fall in, but from *their* point of view everything would

be perfectly normal. If they could somehow survive the gravitational tides and radiation flux, they would emerge in . . . another universe! The explanation of the ascension begins to look less naive.

Regarding the constant interpenetration of our four-dimensional universe by the fifth super-natural, meta-physical dimension, understand that at this very moment you are bathed in showers of neutrinos, impalpable and swift as angels. You're not aware of them, but they're "there," just as real as the ultra-violet light you're not aware of is giving you a sunburn.

Regarding the omnipresence of God—in both the immanent and transcendent spheres of reality—I am intrigued by the speed of light. It takes only eight minutes for light to travel the ninety-three million miles from the sun to us. What if there were an entity "faster" than light? It would be so fast that it would be at rest, everywhere at once. It would be like God—or vice versa. And isn't it a coincidence how many people, no matter what their religion, described the quality of their experiences with the deity in terms of light and fire? I myself spoke of "drowning in light," and when I pray in my later years I pray not to a Father on a throne, or even to a physical Jesus, but to "a person made of light." I may be onto something there.

2. *The Fish.* Picture a fish in a very big fishtank at the bottom of the Pacific Ocean. Even the wisest old fish isn't aware that she's in water; that's just the way things "are." We feel "out of our element" in the water; the fish feels out of her element in ours. When she bumps into the limitations of the glass, she simply turns around and goes in another direction. She isn't aware that there's one helluva lot more water than in *her* tank, but there is. Or that there's an almost limitless ocean of air beyond that. And what fills the whole ocean? What fills the tank? What fills even the fish herself? H_2O.

Clumsy, perhaps, as all analogies are. But in remotely the same way, our four-dimensional physical reality is suspended within God's metaphysical reality, and thoroughly interpenetrated by it.

3. *The Atoms.* Consider (since you can't see them) the atoms which form everything we see: hair, skin, air, hydrogen, the host-wafer, the body of Jesus, and the bodies of all the members of his Mystical Body. We don't see those atoms, but they're there—not *beneath* everything we see, but *within* everything we see—binding us all into union. In

a similar way, the Reality of God thoroughly saturates the realities of all that we see and goes immeasurably beyond all we see. God is the well of existence out of which everything that is draws its existence.

4. *The Cave.* Plato pictured our world as a group of men sitting in a cave watching the shadows that the fire made on the wall. Someone comes running in to tell them, "Hey! There's a more real world outside! It's all around us. Those are only shadows of imitations of reality. Come out and see!" But the men have been there all their lives; they stayed with the shadows they *could* see rather than go out and try to grasp realities they could not yet see. A Christian looking at this myth says that the man who came into the cave from the real world was Jesus Christ.

Christianity claims that a Visitor came from that Fifth Dimension, and the consequences to our civilization have been stunning—although not universally well received. Some in fact treated the Visitor's claims in the same way the Inquisition treated those of Galileo. But the Visitor was the final step in the process of human evolution—from inert matter, to living matter, to vegetation, to animality, to humanity, to participation in the life of the divinity. He was the ray of transcosmic Light which sparked a supernatural life in us. And it starts now.

5. *Helen Keller.* For Helen, reality was confined to what *she* knew: herself and the nameless, faceless, personality-less bodies she bumped into. The larger world in which she was actually existing was actually richer and more real than the one she was capable of immediately perceiving. But Helen had suspicions of it—all those "why's" when some strange body interfered, her own inner yearning to share with someone else, and above all Annie's game in her hand.

Just so, we are living in our own solid world but also within God's way-of-existing. We don't see it, but we get appetizing suspicions of it—the questions "why," the yearning for permanence and ultimate value, the testimony of others that they have communicated beyond time and space and death. God's way-of-existing is all around us, but we can begin gradually to realize it only when we've had a realization like Helen's at the pump, a conversion: I am *not* alone!

So when we talk to God we are not talking across the abyss of space. The division is not spatial; it is a division between ways of existing, a division we cross over forever in death. And yet, we can cross over it now, merely by talking to God. Like Helen Keller's attempts at communication from her darkness, it is a calculated risk, an act of faith—that Someone is actually listening. But if we don't try, we will always be taking someone else's word for it, either way.

The Transcendent Now

For some odd reason, I used to think of that new dimension of reality as merely an *after*-life. Typically, self-centeredly, I kept thinking of it as becoming real only when *I* get there. But it exists now, not just for those who are already fully in it, but for us. Even at this moment, if we are able to live in that dimension in moments of ecstasy or prayer or awe, if it has no reverence for the limits of time and space, then it's as much "here" as any "place" else! In those moments, we are in touch with the incandescent aliveness of God, an aliveness before which my human aliveness, beautiful as it is, is still an imitation.

Then the true "I" within me, which rises out of the body and mind like their flowering, *can't* be measured by seventy years on a time-line or a speck on a cosmic map or a small heap of human accomplishments or failures. At this very moment, I have an importance that *transcends* the measurements of time and space! It wasn't hell that began the day we were born. It was heaven!

Forgive all the exclamation points, but that is Good News indeed!

Question for the Notebook

Page 27. Have you ever had a moment in your life when you truly felt God was "touching" you? Can you describe what the experience was like—and what it told you about the living God?

A Prayer

God, you are not distant. You're in this room with me, caring. Help me not to be afraid to come out of the darkness into your light. Amen.

The God of Other Religions

He not only created the whole human race
so that they could occupy the entire earth,
but ... he did this so that all nations might
seek God and, by feeling their way toward
him, succeed in finding him.

—St. Paul in Athens, Acts 17:26–27

One day in a park in India, six old blind men were being taken for an outing by their guide. Suddenly, silent as a shadow, a twenty-foot boa constrictor slithered out of a tree and gobbled up the guide. Confused, the old men stumbled around with their arms outstretched trying to find the guide or a gate or help. Finally, one old man cried out, "Ah! It's the wall! There must be a gate!" But another said, "No. We're still lost. I can feel the trunks of the trees." The third reached up high and said, "You're right. I can feel the big palm leaves." The fourth said, "There's a guard here. I can feel his spear. Help us!" The fifth screamed, "Ayee! There's a snake in the tree!" And the last, who'd gotten himself a bit disoriented, said, "There's a rope coming out of the wall, and it's very smelly."

With their limited resources, they had perceived what each could, digested it, and come up with varying conclusions.

Even combining them all and rearranging them, you're still about a mile away from the elephant they had stumbled on.

What is God really like?

Each of the blind men in the above story was partly right. But they were all wrong, not completely but pretty far off. Even if they exchanged places and individually experienced what the others had experienced, they ultimately would come up with a picture as confusing as the drawing. And yet, listening to one another, switching places, they could get *more* than they had alone. And if they'd found someone with clearer vision, they might have found even more.

Throughout history, people have seen God from different angles. It's the same God, but seen from a particular bias, a particular point in history. Deists emphasize God's transcendence—putting him outside matter completely; aborigines emphasize his immanence—seeing him *in* every tree and brook; Zoroastrians split him in two—making one evil God and one good God; and the Greeks and Egyptians split him into a thousand pieces. Even the Hebrews' view varied with their history: when they were desert nomads, God was a sheik; when they had a monarchy, he was a king; when they were overthrown and in exile, he was a suffering servant like them.

In other words, God spoke *through* the times about different aspects of himself. The philosophical Greeks saw him as the Prime Cause; the practical Hebrews saw him as a reliable friend. Puritans saw the unsmiling judge; romantics saw the welcoming Good Shepherd. Manicheans, Buddhists, and Jansenists saw a God who condemned the body, the Mithraic cults thought he got a kick out of temple prostitution as a form of worship.

Like the elephant, God is like all the things these religions saw. And more. Like the blind men, we can profit from the experience other men and women have of the same God. We have asked creation itself, "Tell me about God." Now we ask the world's great non-Christian religions, "Tell me about God."

Every experience of God is conditioned by the receiver, first by his comparative blindness, and second by his unique position "around the elephant." Just so, everyone's view of God—even within the same religion or belief-system—is conditioned by his or her own receptivities and past experience. What's more, the whole belief-system is conditioned by time, place, culture, social conditions, and even by the language and analogies available to them (as we saw in the ascension). Even the Son of God himself was limited to preaching in a specific language to people highly influenced by their culture and their particular place in history. This is why each new era must reinterpret his preaching in its own idioms.

Thus, my ability to form an *opinion* of those religions' pictures of God's nature is also somewhat limited by the fact that I have a "Western mind," trained to deal with hard facts, clean logic, and clear verbal formulations. Some of the Indian religious formulations simply baffle me. It is further limited by the fact that my parents were practicing Christians and my education has been mostly Christian. Finally, my ability to judge is conditioned by *my* personal experiences in the past of God's personality.

Nonetheless, one can range the great world religions objectively, based on their own judgments of themselves, along a spectrum from a God who is perceived as very *immanent,* with hardly any other-world dimension, to a God who is perceived as very *transcendent,* with hardly any involvement in this world. The spectrum runs from "hot-blooded" pantheists and pagans (and even black magic) at one end, to "cool-headed" deists at the other. One can only report them as honestly as possible, and let the reader judge which comes closer to his or her experience of God. Admittedly, it's unfair to sum up each of the world's great faiths in a paragraph or two. Men and women for centuries have enriched their lives with these creeds; whole civilizations have been built around them. But in order even to begin to understand them, we have to try to distill out their essences just as we did with Christianity earlier.

The God of Immanent Religions

Pantheism. The earliest people to walk the jungles and prairies of the earth were not burdened with Ph.D's. They were primitive people whose lives depended utterly on the caprices of nature. Therefore the god was basically a provider of food. In the earliest stages of hunting and foraging, his power was symbolized by some beast, and clans named themselves for their provider and sacrificed the best parts of their catch to him or her. Later, when peoples settled into farming communities, they depended on the fickle powers of earth, sun, and clouds for their lives, and thus offered appropriate—often sexual—sacrifice to secure fertility. Such were the Canaanites who surrounded the Israelites—tantalizingly—in the years when they settled in Palestine.

Polytheism. As peoples merged through conquest, they often merged their pantheons of gods as well, more often than not finding obvious mirror-images or more sophisticated pictures of their own gods. Thus Greece's Poseidon, lord of the seas, merged easily into Rome's Neptune, and so forth. But always, in connection with the people's creation myths, there was an original pair (Tiamat and Apsu in Babylon, Zeus and Hera in Greece) who were the first gods and begat all the others. Often, when questions arose such as "But who begat the first pair?" there were suspicions of still another power even beyond them.

In a sense, polytheism "puts one chip on each of the roulette squares," moving from shrine to shrine, just in case. Also, it was very much of this world; the gods were no "higher" above the people than the top of Mount Olympus. What's more, the gods were very unpredictable and arbitrary, playing favorites, holding grudges, not only against

204 / Meeting the Living God

humans but against one another. Stories of their constant meddling and cross-purposes, of course, were an attempt to justify one's favorite god's "inability" to pay off on one's offering; some other god had interfered.

As civilization and philosophical speculation grew, nature religions began to appear naive even to such early thinkers as Socrates and Plato, who saw that the Mind behind it all really ought to be at least more self-disciplined than humans. Nonetheless, the polytheists—though they might seem too immanentist to us—can remind us of aspects of the infinitely-faceted God which can get lost in our lofty theologizing. God is not *just* the rarefied "Prime Mover" or "Uncaused First Cause"—thinner than thought, colder than calculation. He is also alive, energizing everything we see. In our rush toward clear definitions we often dash right by the God who is hiding in plain sight.

The Strange "God" of Hinduism/Buddhism

Hinduism (or *Brahmanism*). In the *Veda,* the scripture of Hinduism, human life is pictured—as it is in *The Myth of Sisyphus*—as one dreary iron round of pain and disappointment after another, alleviated only infrequently and very temporarily by beauty, success, sexual ecstasy, and so on. In the end, they are all illusions. Even death gives no release, since each individual is reincarnated endlessly in some other form, either better or, more often, worse than one's present lot. But there is a possibility of affecting one's next reincarnation by *karma,* i.e., all the positive and negative consequences of one's good and bad choices in life. By working on one's *karma,* he or she can try to *fix* the condition of the next rebirth. Thus, by strict mortification of desire (the cause of all unhappiness) and absorption into one's own soul in meditation (yoga), one can move gradually into absorption into Brahma, or the Oversoul, and a release from the paralyzing limitations of one's "I." At last one is freed from consciousness, feeling, love, and individuality—at one with the All. For those who do not discipline themselves by mortification and prayer, bad *karma* leads to rebirth on a lower plane—as an animal or a member of a lower caste, or of no caste at all: a pariah.

Strictly speaking, there is really *no* God in Hinduism, not in the sense in which we have used the word: the caring Creator who gives meaning to it all. Whatever the "Oversoul" or "All" is, it does not seem to be a mind or personal in any way, but rather an "Emptiness." One is almost tempted to call it an atheism.

Buddhism arose from Hinduism, somewhat as Christianity did from Judaism. Siddhartha Gautama (d. 480 B.C.), after years of Brahman penance, received a vision that humans could break *out* of the cycle of rebirths and achieve Nirvana (Dissolution) even before physical death by following "the Middle Way"—an equilibrium between hedonism and excessive penance, which brings serenity and peace, here and now.

As with Hinduism there seems no doctrine at all of a personal God. Rather both belief-systems seem focused on the self—with the sole purpose of *dissolving* the self. Even kindness to others is seen by some Buddhists not as generosity to the other but rather as a means to one's own inner tranquility. Moreover, both are very *fatalistic,* teaching each person to bow unquestioningly to his or her own fate. Even though we are urged to attempt to sway that fate by prayer and self-denial, fate has the last word. True enough, the disciplined individual is less *aware* of life's wretchedness, but the wretchedness goes on, in fact is allowed to go on since it is "the way things are." Thus the Buddhist is resigned to non-development, of himself or of society, which *seems* unnatural.

In the end, there is no God, only the All. And there is no love (which requires two self-aware individuals), only absorption and the cessation of self. Even in the best of cases, after all the rebirths, one achieves what the atheist has been claiming all along awaits us at death: annihilation.

The God of Transcendent Religions

Deism has a picture of God who seems almost too "refined" and transcendent to call that belief a religion. It is, rather, "a view of God," which sees him as the Mind behind it all, like the clockmaker, who set all the pieces in place and then let it run on its own. It has the advantage, on the one hand, of solving the logical necessity of having a Mind as the source of the order and variety of the universe while, on the other hand, relieving us of any need to deal with such an aloof personage in prayer or worship. It also relieves us of the need for organized religion and meddlesome priests.

But there is a further appeal to Deism. Unlike the Allah of Islam (as we will see momentarily), the God of Deism is not intrusive. He does not directly cause every trivial incident in our days or even major tragedies like hurricanes or airplane crashes. There is no need to question "how a good God could allow" my friend to die so young. However, one is still left with the question of how a good God could choose such a *universe* where, as a matter of course or accident, such tragedies could occur.

Islam (the religion of Moslems) is a one-transcendent-God religion which arose about 600 A.D. as the last revelation of the living God, beginning with Abraham, then Moses, then Jesus, and finally Mohammed: "the Seal of All the Prophets." In Islam, Allah (God) exists from forever and is unquestionably supreme over all; "there is no God but Allah." Whatever happens—each single birth and death, each accident, each toe-stubbing—is the direct intervention of Allah. No object has a causality of its own; rather, it is manipulated as Allah wills.

It is his will that each Moslem pray five times each day facing Mecca, give alms to the poor, fast each day in the month of Ramadan from sunup to sundown, and make a pilgrimage to Mecca once in a lifetime. All physical images of God—or any living thing—are strictly forbidden, lest the picture become an idol of Allah rather than only a symbol.

The most striking aspect of Islam is its profound inner yielding before God's transcendent and unquestionable power. If Allah's will changes in a moment, arbitrarily, one bows to it. There is no fellowship between the human and God, who utterly transcends his creation. In a sense, he is a "personalized fate" who determines the lot in life of rich and poor, to which each must bow without objection. There is not only no use in trying to alter one's state (the will of Allah); it would, in fact, be blasphemous to try.

It would not be at all unfair to ascribe the misery of the poor in India and the Arab countries to the fatalism of their religions' views of God's nature and therefore the essentially *passive* response of the individual to fate. The God questions, again, are not sheerly academic.

However, as with their opposities, the polytheists and pagans, the deists and Moslems can remind us of aspects of the infinitely-faceted God which can get lost—even if, to oneself, they may seem "too transcendent." God may indeed be "the buddy at my elbow," but he is not a patsy. He is not answerable to us.

The God of Israel

It has seemed all along that the truth has appeared for us more often at the balance than at the extremes. For the Jew, this is where the best image of the God they experienced could be found. On the one hand, he was unutterably holy, so much so that even touching the box which held the tablets of the Ten Commandments would strike one dead. On the other hand, the community of Israel was Yahweh's darling, his pet; Yahweh's home—his temple—was right in the middle of their own capital city, and his glowing presence—the *shekinah*—hovered in its Holy of Holies.

Yahweh's Nature

Yahweh's *nature* is nowhere more clearly (or obscurely) focused than in his encounter with Moses on Mount Horeb. Before the burning bush out of which God had spoken, Moses hid his face in terror, for he was afraid to look on God. But he was not so fearful that he did not ask, when God commanded him to lead out the people, "But when they ask me who you are, what your name is, what shall I tell them?" God answered, "*Ehyeh asher ehyeh.*"

Realize first that a Hebrew's name was not a mere arbitrary word. It was more like a *definition* or a description of the person's function in the community, just as later Carpenter or Smith or Cooper was not only a name but a job-description. So the name *ehyeh asher ehyeh*—which is usually translated, "I am who am"—somehow captures what God is. So holy was that name that no Jew could pronounce it; rather, he or she had to resort to synonyms like "*Adonai*" or "*Elohim,*" the "Lord." When Jesus answered, "I am," he was executed for blasphemy for taking God's name to himself.

There are several levels of meaning in that name:

1. *"I am existence."* God's very name is *being;* he is the ground of all being, the source of all reality, the power behind all that comes to be. Each of the realities around us, like the tip of an iceberg, is leading us further to discover an immeasurably greater way of being real.

2. *"I am with you."* For the Hebrews, "to be" in isolation had no meaning; one had reality only in relation to the whole community of Israel. "To be" automatically meant "to-be-with," to be *there,* concretely and reliably. Thus, when God says *ehyeh asher ehyeh,* he is saying that he is *Emmanu-el:* God-with-us. God's name really means: "Here I am."

3. *"I am beyond your definitions."* There is a note of transcendence hidden in God's Hebrew name. For a Hebrew, to know a man's name was in some sense to grasp his identity, character, power. To know a man's name was to have a kind of claim on him as a fellow member of the same community. God says to Moses, almost playfully, "I am . . . who I am." God is saying that if Moses wants to know God's name so that he can capture him in a word, it's impossible. "Who I am" is beyond the power of words to contain it. There's no receptacle big enough.

Thus, God's name—*ehyeh asher ehyeh*—is a declaration of his nature: he is the underlying source of all being and power; he promises to be-with his people in their midst, reliably; and words are inadequate to capture him.

Yahweh's Personality

Unfortunately, most of us get our idea of what a Hebrew thought of God not from the Hebrew Scriptures but from movie remakes of "The Ten Commandments." As children, we saw Charlton Heston, or somebody else bearded and furious, and—putting that together subconsciously with pictures in church of "God the Father"—we concluded that, to the Jew, God is like a gouty, grumpy grandfather.

On the contrary, there are many "faces" of God in the Old Testament: wrathful, fond, threatening, promising, wooing. Leviticus, Deuteronomy, and some of the more hot-tempered prophets emphasize the lawgiver and judge; Hosea, the Canticle, Isaiah and many others emphasize the lover and the savior.

At the innermost core of all Israel's views of Yahweh is the realization of the covenant: "I will be your God; you will be my people." In the covenant, the people were called to be-with one another as a holy entity because Yahweh is-with them in their community. For his part of the covenant, Yahweh was a person, dependable, loving, and merciful to the people; for their part, the people must also be dependable, loving, and obedient to Yahweh.

More often than not, the picture of Yahweh which emerges from the Old Testament is the husband of Israel—who is again and again betrayed and cuckolded by his falsehearted wife, Israel, who at every chance runs whoring after the fertility gods of Canaan. Their love in good times is captured in The Canticle of Canticles, in which Yahweh is the Prince and Israel is his Beloved—a biblical poem which is, to be perfectly honest, pretty hot stuff. "Feed me with raisin cakes, comfort me with apples, for I am sick with love. . . . Your breasts are two fawns, feeding among the lilies. . . . Your lips, my promised one, distill wild honey. Honey and milk are under your tongue" (2:5; 4:5–11). Not exactly your gouty, grumpy grandfather.

More frequently, Israel had run away from her Spouse, who had never been unfaithful to her, and always Yahweh goes looking for her:

> The fame of your beauty spread through the nations, since it was perfect, because I had clothed you with my own splendor—it is the Lord Yahweh who speaks. You have become infatuated with your own beauty; you have used your fame to make yourself a prostitute; you have offered your services to all comers. . . . Well then, whore, hear the word of Yahweh. The Lord Yahweh says this: for having undressed and let yourself be seen naked while whoring with your lovers and with your filthy idols, and for giving them your children's blood—for all this, I am going to band together all the lovers who have pleasured you, both those you liked and those you disliked; I am going to band them together against you from all around. I will strip you in front of them, and let them see you naked (Ezekiel 16:14–15, 35–37).

But invariably, Yahweh cannot be content with wrath; it is against his own nature and against his covenant: the agreement was not *if* you be my people, I will be your God. No matter how unfaithful Israel was, Yahweh could not be unfaithful:

> Then she will say, "I will go back to my first husband; I was happier then than I am today." That is why I am going to lure her and lead her out into the wilderness and speak to her heart. . . .There she will respond to me as she did when she was young (Hosea 2:7ff).

The "Masculine" God

With the recent and, to me, long overdue demand for the equality of women with men, there has arisen a problem with which even the fairest mind cannot cope: the sexist language of the Scriptures and all our statements about God. There has been a slow move to change such (perhaps unconsciously formulated) sexist language as "(this blood) will be shed for you and all *men.*" Most writers and homilists now—while avoiding the ugly "he/she" and the clumsy "each boy or girl will have himself or herself ready for his or her test"—try also to avoid such sexism by using indifferent terms like "letter carrier" or "police officer." (At times, though, it can become ludicrous, as in "personhole cover.")

But when we come to the divinity, we—I—have to bite the bullet. At least I cannot tolerate the person I worship being neutered down to "Our Parent who art in heaven," nor am I at all comfortable with those, even more aggressive, who want me to call the God I've known for fifty years "Our Mother who art in heaven." God may be as much feminine as masculine, but—as I must have demonstrated throughout these pages—I am, on the one hand, impatient with fence-straddling and, on the other hand, wary of those who try to effect change by infuriating congregations and students, both male and female. Believe me, if I could *honestly* avoid this topic, I would. But in fairness I cannot, even if my attempt comes out badly. What I say here, I believe, is not at all callous to women's rightful sensitivity even to inadvertent sexism; what I would question is the possibility of *over*-sensitivity in an area which is one of those "things that can't be changed."

It would be self-serving to deny that the Scriptures and rituals of *all* religions arose originally out of cultures with unbending male bias. (Even in the enlightened United States, females were not considered legal persons—although ships and corporations were—until August 26, 1920.) Of course, if Yahweh is a *spirit* he has no physical genitals and therefore no gender, neither male nor female. However, no language I know of has pronouns that cope with someone who has the character of a person and yet who is neither male, nor female, nor neuter, nor hermaphrodite. It is not the fault of God, nor of ill will, nor at least today of male chauvinism. It is the fault, once again, of our inadequate word-boxes.

Let me make a distinction which, if it does not settle the question, might offer a path to peace. I take the difference between "male" and "female" to be a genital difference, a matter of physique and quite easily certifiable. "Masculine" and "feminine," however, are more vague and for that very reason are perhaps more serviceable here. By "masculine" (not "mannish" or "macho" or "virile" or "hairy") I mean all those qualities which, *wrongly,* have always been restrictively associated with the *male:* activity, decisiveness, reason, calm, justice; by "feminine" (not "girlish" or "kittenish" or "ladylike" or "foxy") I mean all those qualities which, *wrongly,* have been restrictively associated with the *female:* passivity, creativity, intuition, enthusiasm, mercy. It is precisely the attempt to *isolate* these qualities from one another into "male" and "female" *bins* which has caused so many parents so much foolish pain when a girl likes to take apart cars and a boy wants to dance ballet.

If, until some better solution is found, we would separate "genitality" (male/female) from "gender" (masculine/feminine) in the God description, we might have a first step toward what I believe will always be an inadequate compromise. Let's face it: we still speak of the sun "rising," of my desk being oak-solid and stable, of an encounter with God as "like drowning in light," of God as "Our Father."

Many women have what I have (nervously) called "masculine" qualities in a degree many males will never attain: clear-thinking, imperturbability, "take-charge" courage. Many men have what I have (equally nervously) called "feminine" qualities: tenderness, compassion, "go-with-the-flow" endurance. God has *all* those qualities: he thunders at Israel's prostitution, and yet he waits resignedly outside the whorehouse door to take her back.

But God *is* the ultimate "in-charge." At least in that sense there is some vague justification for yielding to masculine pronouns about him rather than "neutered" or "female" pronouns. More importantly, the only analogy I know which can in the remotest way capture the love relationship between God and the Church or between God and the individual (male and female) is a comparison to a marriage. Assuredly, any marriage is a *cooperative* venture. Such I believe would be the usual relationship between God and ourselves, with one partner not unquestionably dominant and the other not unquestioningly submissive. Such an active/passive relationship would mirror the Islamic concept of the relationship both of wife to husband and individual to God. Nonetheless, there are times in one's dealings with God—like the seemingly unreasonable death of a child—when one has no alternatives but submissive trust or desertion. It goes against the grain. But he is not the God we choose; he is the God we find.

Can I plead, then, with the men and women on both sides of this question to yield to the limitations of the language until the linguists come up with a solution? "Our Parent" seems to me only one step away from "Our Thing"; "Our Mother" serves no purpose other than to rile listeners into closed-mindedness. Let us settle for our inadequacy, for the moment. To quibble over pronouns is to miss the *whole* point, like nations waging civil war over crosses with Christ's body on them or without. When the difference is whether Jesus is God, there is a point in at least a heated argument. But to argue over the divine gender seems, to me, a question which has not only no point but no solution.

Judaism

Thus, no matter its pronouns, Judaism balances the two more radical questions of the unspeakably holy God and the caressing lover. God's judgments are not condemnations but a call. He who calls is utterly reliable, the reason beyond our reasoning, the generosity that not only answers our need for a love which will not fade but challenges us to fulfill our natures by loving the unloved as he loves us, even when we feel utterly unlovable.

Question for the Notebook

Page 28. In your own dealings with God, is your image of him "overbalanced" in any way? Do you, on the one hand, treat him most often as far away, judgmental, someone to be appeased? Or do you, on the other hand, take him for granted, a pushover, your servant?

A Prayer

More delightful is your love than wine. Your name spoken is a spreading perfume—that is why maidens love you. Draw me! We will follow you eagerly. How rightly you are loved. Amen.

(Canticle 1:2)

The God of Jesus Christ

In our own time, the last days, he has spoken to us through his Son, the Son that he has appointed to inherit everything and through whom everything was made. He is the radiant light of God's glory and the perfect copy of his nature.

—Hebrews 1:2–3

In Jesus Christ, humanity and God met, definitively. If we want to know "what is God like?" we have the answer *embodied* in him. By studying Jesus, we learn about God's personality—his attitudes, his likes and dislikes, his ways of dealing with people and with material goods, and so on. Conversely, since *we* are made in the image of that God whom Jesus embodies, we find in Christ the model of how *our* lives should be lived if we are to fulfill the call of our God-given nature and if we dare to consider ourselves Christians.

Jesus' Physical Appearance

If Jesus actually looked like the abnormal being pictured in so much inexpensive religious art, I would not be at all surprised that both men and women might hesitate to spend much time listening to anything he had to say. Most of us would be a touch reluctant even to invite someone so distant and "out of it" home for one Sunday dinner. It's not that he looks so effeminate (though he does); the problem is that he doesn't even look *human,* much less male. You've all seen the pictures: long tapering fingers, skin pale as smoke, eyes glistering back into his head. Even in recent and otherwise well-made Gospel movies, Jesus still seems "disconnected" and aloof among those smelly, stubbly disciples, almost as if he were an Oxford professor embarrassed to be caught slumming.

Religious art is at times propaganda, and the religious "art" I have been speaking of is false—or at least misleadingly unbalanced. I believe it is caused by two factors: a warped view of Jesus' *nature* and of his *personality.* First, it overemphasizes the transcendence of Jesus/God, making him so otherworldly that he seems more ghost than man. Second, that fragile face and form overemphasize only one attitude of Jesus, excluding the others: his gentleness. What's more, prissy though such images may be, they make Jesus easier to cope with—that is to say: avoid. On the one hand, he is *so* unworldly that no one could in any realistic way use him as a model for *human* living; it would be like trying to live as an angel. On the other hand, we are more comfortable with the pushover Jesus than we are with the hot-eyed peasant thrashing the moneychangers out of the temple, the Jesus who challenges their (and our) bluffs, and compromises, and self-deceptions.

The real flesh-and-blood Jesus simply could not have looked like that spindly mutant on so many holy cards. In the first place, he was a Jew; in the second place, he was a carpenter for twenty years. Look at a carpenter's hands sometime; they aren't those concert pianist's fingers you see in the pictures. Nothing wrong with long slender fingers, except in Jesus' case—because they're a lie. Look at the skin of Israelis or Arabs who live outdoors in Palestine; only delicate Roman ladies under sunshades could have had the skin the holy-card Jesus has. Finally, although it is possible, it is hard for me to imagine that any carpenter after two decades of pulling handsaws and hauling roofbeams could have had that bare-boned, emaciated body. The artists seem to deny the Gospel evidence that Jesus' enemies called him "a glutton and a drunkard." Moreover, it is even more difficult to imagine the man pictured being flogged with leaded whips, roughed up by soldiers, cuffed through the screaming crowds, enduring spikes in his wrists and ankles—and taking three more hours to die.

Just as with our image of Yahweh, our images of Jesus are conditioned by second-rate, simplistic art which, almost unavoidably, skews our opinions and feelings of the man himself and his message.

Jesus' Attitudes

To do justice to the people who hanged Christ, their motive was not that he was a gentle preacher who wanted everybody just to be nice. Even Hitler wouldn't have troubled to execute anyone so irrelevant. Jesus' executioners did not think he was a bore; they thought him too dynamic to have around. One time when his scandalized audience was about to stone him, they said, "We are not stoning you for good work but for blasphemy; you are only a man, and you claim to be God!" The people of Gadara were so afraid of what he was that they "implored him to leave the neighborhood." He was, indeed, too dangerous to associate with. At the end, Peter found it too dangerous even to admit he knew Jesus.

If you look for the personality of the God/Man not just in made-for-TV movies but in his actions and statements in the Gospels, you will surely not find "the grammar-school Jesus." To those who loved him and those who hated him, he was *unnerving*. Of course, he was compassionate to the needy, especially the outcasts. And there's the clue. Jesus and his disciples had been brought up as strict orthodox Jews; their religion was the very marrow of their lives. According to their deepest beliefs, there were certain people who, because of their physical contagion or their unethical professions or their defiance of the Law, were pariahs, untouchables. Since the days of Moses, they had been taught that to deal with such outcasts or touch them was to risk physical and spiritual infection, expulsion from the temple, and the wrath of God. But Jesus, in defiance of the leaders and teachings of his own religion, went *searching* for such people: lepers, whores, grafters, epileptics, incurables, lunatics. He even violated the sabbath to help them. Surely, it took more than a little courage for the apostles to stay with him. But it hardly seemed to trouble Jesus. "It is not the healthy who need a doctor," he said, quite simply, "but the sick. I have not come to call the virtuous, but sinners."

Those same pious clergymen whom he affronted he routinely called "hypocrites," among other uncomplimentary things. Imagine going into some modern equivalent, like the diocesan priests' senate, and shouting at them what Jesus shouted at the Jewish leaders of his day in Matthew 23: frauds, self-aggrandizers, "fit for hell," "blind guides," "whitewashed tombs," "brood of vipers!" Not calculated to win friends among the influential. He showed no proper deference to social position or economic power. He called King Herod "that fox"; he thought nothing of upbraiding his wealthy host at dinner for discourtesy and, in his host's presence, praising a whore who had broken in on the party. Other than evil spirits and the wind at sea, in fact, I can recall nowhere in the Gospels where Jesus bawls out any other human being, no matter how depraved, *except* priests, and his own apostles, whom he was training to be priests.

More than a few other times Jesus proved in action that his sole doctrine was *not* "turn the other cheek." Faced with his own apostles' greed for the first place and rewards for all they'd given up, with their petty fears for themselves and distrust of him, with their truth blindness—in short with their unerring ability completely to miss his point—he said, again and again, "Do you still not understand? Have you no perception? Are your minds closed? Have you eyes that do not see, ears that do not hear? Or don't you remember?" And so many times, "Oh, you have such little faith!" And no one got the sharp edge of Jesus' tongue more often than his favorite, Peter: "Get behind me, you Satan. You are an obstacle in my path, because what you think is man's way and not God's way." And yet Jesus still washed their feet, even Peter's feet, even Judas' feet.

Jesus' love—like all love—is shown in tenderness, but not *only* in tenderness. Sometimes truly loving means being harsh. There is no trace of hesitancy or of planning, no cautious hedging of bets, no diffidence. Jesus was a man of power, perfectly under his own control. He did not attempt to prove anything. He *declared* it. This was no mere "great man." No mere man has ever spoken or acted with such power. And no mere man has ever made the claims he made and made good on them. Precisely because of that refusal to pussy-foot, "many of his disciples left him and stopped going with him."

I do not need to detail here the instances of Jesus' compassion. If I seem to overstress his "spine" it is that I believe it is an essential aspect of his character and preferences, which is woefully underplayed—often even hidden away. It is easier to pretend he wasn't like that. But he was.

There is also a certain serenity in Jesus' fearlessness, which the Gospel seems to indicate Jesus wanted to be a quality of all those who call themselves Christian: "You are the light of the world! A city built on a hilltop cannot be hidden. . . .Your light must *shine* in the sight of men, so that, seeing your good works, they may give the praise to our Father in heaven." Such a call to forthright self-confidence—based not on arrogant preening but on the fact that, despite our supposed burden of shortcomings, God has *chosen* us—seems to me often lost in a flurry of pious nit-picking and sin-mongering. "As for human approval," Jesus says, "this means nothing to me." Think back on the sections about propaganda.

Always he kept telling them to stop worrying. Could anyone add a foot to his height by gritting his teeth? Why not just accept the facts and forget it, and go on from there? Did the ravens or the wildflowers fuss and fret? And every time he entered a room, his first word was "peace."

Unlike most preachers, Jesus did not profess a religion of un-sin—although many churchfolk since Jesus have tried to change his message into that and only that. He said that the *only* question one would be asked at the judgment about fulfilling the invitation of our nature was not "Did you practice birth control?" or "Did you masturbate?" but rather: "I was hungry, I was thirsty—did you even notice me?"

Jesus spoke working-people's language. He had lived his entire life with fishermen, housewives, carpenters, farmers, and they gave a particular tang to his speech. All his talks to people are about the material things that filled their days: lilies and mustard seeds, farmers and shepherds, patching old cloaks and new wineskins, corn, bread, salt, lamps. In a land parched by the merciless desert sun, he spoke of himself not as a channel of sanctifying grace but as a spring of living waters which would never run dry.

He was not set against material things. He was not a monk; he did not live the life of John the Baptist or preach about the things John inveighed against. On the contrary, he was accused of being a glutton, of eating and drinking with sinners. He traveled some distance to attend a wedding party at Cana, and he thought enough of the fun-value of alcohol at a party that he performed his first miracle to keep a party going. And he used wine at the core of the Mass!

You can tell something about anyone's personality by the way others react to him or her. Despite Jesus' intimidating honesty—or because of it—they still followed him. A case-hardened grafter like Zacchaeus promised on the spot to give away triple what he had extorted. A whore like Magdalene thought nothing of the humiliations of confession at his feet at a dinner. Children seem to have flocked around him—and children can spot a phony a mile off. The Samaritans begged him to stay with them. And always there were the poor and sick, devouring him with their eyes and ears. Even his opponents returned again and again to "try" him, like a finger to a loose tooth. He just couldn't be all that he seemed to be. He had come to cast fire on the earth. He was somehow intriguingly dangerous.

Jesus' Doctrine

We have seen earlier at least one version of the irreducible core of Jesus' teachings: the Son of God rose from death to prove to us the permanence of the human spirit; at death, we enter a Kingdom (a "banquet") that will never end. But that eternal Kingdom *begins,* as a mustard seed, *now.* If you want to declare yourself for the Kingdom—the Christian community, the embodiment of Christ—you must be converted 180° around from the self-seeking values of "the world," to the self-forgetful values of the Gospel: love God more than you love any creature or possession, and show that love for God by loving the neighbor, especially the outcasts. We celebrate our belonging to the Kingdom each week at a "banquet" which Jesus instituted, in which the aliveness of the God/Man focuses into bread and wine and thence into ourselves.

It all sounds quite positive and inviting—in the abstract. But every "is" involves an "ought." Just as our belief in God should be visible in our concrete life-choices, so our belief in Jesus Christ should be visible in them as well. It is not a matter of merely "being" a Christian, like being a non-voting citizen; it is *acting* Christian—no matter what any-one else thinks or says or sneers. And that is *not* easy.

The tragedy of formal Christian education is that ordinarily it *ends*, to all intents and purposes, when we are children—or adolescents whose childhood has been protracted by protective adults. Thus, the only side of the Christian message we are exposed to is the side which children are capable of understanding: the gentle Good Shepherd who just wants us to be good girls and boys. No, that's just where the Gospel *starts*. The message of Jesus is far more intimidating than that.

The call of Christ moves in precisely the *opposite* direction from most of the values we saw in the earlier sections on propaganda: scrab-bling to the top of the Plastic Paradise, all the goods we are taught by advertisers to covet, the *Playboy/Playgirl* loveless love, the escape to booze, the opinions of our worth from grades or peers or even parents. The core of Jesus' doctrine calls to task even elements of the un-ideal Christian Church: the listlessness of so many liturgies, the shyness of the laity, the joylessness of a people who claim not to fear death any-more.

The Gospel challenges some of our most comforting opinions, opinions bolstered not only by so many powerful and convincing propa-ganda voices but even more by our own inner voices warning us that we are nobodies, that this conversion may not be worth the considerable cost. Its challenge is this: if you can look at a crucifix, *the* symbol of the Christian message, and say, "*That* is what a *real* winner looks like. He is *the* world-beater. He is the most perfectly fulfilled human being who ever lived. I will never catch up with him. But I'm going in *his* direc-tion."

The Gospel of Jesus Christ does offer us the consolation of forgive-ness, of companionship, of final answers, of surviving death. But let no one kid you; being a Christian costs. If the Gospel doesn't make you even the slightest bit uneasy, you haven't really *heard* it yet.

Jesus' Consciousness of Divinity

Jesus was not merely the unsurpassable human being. He did not leave us that option. He did not intend to. He claimed in no uncertain terms that he and the Father were on an equal plane. In Jesus, God's way-of-existing focused itself into our way-of-existing. He was the Word of God made flesh.

I have always had great problems in forming even an inadequate picture of how he could be both at the same time. In a trivial way, when he was a boy did he just pretend he did not know how to make tables better than Joseph did? In a more serious way, if he had the fullness of the divine knowledge, why did he cry out in abandonment from the cross? Was he just quoting a psalm? Was he faking doubt? With the fullness of the vision of God, didn't he *know* he was not abandoned? Further, if he was fully *human,* how did he handle that superior, that infinite knowledge? For every other human being ever born the greatest difficulty in *being* human is in coping with imperfection, uncertainty, doubt—all we've been considering throughout this book about calculated *risks.* How could Jesus be authentically human if he always had Cartesian certitude?

I start from the conviction that Jesus did not lie and that he was not a self-deluded visionary. The rest of his message is too true-to-life and sane for that. Therefore, I believe he *was* both God and man, and at the same time. But how did the God/Man grow?

Growth is the law which God implanted in human nature. That's obvious. If Jesus was *fully* human, then, he must have known what it is to grow—not just physically like animals but mentally and emotionally, as all human beings must. The Gospel itself says explicitly, "And Jesus *increased* in wisdom, in stature, and in favor with God and men."

One of the greatest crises of human life comes in adolescence with the search for and discovery of who-I-am. Not the smallest part of this crisis is bewilderment with sexuality. As McBrien says, "To accept a Jesus who is at once human—and yet immune from sexual desires—is to stretch not only one's imagination but also one's theological convictions about the incarnation and the fundamental goodness of creation, the human body, and human sexuality."

Jesus must have faced it, too. But in his case, it was not just a gradual realization of his human self (as we all have) but also a gradual human realization of his *divinity*—more than a little difficulty to cope with.

This is *not* a case of "creeping divinity"—Jesus slowly *becoming* more and more divine, just as he became more and more tanned or more and more tall. He was God from long before the moment of his human conception. But just as I was male when I was born—but had no understanding of that fact or what it meant until much, much later, so it is very probable, at least to me, that Jesus' human consciousness became only gradually more solidly aware of just who-he-was.

But how? How could God *learn?* I believe I found my answer in St. Paul's Letter to the Philippians (2:6–10).

He had always the nature of God
but he did not think that by force he should try to remain equal
    to God.
Instead, of his own free will he gave it all up
and took the nature of a servant . . .
    and walked the path of obedience to death—
    his death on the cross.
For this reason God raised him back up to the highest place
    above,
and gave him the name that is greater than any other name.

Two things must be made very clear: (1) He didn't *stop* being God. It was more like a king who came down and became fully one of his people; everything he did, he did as a peasant. But he couldn't stop being king. After all, that's what he was: a king/peasant, a God/Man. (2) The name returned to Jesus at his resurrection which is "greater than any other name" is *ehyeh asher ehyeh*—I am existence, I am with you, I am beyond definition. He had it; he surrendered it—not the *reality* of it, but the *privileges* of it. In a sense, at his incarnation Jesus became *amnesiac* about his divinity.

As this theory of the gradual human realization by Jesus of his divinity goes, he certainly must have known there was something special about him all along—the circumstances of his birth, the urge to speak to the teachers in the temple and their wonderment at his precocious wisdom, the "call" built right into his giftedness. Then, at his baptism, the thunderous realization: "You are my own dear Son. I am well pleased with you." Just as we in early adulthood come to the realization of who-we-are, Jesus came to a realization of the stunning fact of who-he-is.

Immediately afterward, in the desert, it is on precisely this newly raised conviction that Evil works his temptation: "If you *are* the Son of God . . ." And they were real, tantalizing temptations to a prophet at the outset of his mission: give them the bribe of bread, coerce their assent with miracles, seduce them with tricks. But he would have none of it; he would work it out as all humans do, step by precarious step. After that, with Jesus' relentless attacks on the Pharisaic establishment, it took no supernatural insight to know that, if he continued, he would be imprisoned and executed just as predictably as the Baptizer had been. But he went on, without all the answers, without knowing *why* God was impelling him to go on.

In Mark's Gospel, Jesus testifies in support of the explanation we are now unraveling: "As to the exact day or hour [of the Second Coming] no one knows it, neither the angels in heaven *nor even the Son,* but only the Father."

The agony in the garden proved that, like all of us, Jesus dreaded pain and death. But the man who does not dread suffering is not a hero, he is a fool. Finally, on the cross, he was tempted to the ultimate doubt. He gave the cry which so tortured Camus: "My God! My God! Why have you abandoned me?" But his last words were an act of *faith:* "Father, into your hands I commend my Spirit."

This explanation of Jesus' growing *awareness* (of a divine *nature* he never surrendered) is neither explicitly approved nor condemned by the Church. But I personally find it profoundly appealing not only because it solves the apparent contradictions I spoke of before (divine learning, doubt, ignorance) but also and even more importantly because it makes the person of Jesus so much more "approachable," so much less intimidating as a model for his Christian followers.

For years I suppressed a very real *resentment* at Jesus' divinity. "Easy enough for *him!* He was God!" I felt unfairly put-upon to be called into the footsteps of someone who knew everything long before it happened, who never felt a twinge of doubt or of regret that he'd ever gotten involved, who never wanted to run away from it all. He never felt his heart pound with fear and doubt; he never even worked up a sweat. But he *did.* He *knows* how I feel; he wanted to quit too; like me, he wondered at times if he were a self-deluded fool; he felt, as I have felt, betrayed and abandoned by a God into whose hands he still committed his life, to the death.

If Jesus Christ is dull, I don't know who in God's name is worthy to be called exciting!

Jesus' Resurrection

We are back at another crossroads: either Jesus is the God/Man or he is not. And it all hinges on the resurrection. St. Paul was absolutely right when he said: "If Christ did not rise from the dead, then your faith is a delusion."

There was no one to witness it. The guards were asleep or passed out in fear or off in the local tavern. There was only circumstantial evidence at first that he had risen: the empty tomb, the gravecloths. In passing, however, one might note that, if the disciples were faking the whole thing, nothing would have been easier than to make up some guard's name and *say* that he'd seen the whole thing, become a Christian, and then suddenly died.

Just as we have proof of the existence of atoms or the inner reality of persons only from the *effects* they produce, I think the only way to "prove" the resurrection is from its undeniable effects.

Fact: the religious movement begun by Jesus apparently ended with his death. He was deserted by his disciples, who barricaded themselves in a hideout. Their leader, within an hour or two of his First Communion, denied ever even knowing Jesus. It was a demonstration of absolute lack of faith and courage.

Fact: within a *month* of Jesus' death, these same men who had exhibited the most shameful lack of faith and courage, who had admitted utter defeat, were out preaching from the rooftops! In defiance of torture and death.

What had happened to explain this 180° conversion? Well, something pretty *startling* must have happened to change abysmal cowards into heroes. The death of Jesus had been a spectacularly crushing event in their lives. Something totally opposite to death and just as spectacular must have occurred in order to cancel that smothering experience. The disciples claimed that it was precisely that: Jesus' triumphant return to life.

Contrary to what one would expect from frauds, in recording the resurrection they don't show themselves in a good light: instant believers. On the contrary, they were openly skeptical: they thought it was only the silly talk of the women who went to embalm him; Thomas had to put his fingers into the nail holes; the disciples at Emmaus never dreamed the stranger who walked with them could be Jesus until he broke the bread with them.

Their credibility as witnesses begins to build.

However, the fact that, after a certain initial skepticism, the disciples died horribly for their belief is very impressive but not enough to compel belief. After all, on November 18, 1978, 911 men, women, and children willingly submitted to convulsive suicide at the order of a madman named Reverend Jim Jones.

But there is a great difference. The Gospel is an open record of what Jesus and his disciples believed: it is calm, life-giving, and self-sacrificial only to give one's *living* for the neighbor. Moreover, the descriptions in Acts of the disciples' frequent escapes from authorities is evidence enough that they did not run suicidally to their martyrdoms.

One further element is worth explicitating: the disciples proclaimed not just that Jesus was a prophet, nor even "just" *the* Messiah; they claimed he was *God.* Remember: they were strict orthodox Jews; there was only *one* God. Such a conversion was even more unthinkable than the change from cowards to martyrs. It was as utterly unthinkable to them as the election of a black Jew as Grand Dragon by the Ku Klux Klan would be to us. This was not just a change of heart; it was a total recasting of *everything* they'd believed all their lives.

They weren't about ready to explain how the Father could be God, and Jesus could be God, and the Spirit could be God, but they believed it, to the death. Something *very* disturbing had happened to them, something that went to the root of their very souls. I can find no other sufficient cause, over so short a time, other than the one they claimed: they had truly experienced Jesus, risen from the dead.

Jesus of Nazareth was a great and dynamic and good man. No doubt about that. But he also made far greater claims than any man ever made: "I and the Father are one. . . . He who has seen me has seen the Father." He came not only to free us from the fear of nullifying death, but to share with us the aliveness of God, to make us sons and daughters just as he is Son.

To believe in him or to disbelieve in him is a calculated risk. As far as I can see, there are only two honest alternatives open to any thinking person: either the sad self-delusion of Camus or the joyous risk of Christ.

Take it. Or leave it.

Question for the Notebook

Page 29. If the Jesus described in this section is in some part indicative of the true Jesus Christ—and therefore of the will of God for you, as a human being and as a Christian—then he is not merely someone who cherishes but also someone who challenges. As John Shea writes, "He visits our dreams and his opening line is always the same: 'I have something for you to do!'" What does he ask *you* to do—however reluctant you might be to face it? Not some "general you" but you as a unique individual. And hear the voice *concretely,* specifically—not what he calls you to do with your life, but what he calls you to do with your *week.*

A Prayer

God, you lay on me challenges I'd just as soon not accept—or even acknowledge. You trust me more than anyone else ever has, more even than I trust myself. Help me to understand how you can be God—and still so unaware of what seems to be my helplessness before the challenges I'm afraid you're offering me. Amen.

Real Knowledge

Meeting the Living God

This is a book about freedom. It tries to pose the most crucial pair of alternatives any human being can face: either God exists, or he doesn't. If he doesn't, then I am *totally* free; if he does, then I am free, but obligated. And growing out of the answers to that question of God's existence is a corollary pair of alternatives: either I am immortal, right now, or I am just so much potential garbage.

There are obstacles to my knowing the truth about God—or any truth. And if they are obstacles to seeing truth, they are obstacles to my freedom. Some of the obstacles I provide for myself: there is my ordinary carelessness in observing and judging, resulting in false or quite inaccurate conclusions; there are also my self-inflicted blindnesses, particularly my masochistic blindness to my own worth. Other obstacles are imposed from outside myself, but nonetheless often cheerfully accepted as an alternative to the burdensome effort of thinking for oneself. Thus, the System and the counter-culture answer the three God questions simply by negating their relevance. There are plenty of readily available, this-world fulfillments—money, fame, sex, power, partying. The trouble is that they don't fulfill or satisfy or pay off for very long. There is always more that I still don't—perhaps even can't—have. Most persuasive of all restrictions on freedom are the opinions others have of my worth. But on the one hand they contradict one another in their expectations of me, and on the other hand they're never satisfied with me—and therefore I can never be satisfied with myself.

Wipe them out, then, at least for the moment, at least until I can find the truth about myself and then come back to the propaganda and accept what is true in it and reject what is corruptive. I am human; my nature impels me to know, to love, to grow. Since the very fact of growth negates the possibility of perfection, I will always be *im*perfect, and yet always worthy of the effort to improve. Further, I am *myself,* a collection of potential and limitations and experiences never again to be duplicated; I need spend very little time in the future counting over my shortcomings once again, like a miser with his treasury. I have done altogether too much mirror-gazing for faults ever to worry about becoming arrogant, but I *am* always in danger of becoming narcissistic— about the perfection of my worthlessness. To be free costs, and one of the costs is surrendering the masochistic pleasures of the mirror. Time to smash that, assess what I *do* have, and get on with it.

Another cost of freedom is trust. In order to *see* the inside of things and people, I have to take the risk of being "taken in," in both senses. Conversely, I have to trust that I am worth knowing and loving; I have to be unafraid to "give myself away," in both senses. I have to trust that outside the safe darkness of my cocoon there are people, and a universe, and perhaps even a God who can fulfill my life beyond my wildest hopes. The price of the light is to surrender the safe security of the darkness, a risk backed up not by a money-back guarantee but by only . . . a promise.

At bottom, the price for freedom is *faith*—that I have fewer limitations than I'd suspected, that there is more, that conversion is worth the cost, that I am not alone.

There is only one way to answer the God questions, upon which my own meaning so completely depends: evidence. On the one hand, I will never have evidence sufficient to *compel* my assent, one way or the other. I will never have Cartesian certitude. There will always be an element of risk, either way. But on the other hand, the answer doesn't come with the flip of a coin. This is important; we're talking about the value of my life. We're not just mulling over some vague theory of arbitrary ethics; we're talking about *my* concrete choices and limitations on *my* freedom: should I be honorable or chaste or sober or hard-working, when "everybody else" seems to be getting away with the opposite— and enjoying it?

And there is death: the moment that separates the wise ones from the suckers. If there is no God, the "saints" were the saps and the "sinners" were winners. But if there is a God, then all the "world's" values have been wrong—by 180°.

There are atheists who say "no" to God's existence—and not all of them subsequently become hedonists; some freely choose to be honorable, chaste, sober, and hardworking. But to them the question seems unanswerable. Unlike other invisible realities that can be manipulated and proven to be "there," the atheists assert that you can't set up an experiment and prove God is there. Thus, it is naive to base one's life and ethical decisions on a God whose existence can't be proven.

The consequences are bleak, but atheism may well be the truth—just as the consequences of theism are joyous, but they may well be a delusion. If there is no God, my seventy years (if I have that many), all my possessions, all my human accomplishments are annihilated by death, because I and my awareness of them will be annihilated. There are ways of kidding myself, immersing myself wholly in a freely chosen cause—even the cause of sheer bitchery, refusing to surrender. But I will be beaten. There is "No Exit."

There are theists who say "yes" to God's existence—and not all of them are subsequently joyful; some of them try to play both ends against the middle, to have God and the pet self-indulgences on their plates, too. But there is still no proof—only, theists claim, a strong convergence of probabilities, evidence enough for a *calculated risk* without any *reasonable* doubt. But there will always be occasions to doubt: "How could a good God have a reason for . . . ?" And yet if there is no God, there are no reasons, for anything, and surely no reasons for hope.

There is evidence of a Mind behind it all: my intelligence itself, the laws of the physical universe, the apparent "plan" of evolution seem to be effects which elude a mindless cause. To deny God, I have to deny the existence of my own intelligence—not the evidence of my senses, as I do in accepting atoms, but the evidence of the very intelligence which *makes* me human.

Further, my hungers for answers, for permanence, for justice are *curses* without God, since without him there are *no* final answers or permanence or justice. That could well be the case. But if it is the truth, I am the only being so cursed *by my very nature;* in me, evolution has gone one cruel step too far. It would be better to be a pig.

Fundamentally, though, the God questions have no meaning if they are merely "head-rush" questions. The only way the existence of God has any real importance—outside of giving some rationale to my mind—is if God does not merely exist but exists as a *person . . . here . . . now . . . accessible to me.*

What's more, if God is a person, the only way I can "prove" him is not by a series of soul-searchings or arguments or testaments. What if all the philosophers, and pantheists, and polytheists, and Brahmans, and Buddhists, and deists, and Moslems, and Jews, and Jesus were all terribly inspiring, and terribly good, and terribly well-intentioned, and terribly *wrong?* For twenty-six hundred of the world's three thousand years of recorded history, all people and nearly all the most brilliant minds who ever lived thought the earth was flat. And they were . . . wrong.

In the end, the *only* way to "prove," for oneself, that God exists is exactly the same way as I "prove" any of my other friends: trying to meet him.

Meeting the Living God

There is only one way to real knowledge in the God questions: meeting. Everything else is notional and therefore precarious. The only way to be sure is to set up experiments—which the atheist says is impossible—and see if God is "there." Two cautions: first, no scientist sets out in a search to find something he or she knows is *not* there; there is an educated hunch that something—or someone—is lurking just beyond the scope of one's vision; second, except in some pre-fab, cookbook school science lab, no scientist expects the first experiment to work; it's going to mean going back again and again.

Many prefer to wait for God to seek *them* out, and, in tragedy, he will. He is persistent; count on it. But he is also patient; he is not ordinarily, day-by-day intrusive. He respects our freedom. He waits till *we're* ready. He doesn't often impose himself in the good times; it's only when the Prodigal is hungry that he heads for home.

From the start, there are obstacles to taking time to be alone with God—to praying, as opposed to saying prayers. We can pass by all the obvious alibis: I'm too busy; there are so many other more pressing things; I forget to take time. Few of us find a day so hectic that we have no time for a shower, that we forget to brush our teeth. We're forced to make time for the "important things."

There are other more substantive reluctances to give God time to "prove" himself, voiced by people who have really tried. Some we can

230 / *Meeting the Living God*

dismiss rather quickly: "God doesn't give me the things I ask for": neither do your other friends. "I pray and it doesn't 'work'; nothing happens": perhaps the problem is with your expectations. You're saying, "I give him the time; he ought to show up." That is not unlike: "I love *her;* why doesn't she love me back?"

Deep communications, even between the best and longest-standing friends, are rare; go for a long car ride with an old friend and find out how rare. Most conversations even between old friends are not worth recording in a book, much less being carved in tablets of stone. All the more reason that most beginning friendships (even with God) have to start with "meaningless" chit-chat. And yet the words and topics are not what's important. They are only an *excuse;* the real communication is going on *underneath* the words; it says, "I want to prolong our being-together." Most times we go to parties with "open expectations," and we don't sit down afterward for an "assessment session" to analyze "how much I got out of that conversation." Then why with God?

One objection of those who have tried praying without apparent success is less easy to dismiss: there's no connection; it's a monologue; no one's listening. I can only answer that if it's a monologue, perhaps it's that *I* don't *shut up.* Perhaps *I'm* the one who's not listening. We are great talkers but rather poor listeners. Even in prayer we want to dominate, to tell God what he doesn't know, and then be sure the conversation has the desired results. We're not praying to "change God's mind" about the way things are going; we're praying to *understand* God's mind.

There are many books about praying; no need to duplicate them here, except to say that the *attitude* with which one enters praying is the most important—and least considered—element of this attempt to establish contact.

Come to prayer with no expectations. Be empty and expectant before him. It is not up to you to manufacture the light; all you have to do is open your protective shutters and raise the blinds. Those who approach prayer with their intelligence only seem almost to expect to "conquer God," like mastering the theory of relativity. But prayer is an opening of the self, making a place for him in your day and in your spirit, and calling God into that opening. When one does that, he or she often finds that God was already there, waiting to be noticed.

No voice will thunder from your ceiling, but you will find him manipulating *your* thoughts in directions you'd never considered—at times in directions which before were literally unthinkable. If you'll just shut up and *listen.*

More than anything else, opening to God and letting him "prove" himself requires short-circuiting the calculating intelligence, the part of us that counts the costs, weighs the risks, balances budgets, meets deadlines, "figures God out." We are not in prayer to know *about* God but to know *God,* and not as a character in a novel or a personage in history, but as a friend—here, now. For some, that is a dreadful price: to acknowledge that, for the moment, I am not in *charge.* But how are you ever going to find *if* Someone Else is in charge unless you're willing to surrender that responsibility for a while—and see if the universe collapses? It is not overdramatizing to say that it is a fearsome moment. There is only one requirement, the most threatening risk of them all: to be utterly vulnerable.

Don't expect instant-friend. No other friendship works that way. It takes, first, noticing—the tribute of awareness. It takes time and talk, mostly pretty surface chatter, but nonetheless a step without which nothing further can happen. *Only* then do you attach yourself to one another, gravitate toward one another, begin to have confidence in one another. It's the same with God.

But what am I telling *you* all this for? You've been through it. You know how friends "prove" themselves to one another. All I ask is that you give *God* the same chance you'd give an acquaintance who looks somewhat promising.

And with that, like any respectful matchmaker, I leave the two of you alone together and withdraw.

Question for the Notebook

Page 30. Try to gather together the most basic insights you've found here. Maybe it would help to page back through the notebook. If you've found very little, try to explain to both of us why. Don't merely say (if such is true), "Because I didn't really work at it." The more important question is *why.*

A Prayer

O God, I want to believe. Help my unbelief. Help me to be unafraid to give you time to "prove" yourself. Give me the courage to shut up—and listen. Amen.